Anonymous

Sacred Hymns and Spiritual Songs

For the Church of Jesus Christ of Latter-Day Saints

Anonymous

Sacred Hymns and Spiritual Songs
For the Church of Jesus Christ of Latter-Day Saints

ISBN/EAN: 9783337083984

Printed in Europe, USA, Canada, Australia, Japan

Cover: Foto ©Lupo / pixelio.de

More available books at **www.hansebooks.com**

SACRED HYMNS

AND

SPIRITUAL SONGS

FOR THE

CHURCH OF JESUS CHRIST OF
LATTER-DAY SAINTS.

Twentieth Edition.

SALT LAKE CITY, UTAH:
THE DESERET NEWS CO., PRINTERS AND PUBLISHERS.
1891.

PREFACE

TO THE FIRST ENGLISH EDITION.

THE Saints in this country have been very desirous for a Hymn Book adapted to their faith and worship, that they might sing the truth with an understanding heart, and express their praise, joy, and gratitude in songs adapted to the New and Everlasting Covenant.

In accordance with their wishes, we have selected the following Volume, which we hope will prove acceptable until a greater variety can be added.

With sentiments of high consideration and esteem, we subscribe ourselves your brethren in the New and Everlasting Covenant,

BRIGHAM YOUNG,
PARLEY P. PRATT,
JOHN TAYLOR.

Manchester, 1840.

PREFACE

TO THE TWENTIETH EDITION.

No BOOK published by or for the Latter-day Saints has run through so many editions or been sold so extensively as the Hymn Book, of which this is the twentieth edition. The demand for it continues unabated, and since the publication of the Latter-day Saints' Psalmody, which contains music for every hymn in this book, a new interest has been added to it and its usefulness enhanced. In this edition will be found a metrical index which the book, as previously published in America, has not contained. This feature will be especially valuable to choirs. A few hymns have also been added to the end of the volume. That these additions may prove acceptable to the public, and that the book may continue its cheering and consoling mission indefinitely, is the desire of

THE PUBLISHERS.

SALT LAKE CITY, UTAH,
September, 1891.

SACRED HYMNS
—AND—
SPIRITUAL SONGS.

HYMN 1. (L.M.)

1 The morning breaks, the shadows flee
   Lo! Zion's standard is unfurled!
   The dawning of a brighter day
   Majestic rises on the world.

2 The clouds of error disappear
   Before the rays of truth divine;
   The glory, bursting from afar,
   Wide o'er the nations soon will shine.

3 The Gentile fulness now comes in,
   And Israel's blessings are at hand;
   Lo! Judah's remnant, cleansed from sin,
   Shall in their promised Canaan stand.

4 Jehovah speaks! let earth give ear,
　And Gentile nations turn and live;
　His mighty arm is making bare,
　His covenant people to receive.

5 Angels from heaven and truth from earth
　Have met, and both have record borne;
　Thus Zion's light is bursting forth,
　To cheer her children's glad return.

HYMN 2. (C. M.)

1 Let every mortal ear attend,
　　And every heart rejoice;
　The trumpet of the Gospel sounds
　　With an inviting voice.

2 Ho! all ye hungry, starving souls,
　　That feed upon the wind,
　And vainly strive with earthly toys
　　To fill an empty mind;

3 Eternal wisdom has prepared
　　A soul-reviving feast,
　And bids your longing appetites
　　The rich provision taste.

4 Ho! ye that pant for living streams,
　　And pine away and die,

Here you may quench your raging thirst
  With springs that never dry.

5 Rivers of love and mercy here
    In a rich ocean join;
  Salvation in abundance flows,
    Like floods of milk and wine.

6 The gates of glorious Gospel grace
    Stand open night and day;
  Lord, we are come to seek supplies,
    And drive our wants away.

HYMN 3. (8's & 7's.)

1 Glorious things of thee are spoken,
    Zion, city of our God!
  He whose word cannot be broken,
    Chose thee for His own abode.

2 On the Rock of Ages founded,
    What can shake thy sure repose?
  With salvation's wall surrounded,
    Thou may'st smile on all thy foes.

3 See! the streams of living waters,
    Springing from celestial love,
  Well supply thy sons and daughters,
    And all fear of drought remove.

4 Who can faint, while such a river
   Ever flows their thirst t'assuage?
Grace which, like the Lord the giver,
   Never fails from age to age.

5 Round each habitation hov'ring,
   See the cloud and fire appear,
For a glory and a cov'ring,
   Showing that the Lord is near.

6 Thus deriving from their banner
   Light by night and shade by day,
Sweetly they enjoy the Spirit,
   Which He gives them when they pray.

7 Blest inhabitants of Zion,
   Purchased with the Savior's blood;
Jesus, whom their souls rely on,
   Makes them Kings and Priests to God.

8 While in love His Saints He raises
   With Himself to reign as King;
All, as Priests, His solemn praises
   For thank-off'rings freely bring.

9 Savior! since of Zion's city
   I through grace a member am;
Though the world despise and pity,
   I will glory in Thy name.

10 Fading are all worldly treasures,
  With their boasted pomp and show;
  Heavenly joys and lasting pleasures,
  None but Zion's children know.

HYMN 4. (L.M.)

1 The time is nigh, the happy time,
  That great, expected, blessed day,
  When countless thousands of our race
  Shall dwell with Christ, and him obey.

2 The prophecies must be fulfilled,
  Though earth and hell should dare oppose;
  The stone out of the mountain cut,
  Though unobserved, a kingdom grows.

3 Soon shall the blended image fall—
  Brass, silver, iron, gold, and clay;
  And superstition's dreadful reign
  To light and liberty give way.

4 In one sweet symphony of praise,
  The Jews and Gentiles will unite;
  And infidelity, o'ercome,
  Return again to endless night.

5 From east to west, from north to south,
  The Savior's kingdom shall extend,
  And every man in every place
  Shall meet a brother and a friend.

HYMN 5. (C. M.)

1 Great is the Lord! 'tis good to praise
His high and holy name:
Well may the Saints in latter days
His wondrous love proclaim!

2 To praise Him let us all engage,
That unto us is given
To live in this momentous age
And share the light of heaven.

3 We'll praise Him for our happy lot
On this much-favored land,
Where truth and righteousness are taught
By His divine command.

4 We'll praise Him for more glorious things
Than language can express;
The "Everlasting Gospel" brings
The humble soul to bliss.

5 The Comforter is sent again;
His power the Church attends,
And with the faithful will remain
Till Jesus Christ descends.

6 We'll praise Him for a Prophet's voice,
His people's steps to guide;

In this we do and will rejoice,
   Though all the world deride.

7 Praise Him! the time, the chosen time
   To favor Zion's come;
And all the Saints from every clime
   Will soon be gathered home.

8 The opening seals announce the day,
   By prophets long declared,
When all, in one triumphant lay,
   Will join to praise the Lord.

HYMN 6. (S. M.)

1 See! all creation joins
   To praise th' Eternal God;
The heavenly hosts begin the song,
   And sound His name abroad.

2 The sun with golden beams,
   The moon with silver rays,
The starry lights and twinkling flames,
   Shine to their Maker's praise.

3 He built those worlds above,
   And fixed their wondrous frame,
By His command they stand or move,
   And always speak His fame.

4 The fleecy clouds that rise,
   Or falling showers, or snow,
The thunder rolling round the skies,
   His power and glory show.

5 The broad expanse on high,
   With all the heavens afford,
The lightning's fire that streaks the sky,
   Unite to praise the Lord.

CHORUS.

By all that shines above,
   His glory is expressed;
But Saints, who know His endless love,
   Should sing His praises best.

HYMN 7. (4-6's & 2-8's.)

1 O happy souls, who pray
   Where God appoints to hear!
O happy Saints, who pay
   Their constant service there!
     We'll praise Him still,
       And happy we
     Who love the way
     To Zion's hill.

2 No burning heat by day,
   Nor blasts of evening air,
Shall take our health away,
   If God be with us there.
      He is our sun,
        And He our shade
        To guard our head
      By night or noon.

3 God is the only Lord,
   Our shield and our defense;
With gifts His hands are stored,
   We draw our blessings thence.
      He will bestow
        On Jacob s race
        Peculiar grace,
      And glory too.

HYMN 8. (7's.)

1 Praise to God, immortal praise,
For the love that crowns our days ;
Bounteous source of every joy,
Let Thy praise our tongues employ.

2 For the blessings of the field,
For the stores the gardens yield,
For the vine's enlivening juice,
For the gen'rous olive's use.

3 Flocks that whiten all the plain,
Yellow sheaves of ripened grain,
Clouds that drop their fat'ning dews,
Suns that temp'rate warmth diffuse.

4 All that spring, with bounteous hand,
Scatters o'er the smiling land,
All that liberal autumn pours
From its rich o'erflowing stores.

5 Thanks to Thee, our God, we owe,
Source from whence all blessings flow!
And for these our souls shall raise
Grateful vows and solemn praise.

HYMN 9. (C.M.)

1 We're not ashamed to own our Lord,
　And worship Him on earth;
We love to learn His holy word,
　And know what souls are worth.

2 When Jesus comes in burning flame,
　Then to reward the just,
The world will know the only name
　In which the Saints can trust.

3 When He comes down from heaven to earth,
　With all His holy band,

Before creation's second birth,
   We hope with Him to stand.

4 Then will He give us a "new name,"
   With robes of righteousness,
And in the New Jerusalem
   Eternal happiness.

HYMN 10. (C.M.)

1 Joy to the world! the Lord will come
   And earth receive her King:
Let every heart prepare Him room,
   And Saints and angels sing.

2 Rejoice! rejoice! when Jesus reigns,
   And Saints their songs employ; [plains,
While fields and floods, rocks, hills and
   Repeat the sounding joy.

3 No more will sin and sorrow grow,
   Nor thorns infest the ground;
He'll come and make the blessing flow
   Far as the curse was found.

4 Rejoice! rejoice in the Most High!
   While Israel spreads abroad
Like stars that glitter in the sky,
   And ever worship God.

HYMN 11. (4-6's & 2-8's.)

1 To Him who made the world,
  The sun, the moon and stars,
  And all that in them is,
    With days and months and years.
      To Him who died,
      That we might live,
      Our thanks and songs
      We freely give.

2 Our hope in things to come,
  The Spirit's quick'ning powers
  Should turn our hearts to Him
    Who makes His blessings ours;
      That we may sing
      Of things above,
      And always know
      That God is love.

3 When He comes down from heaven,
  And earth again is blest,
  Then all the ransomed heirs
    Will find their promised rest.
      With all the just
      Then we may sing,
      God is with us,
      And we with Him.

HYMN 12. (L.M.)

1 Ere long the vail will rend in twain,
The King descend with all His train;
The earth shall shake with awful fright,
And all creation feel His might.

2 The angel's trumpet long shall sound,
And wake the nations under ground;
Throughout the vast domain of space
'Twill echo forth from place to place.

3 Lift up your heads, ye Saints, in peace
The Savior comes for your release;
The day of the redeemed has come,
The Saints shall all be welcomed home.

4 Behold the Church! it soars on high
To meet the Saints amid the sky,
To hail the King in clouds of fire,
And strike and tune the immortal lyre.

5 Hosanna! now the trump shall sound,
Proclaim the joys of heaven around,
When all the Saints together join
In songs of love, and all divine.

6 With Enoch here we all shall meet,
And worship at Messiah's feet;
Unite our hands and hearts in love,
And reign on thrones with Christ above.

7 The city that was seen of old,
Whose walls were jasper, streets were gold,
We'll now inherit, throned in might,
The Father and the Son delight.

8 Celestial crowns we shall receive,
And glories great our God shall give;
While loud hosannas we'll proclaim,
And sound aloud the Savior's name.

9 Our hearts and tongues shall join in one,
To praise the Father and the Son,
While all the heavens shall shout again,
And all creation say, Amen.

HYMN 13. (S.M.)

1 Let sinners take their course,
    And choose the road to death;
But in the worship of my God
    I'll spend my daily breath.

2 My thoughts address His throne
    When morning brings the light;
I seek His blessings every noon,
    And pay my vows at night.

3 Thou wilt regard my cries,
    O my eternal God!
While sinners perish in surprise,
    Beneath Thine angry rod.

4 Because they dwell at ease,
    And no sad changes feel,
 They neither fear, nor trust Thy name,
    Nor learn to do Thy will.

5 But I, with all my cares,
    Will lean upon my Lord;
 I'll cast my burdens on His arm,
    And rest upon His word.

6 His arm shall well sustain
    The children of His love;
 The ground on which their safety stands
    No earthly power can move.

HYMN 14. (C.M.)

Come, all ye Saints who dwell on earth,
   Your cheerful voices raise,
Our great Reedemer's love to sing,
   And celebrate His praise.

His love is great, He died for us;
   Shall we ungrateful be,
Since He has marked a road to bliss,
   And said, Come, follow me?

The straight and narrow way we've found!
   Then let us travel on,
Till we, in the celestial world,
   Shall meet where Christ is gone.

4 And there we'll join the heavenly choir,
   And sing His praise above,
While endless ages roll around,
   Perfected by His love.

HYMN 15. (L.M.)

1 God spake the word, and time began;
He spake, and gave His law to man;
His presence oft did Adam cheer,
Who lov'd the voice of God to hear.

2 But soon the happy scene was changed,
And they became from God estranged;
They broke His law, and guilt and shame
Their state of innocence o'ercame.

3 Impelled by fear, they vainly tried
From God's all-searching eyes to hide;
His well-known voice by them was heard,
And tremblingly they both appeared.

4 So men, from that eventful day,
Far from the God of heaven stray,
Till near six thousand years have passed,
And left a lifeless faith at last.

5 By faith the ancients sought the Lord,
From time to time obtained His word:

Not only they, but so may we,
When faith and works do both agree.

6 From Adam to the present day,
Many have sought a righteous way;
And some have found the narrow road,
And, Enoch-like, have walked with God.

7 God is unchangeable to save,
Though men are changeful as the wave;
While sinners take the downward road,
The faith of man approaches God.

8 Experience and the word agree—
Draw nigh to God, He'll draw nigh thee;
Then, are they wise who do deny
The works of faith beneath the sky?

HYMN 16. (C.M.)

1 Mortals, awake! with angels join,
  And chant the solemn lay;
Love, joy, and gratitude combine,
  To hail th' auspicious day.

2 In heaven the rapturous song began,
  And sweet seraphic fire
Through all the shining legions ran,
  And swept the sounding lyre.

3 The theme, the song, the joy was new
  To each angelic tongue;

Swift through the realms of light it flew,
And loud the echo rung.

4 Down through the portals of the sky
The pealing anthems ran,
And angels flew with eager joy
To bear the news to man.

5 Hark! the cherubic armies shout,
And glory leads the song;
Peace and salvation swell the note
Of all the heavenly throng.

6 With joy the chorus we'll repeat—
"Glory to God on high;
Good-will and peace are now complete;
Jesus was born to die."

7 Hail! Prince of Life, forever hail!
Redeemer, Brother, Friend!
Though earth and time and life should fail,
Thy praise shall never end.

HYMN 17. (4-11's.)

1 O Jesus! the giver
Of all we enjoy,
Our lives to Thy honor
We wish to employ;
With praises unceasing
We'll sing of Thy name,

Thy goodness increasing,
Thy love we'll proclaim.

2 With joy we remember
   The dawn of that day,
When cold as December,
   In darkness we lay!
The sweet invitation
   We heard with surprise,
And witnessed salvation
   Flow down from the skies.

3 The wonderful name
   Of our Jesus we'll sing,
And publish the fame
   Of our Captain and King.
With sweet exultation
   His goodness we prove;
His name is salvation,
   His nature is love.

4 We now are enlisted
   In Jesus' blest cause,
Divinely assisted
   To conquer our foes:
His grace will support us
   Till conflicts are o'er,
He then will escort us
   To Zion's bright shore.

HYMN 18. (C.M.)

1 Beloved brethren! sing His praise
   Who formed the worlds on high;
  Who taught the planets where to trace
   Their orbits through the sky.

2 O sing the fervor of His love,
   The wonders of His grace,
  Who sent the Savior from above
   To save a dying race.

3 In songs declare the works and ways
   Of our Eternal God,
  Whose kingdom in these latter days
   Is spreading far abroad.

4 In Zion let His name be praised,
   Who has a feast prepared,
  The glorious Gospel standard raised,
   The ancient faith restored.

5 Swift heralds, the glad news to bear
   O'er land and ocean, fly;
  And to the wond'ring world declare
   The message from on high.

6 Ye nations of the earth attend!
   Let kings and princes hear,
  And let the powers of darkness bend—
   Messiah's reign is near.

7 The Savior comes! Ye Saints, be pure,
   And fix your hearts on high;
  Lift up your heads, rejoice, for your
   Redemption draweth nigh.

8 Sing, brethren! sing, in strains divine;
   Let all your voices raise;
  Let heaven and earth their anthems join
   In these the latter days.

HYMN 19. (C.M.)

1 Jehovah, Lord of heaven and earth,
   Thy word of truth proclaim!
  O may it spread from pole to pole,
   Till all shall know Thy name.

2 We long to see Thy church increase,
   Thy own new kingdom grow,
  That all the earth may live in peace,
   And heaven be seen below.

3 Roll on Thy work in all its power!
   The distant nations bring!
  In Thy new kingdom may they stand,
   And own Thee God and King.

4 One general chorus then shall rise
   From men of every tongue,
  And songs of joy salute the skies,
   From every nation sung!

HYMN 20. (L.M.)

1 Arise! arise! with joy survey
The glory of the latter day:
Already has the dawn begun
Which marks at hand a rising sun.

2 Behold the way! ye heralds cry;
Spare not, but lift your voices high;
Convey the sound from pole to pole—
Glad tidings to the captive soul.

3 Behold the way to Zion's hill,
Where Israel's God delights to dwell!
He fixes there His lofty throne,
And calls the sacred place His own.

4 The north gives up; the south no more
Keeps back her consecrated store;
From east to west the message runs,
And either India yields her sons.

5 Auspicious dawn! thy rising ray
With joy we view, and hail the day:
Great Sun of Righteousness! arise,
And fill the world with glad surprise.

HYMN 21. (6-8's.)

1 The Lord my pasture shall prepare,
And feed me with a shepherd's care;
His presence shall my wants supply,
And guard me with a watchful eye;
My noonday walks He shall attend,
And all my midnight hours defend.

2 When in the sultry glebe I faint,
Or on the thirsty mountain pant,
To fertile vales and dewy meads
My weary, wand'ring steps He leads,
Where peaceful rivers, soft and slow,
Amid the verdant landscape flow.

3 Though in the paths of death I tread,
With gloomy horrors overspread,
My steadfast heart shall fear no ill,
For thou, O Lord, art with me still;
Thy friendly rod shall give me aid,
And guide me through the dreadful shade.

4 Though in a bare and rugged way,
Through devious lonely wilds I stray,
Thy presence shall my pains beguile;
The barren wilderness shall smile,
With green and beauteous herbage crowned,
And streams shall murmur all around.

HYMN 22. (C.M.)

1 God moves in a mysterious way,
   His wonders to perform;
He plants His footsteps in the sea,
   And rides upon the storm.

2 Deep in unfathomable mines
   Of never-failing skill,
He treasures up His bright designs,
   And works His sovereign will.

3 Ye fearful Saints, fresh courage take!
   The clouds ye so much dread
Are big with mercy, and shall break
   In blessings on your head.

4 Judge not the Lord by feeble sense,
   But trust Him for His grace;
Behind a frowning providence
   He hides a smiling face.

5 His purposes will ripen fast,
   Unfolding every hour;
The bud may have a bitter taste,
   But sweet will be the flower.

6 Blind unbelief is sure to err,
   And scan His work in vain;
God is His own interpreter,
   And He will make it plain.

HYMN 23. (7's & 6's.)

1 Arise, O glorious Zion,
  Thou joy of latter days,
 Whom countless Saints rely on,
  To gain a resting place;
 Arise, and shine in splendor,
  Amid the world's deep night;
 For God, thy sure defender,
  Is now thy life and light.

2 Let faithful Saints be rearing
  The city of our Lord,
 On mountain tops appearing,
  According to His word;
 A sought-out habitation,
  By men of truth and faith,
 A covert of salvation
  From ignorance and death.

3 The Temple long expected
  Shall stand on Zion's hill,
 By willing hearts erected,
  Who love Jehovah's will:
 Let earth, her wealth bestowing,
  Adorn His holy seat;
 For nations great shall flow in,
  To worship at His feet.

4 What though the world in malice
   Despise these mighty things,
We'll build the Royal Palace,
   To serve the King of kings;
Where holy men, anointed
   To know His sovereign will,
Each ordinance appointed
   To save us, will reveal.

5 From Zion's favored dwelling
   The Gospel issues forth,
The covenant revealing
   To gather all the earth;
And Saints, the message bringing
   To all the sons of men,
With the redeemed, shall, singing,
   To Zion come again.

6 O hear the proclamation,
   And fly as on the wind!
For righteous indignation
   Shall desolate mankind!
Then, Zion, men shall prize thee,
   And bow before thy shrine;
And they who now despise thee
   Shall own thy light divine.

7 Through painful tribulation
   We walk the narrow road,

And battle with temptation,
  To gain that blest abode,
But patient, firm endurance,
  With glory in our view—
The Spirit's bright assurance—
  Will bring us conquerors through.

8 O grant, Eternal Father,
  That we may faithful be,
With all the just to gather,
  And Thy salvation see!
Then, with the hosts of heaven,
  We'll sing th' immortal theme—
To Him be glory given,
  Whose blood did us redeem.

HYMN 24. (C.M.)

1 O happy is the man who hears
    Instruction's warning voice!
  And who celestial wisdom makes
    His early, only choice!

2 For she has treasures greater far
    Than east or west unfold;
  And her rewards more precious are
    Than all the stores of gold.

3 In her right hand she holds to view,
    A length of happy days;

Riches, with splendid honors joined,
  Are what her left displays.

4 She guides the young with innocence
    In pleasure's path to tread;
  A crown of glory she bestows
    Upon the hoary head.

5 According as her labors rise,
    So her rewards increase;
  Her ways are ways of pleasantness,
    And all her paths are peace.

HYMN 25. (L.M,)

1 Peace, troubled soul! thou need'st not fear;
  Thy great Provider still is near;
  Who fed thee last will feed thee still;
  Be calm, and seek to do His will.

2 The Lord, who built the earth and sky,
  In mercy stops to hear thy cry;
  His promise all may freely claim:
  "Ask and receive, in Jesus' name."

3 His stores are open all, and free,
  To such as truly upright be;
  Water and bread He'll give for food,
  With all things else which He sees good.

4 The ravens daily doth He feed,
  And sends them food as they have need;

Although they nothing have in store,
Yet as they lack He gives them more.

Then do not seek with anxious care
What ye shall eat or drink or wear:
Your heavenly Father will you feed;
He knows that all these things you need.

Without reserve give Christ your heart;
Let Him His righteousness impart;
Then all things else He'll freely give,
With Him you all things shall receive.

Thus shall the soul be truly blest,
That seeks in God his only rest:
May I that happy person be
In time and in eternity.

HYMN 26. (8's & 7's.)

1 Softly beams the sacred dawning
   Of the great Millennial morn,
  And to Saints gives welcome warning
   That the day is hasting on.

2 Splendid, rising o'er the mountains,
   Glowing with celestial cheer,
  Streaming from eternal fountains,
   Rays of living light appear.

3 Swiftly flee the clouds of darkness,
    Speedily the mists retire;
Nature's universal blackness
    Is consumed by heavenly fire.

4 Yea, the fair sabbatic era,
    When the world will be at rest,
Rapidly is drawing nearer;
    Then all Israel will be blest.

5 Odors sweet the air perfuming,
    Verdure of the purest green;
In primeval beauty beaming,
    Will our native earth be seen.

6 At the resurrection morning,
    We shall all appear as one;
O what robes of bright adorning,
    Will the righteous then put on!

7 Eye's not seen the untold treasures,
    Which the Father hath in store,
Teeming with surpassing pleasures,
    Even life for evermore.

8 Mourn no longer, Saints beloved,
    Brave the dangers, no retreat;
Neither let your hearts be moved,
    Scorn the trials you may meet.

HYMN 27. (6-7's.)

1 Hark! ye mortals. Hist! be still.
Voices from Cumorah's hill
Break the silence of the tomb,
Penetrate the dreadful gloom,
Gently whisper, all is well!
Now's the day of Israel!

2 Now the Gentile reign is o'er;
Darkness covers earth no more;
Now shall Zion rise and shine,
Fill the world with light divine;
Angels join—the tidings tell,
Now's the day of Israel!

3 Thrones shall totter, Babel fall,
Satan reign no more at all;
Saints shall gain the victory,
Truth prevail o'er land and sea,
Gentile tyrants sink to hell;
Now's the day of Israel!

4 Jesus now will come again,
Saints with Him shall rise and reign,
Heaven and earth in songs combine,
All the worlds in chorus join;
Every tongue the music swell,
Now's the day of Israel!

5 Ghastly death shall conquered be,
Zion reign, and Saints be free,
Priests and kings shall join in love,
Fill the worlds below, above,
Singing anthems—all is well!
Now's the day of Israel!

HYMN 28. (8-8-6's.)

1 Be it my only wisdom here
To serve the Lord with filial fear,
　With loving gratitude;
Superior sense may I display,
By shunning every evil way,
　And walking in the good.

2 Oh, may I still from sin depart;
A wise and understanding heart,
　Jesus, to me be given;
And let me through Thy Spirit know
To glorify my God below,
　And find my way to heaven.

HYMN 29. (S.M.)

1 Come we that love the Lord,
　And let our joys be known;
Join in a song with sweet accord,
　And worship at His throne.

2 Let those refuse to sing
    Who never knew our God;
But servants of the heavenly king
    May speak their joys abroad.

3 The God who rules on high,
    And all the earth surveys—
Who rides upon the stormy sky,
    And calms the roaring seas—

4 This mighty God is ours,
    Our Father and our Love;
He will send down His heavenly powers,
    To carry us above.

5 There we shall see His face,
    And never, never sin;
And, from the rivers of His grace
    Drink endless pleasures in.

6 Yes, and before we rise
    To that immortal state,
The thoughts of such amazing bliss
    Should constant joys create.

7 The men of grace have found
    Glory begun below;
Celestial fruit on earthly ground,
    From faith and hope may grow.

8 Then let our songs abound,
    And every tear be dry;
We're marching through Immanuel's ground
    To fairer worlds on high.

HYMN 30. (8's & 7's.)

1 What was witnessed in the heavens?
    Why, an angel, earthward bound.
Had he something with him bringing?
    Yes—the Gospel—joyful sound!
It was to be preached in power
    On the earth, the angel said,
To all men, all tongues and nations
    That upon its face are spread.

2 Had we not before the Gospel?
    Yes—had several taught by men.
Then what is this latter Gospel?
    'Tis the first one come again.
This was preached by Paul and Peter,
    And by Jesus Christ, the head;
This we latter Saints are preaching—
    We their footsteps wish to tread.

3 Where so long has been the Gospel?
    Did it never fall away?
What became of those neglected?
    God is just, is all we say.

    Seek no crop where 'twas not planted,
      Nor a day where reigns the night;
    Now the sunshine bright is beaming,
      Let all creatures see aright.

HYMN 31. (L.M.)

1 Happy the man who finds the grace,
   The blessings of God's chosen race,
   The wisdom coming from above,
   The faith that sweetly works by love.

2 Happy beyond description he
   Who knows, "The Savior died for me,"
   The gift unspeakable obtains,
   The heavenly understanding gains.

3 Wisdom divine! Who tells the price
   Of wisdom's costly merchandise?
   Wisdom to silver we prefer,
   And gold is dross compared to her.

4 Her hands are filled with length of days,
   True riches and immortal praise;
   Riches of Christ on all bestowed,
   And honor that descends from God.

5 To purest joys she all invites,
Chaste, holy, spiritual delights;
Her ways are ways of pleasantness,
And all her flowery paths are peace.

6 Happy the man who wisdom gains,
Thrice happy who his guest retains;
He owns, and will forever own,
Wisdom and Christ and Heaven are one.

HYMN 32. (L.M)

1 Happy the souls who first believed,
To Jesus and each other cleaved,
Joined by the unction from above,
In mystic fellowship of love.

2 Meek, simple followers of the Lamb!
They lived and spake and thought the same
They joyfully conspired to raise
Their ceaseless sacrifice of praise.

3 With grace abundantly endued,
A pure, believing multitude,
They all were of one heart and soul,
And heavenly love inspired the whole.

4 Oh! what an age of golden days!
Oh! what a choice, peculiar race!

Washed in the Lamb's all-cleansing blood,
Anointed Kings and Priests to God.

5 Where shall we wander now to find
Successors they have left behind?
The faithful whom we seek in vain,
Are 'minished from the sons of men.

6 Ye different sects, who all declare,
"Lo! here is Christ!" or "Christ is there!"
Your stronger proofs divinely give,
And show me where true Christians live.

HYMN 33. (L.M.)

1 Jesus, from whom all blessings flow,
Great Builder of thy Church below!
If now Thy Spirit moves my breast,
Hear, and fulfil Thine own request!

2 The few that truly call Thee Lord,
And wait Thy sanctifying word,
And Thee their utmost Savior own,
Unite, and perfect them in one.

3 O! let them all Thy mind express,
Stand forth Thy chosen witnesses,

Thy power unto salvation show,
And perfect holiness below.

4 In them let all mankind behold
How Christians lived in days of old;
Mighty their envious foes to move—
A proverb of reproach and love.

5 Call them into Thy wondrous light,
Worthy to walk with Thee in white!
Make up Thy jewels, Lord, and show
Thy glorious, spotless Church below.

6 From every sinful wrinkle free,
Redeemed from all iniquity,
The fellowship of Saints made known,
And, O my God, let me be one!

7 O! may my lot be cast with these,
The least of Jesus' witnesses;
O! that my Lord would count me meet
To wash His dear disciples' feet.

8 This only thing do I require;
Thou know'st 'tis all my heart's desire,
Freely what I receive to give,
The servant of Thy Church to live.

9 After my lowly Lord I go,
And wait upon Thy Saints below,

Enjoy the grace to angels given,
And serve the royal heirs of heaven.

10 Lord, if I now Thy drawings feel,
And ask according to Thy will,
Confirm the prayer, the seal impart.
And speak the answer to my heart.

11 Tell me—or Thou shalt never go—
"Thy prayer is heard; it shall be so!"
The word hath passed Thy lips, and I
Shall with Thy people live and die.

HYMN 34. (C.M.)

1 How will the Saints rejoice to tell
   And count their sufferings o'er,
When they upon Mount Zion dwell,
   And view the landscape o'er.

2 There they will see, upon that land,
   Fair Zion from above,
And meet with Enoch's holy band,
   And sing redeeming love.

3 There no more sickness, pain, or woe
   Shall mar their peaceful rest,
For God shall wipe away their tears,
   And comfort the oppressed.

4 O may I see that glorious day
   And join with all the blest,
To sing aloud the Savior's praise,
   And enter into rest.

HYMN 35. (S.M.D.)

1 Ye simple souls who stray
   Far from the path of peace,
That lonely, unfrequented way
   To life and happiness;
Why will ye folly love,
   And throng the downward road,
And hate the wisdom from above,
   And mock the sons of God?

2 Madness and misery
   Ye count our life beneath,
And nothing great or good can see,
   Or glorious in our death,
As only born to grieve,
   Beneath your feet we lie,
And utterly condemned we live,
   And unlamented die.

3 So wretched and obscure,
   The men whom ye despise,
So foolish, impotent and poor,
   Above your scorn we rise.

We, through the Holy Ghost,
  Can witness better things;
For He, whose blood is all our boast,
  Hath made us Priests and Kings.

4 Riches unsearchable
    In Jesus' love we know;
  And pleasures springing from the well
    Of life our souls o'erflow.
  The Spirit we receive
    Of wisdom, grace and power;
  And, though 'mid scenes of woe we live,
    Rejoicing evermore.

5 Angels our servants are,
    And keep in all our ways;
  And in their watchful hands they bear
    The sacred sons of grace;
  Unto that heavenly bliss
    They all our steps attend,
  And God Himself our Father is,
    And Jesus is our Friend.

6 With Him we walk in white,
    We in His image shine;
  Our robes are robes of glorious light,
    Our righteousness divine.

On all the kings of earth
　With pity we look down;
And claim, in virtue of our birth,
　A never-failing crown.

HYMN 36. (2-6's & 4 & 3-6's & 4.)
Tune: "God Save the Queen."

1 Our God, we raise to Thee
　Thanks for Thy blessings free
　　We here enjoy;
　In this far western land,
　A true and chosen band,
　Led hither by Thy hand,
　　Would sing for joy.

2 Bless Thou our Prophet dear;
　May health and comfort cheer
　　His noble heart;
　His words with fire impress
　On souls that Thou wilt bless;
　Nor gold may they caress,
　　But free impart.

3 So shall Thy kingdom spread,
　As by Thy Prophets said,
　　From sea to sea;
　As one united whole
　Truth burn in every soul,
　While hast'ning to the goal
　　We long to see.

4 O may Thy Saints be one,
   Like Father and the Son,
      Nor disagree;
   United heart and hand,
   So may they ever stand,
   A firm and valiant band,
      Eternally.

HYMN 37. (C.M.)

1 Ye Saints who dwell on Europe's shore,
   Let not your hearts be faint;
  Let each press on to things before,
   And be indeed a Saint.

2 Although the present time may seem
   O'erspread with clouds of gloom,
  The light of faith will shed its gleam
   Until deliverance come.

3 Hold fast the things you have received,
   Be faithful in the Lord;
  You know in whom you have believed,
   He's faithful to His word.

4 Your brethren in America
   Are one in heart with you,
  And they are toiling night and day
   For Zion's welfare too.

5 They even now are driven forth
    To track the wilderness;
  They leave the country of their birth
    For truth and righteousness.

6 But there's a day, 'tis near at hand,
    A day of joy and peace!
  That day will break oppression's band,
    And bring the Saints release.

7 Then, brethren, haste and gather up;
    We shall rejoice to meet;
  When we have drunk the bitter cup,
    We'll share a heavenly treat.

8 And even now the Lord bestows
    More, more than tongue can tell,
  Of that which from His presence flows:
    Yes, brethren, all is well.

HYMN 38. (4-6's & 2-8's.)

1 Let earth and heaven agree,
    Angels and men be joined,
  To celebrate with me
    The Savior of mankind,
  Adore the all-atoning Lamb,
  And bless the sound of Jesus' name.

2 Jesus! transporting sound
   The joy of earth and heaven!
No other help is found,
   No other name is given,
By which we can salvation have;
But Jesus came the world to save.

3 Jesus! harmonious name!
   It charms the hosts above;
They evermore proclaim,
   And wonder at His love;
'Tis all their happiness to gaze,
'Tis heaven to see our Jesus' face.

4 His name the sinner fears;
   But when from sin set free,
'Tis music in His ears,
   'Tis life and liberty;
New songs do then his lips employ,
And his glad heart e'en leaps for joy.

5 Stung by the scorpion, sin,
   My poor, expiring soul
The balmy sound drinks in,
   And is at once made whole.
See there my Lord upon the tree!
I hear, I feel, He died for me!

6 O, unexampled love!
   O, all redeeming grace!
How swiftly Thou dost move
   To save a fallen race!
What shall I do to make it known
What Thou for all mankind hast done?

7 O, for a trumpet voice,
   On all the world to call,
To bid their hearts rejoice
   In Him who died for all!
For all, my Lord was crucified!
For all, for all, my Savior died!

HYMN 39. (C.M.)

1 Jesus, Thou all-redeeming Lord,
   Thy blessing we implore;
Open the door to preach Thy word,
   The great, effectual door.

2 Gather the outcasts in, and save
   From sin and Satan's power,
And let them now acceptance have,
   And know their gracious hour.

3 Lover of souls, Thou know'st to prize
   What Thou hast bought so dear;
Come, then, and in Thy people's eyes,
   With all Thy wounds, appear.

HYMN 40. (P.M.)

1 Come, let us anew our journey pursue,
   Roll round with the year,
And never stand still till the Master appear.
His adorable will let us gladly fulfil,
   And our talents improve,
By the patience of hope and the labor of love.

2 Our life as a dream, our time as a stream,
   Glides swiftly away,
And the fugitive moment refuses to stay.
The arrow is flown, the moments are gone,
   The Millennial year
Presses on to our view, and eternity's here.

3 O that each in the day of His coming may say,
   "I have fought my way through;
I have finished the work Thou did'st give me to do."
O that each from his Lord may receive the glad word:
   "Well and faithfully done;
Enter into my joy and sit down on my throne."

HYMN 41. (7's D.)

1 Who are these arrayed in white,
    Brighter than the noonday sun,
Foremost of the sons of light,
    Nearest the eternal throne?
These are they that bore the cross,
    Nobly for their Master stood,
Suff'rers for His righteous cause,
    Foll'wers of the dying God.

2 Out of great distress they came,
    Washed their robes, by faith below,
In the blood of yonder Lamb—
    Blood that washes white as snow.
Therefore are they next the throne,
    Serve their Maker day and night;
God resides among his own,
    God doth in His Saints delight.

3 More than conquerors at last,
    Here they find their trials o'er;
They have all their suff'rings past,
    Hunger now and thirst no more:
No excessive heat they feel
    From the sun's directer ray,
In a milder clime they dwell—
    Region of eternal day.

1 He that on the throne doth reign;
   Them the Lamb shall always feed,
With the tree of life sustain,
   To the living fountains lead;
He shall all their sorrows chase,
   All their wants at once remove,
Wipe the tears from every face,
   Fill up every soul with love.

HYMN 42. (S.M.)

1 Spirit of Faith, come down,
   Reveal the things of God,
And make to us the Godhead known,
   And witness with the blood.

2 'Tis Thine the blood t' apply,
   And give us eyes to see;
Who did for every sinner die,
   Did surely die for me.

3 No man can truly say
   That Jesus is the Lord,
Unless Thou take the vail away,
   And breathe the living word.

4 Then, only then, we feel
   Our int'rest in His blood,
And cry, with joy unspeakable,
   "Thou art my Lord, my God!"

5 O that the world might know
    The all-atoning Lamb!
Spirit of Faith descend and show
    The virtue of His name.

6 The grace which all may find,
    The saving power impart;
And testify to all mankind,
    And speak in every heart.

7 Inspire with living faith,
    Which whosoe'er receives,
The witness in himself he hath,
    And consciously believes;

8 The faith that conquers all,
    And doth e'en mountains move,
And saves all who on Jesus call,
    And perfects them in love.

HYMN 43. (C.M.)

1 Come, Holy Ghost, our hearts inspire,
    Let us thine influence prove;
Source of the old prophetic fire,
    Fountain of light and love.

2 Come, Holy Ghost; for moved by Thee,
    The Prophets moved and spoke;
Unlock the truth, Thyself the key;
    Unseal the sacred book.

3 Expand Thy wings, celestial dove,
    Brood o'er our nature's night;
On our disordered spirits move,
    And let there now be light.

4 God, through Himself, we then shall know
    If Thou within us shine,
And sound with all Thy Saints below,
    The depth of love divine.

HYMN 44. (6-8's.)

1 Inspirer of the ancient seers,
    Who wrote from Thee the sacred page,
The same through all succeeding years,
    To us in our degen'rate age,
The spirit of Thy word impart,
And breathe the life into each heart.

2 While now Thine oracles we read
    With earnest prayer and strong desire,
O let Thy spirit now proceed,
    Our souls to waken and inspire;
Our weakness help, our darkness chase,
And guide us by the light of grace!

3 Whene'er in error's path we rove,
    The living God through sin forsake,
Our conscience by Thy word reprove,
    Convince and bring the wand'rers back;

Deep wounded by the Spirit's sword,
And then by Gilead's balm restored.

4 The sacred lessons of Thy grace,
   Transmitted through Thy word, repeat,
And train us up in all Thy ways,
   To make us in Thy will complete;
Fulfil Thy love's redeeming plan,
And bring us to a perfect man.

5 Furnished out of Thy treasury,
   O may we always ready stand
To help the souls redeemed by Thee,
   In what their various states demand—
To teach, convince, correct, reprove,
And build them up in holiest love!

HYMN 45. (L.M.)

1 Author of faith, Eternal Word,
   Whose Spirit breathes the active flame—
Faith, like its Finisher and Lord,
   To-day as yesterday the same.

2 To Thee our humble hearts aspire,
   And ask the gift unspeakable;
Increase in us the kindred fire,
   In us the work of faith fulfil.

3 By faith we know Thee strong to save;
    Save us, a present Savior thou!
  Whate'er we hope, by faith we have,
    Future and past subsisting now.

4 To him that in Thy name believes,
    Eternal life with Thee is given!
  Into himself he all receives,
    Pardon and holiness from heaven.

5 The things unknown to feeble sense,
    Unseen by reason's glimm'ring ray,
  With strong commanding evidence,
    Their heavenly origin display.

6 Faith lends its realizing light,
    The clouds disperse, the shadows fly,
  Th' Invisible appears in sight,
    And God is seen by mortal eye.

HYMN 46. (7's.)

1 Give us room that we may dwell,
    Zion's children cry aloud;
  See their numbers how they swell!
    How they gather like a cloud!

2 O! how bright the morning seems!
   Brighter from so dark a night;
Zion is, like one that dreams,
   Filled with wonder and delight!

3 Lo! thy sun goes down no more;
   God Himself will be thy light;
All that caused thee grief before
   Buried lies in endless night.

4 Zion, now arise and shine!
   Lo, thy light from heaven is come!
These that crowd from far are thine,
   Give thy sons and daughters room.

HYMN 47. (P.M.)

1 Come, come, ye Saints, no toil nor labor fear,
   But with joy wend your way;
Though hard to you this journey may appear,
   Grace shall be as your day.
'Tis better far for us to strive,
Our useless cares from us to drive.
Do this, and joy your hearts will swell—
All is well! all is well!

2 Why should we mourn, or think our lot is hard?
   'Tis not so; all is right!

Why should we think to earn a great reward,
  If we now shun the fight?
Gird up your loins, fresh courage take,
Our God will never us forsake;
And soon we'll have this tale to tell—
All is well! all is well!

3 We'll find the place which God for us prepared,
  Far away in the West;
Where none shall come to hurt nor make afraid;
  There the Saints will be blessed.
We'll make the air with music ring,
Shout praises to our God and King;
Above the rest these words we'll tell—
All is well! all is well!

4 And should we die before our journey's through,
  Happy day! all is well!
We then are free from toil and sorrow too;
  With the just we shall dwell.
But if our lives are spared again
To see the Saints, their rest obtain,
O how we'll make this chorus swell—
All is well! all is well!

HYMN 48. (L.M.)

1 O Lord! responsive to Thy call,
  In life or death, whate'er befall,
  Our hopes for bliss on Thee depend;
  Thou art our everlasting Friend.

2 Though life be short, and trials seem
  To darken its protracted gleam,
  Though friends forsake and foes contend,
  Thou art our everlasting Friend.

3 Death may distract our present joy,
  And all our brightest hopes destroy;
  Yet these will in the future tend
  To prove Thee still our faithful Friend.

4 O let Thy Spirit with us dwell,
  That we in future worlds may tell
  How we o'ercame, and, in the end,
  Make Thee our everlasting Friend.

HYMN 49. (8's & 7's.)

1 Sweetly may the blessed Spirit
    On each faithful bosom shine;
  May we every grace inherit;
    Lord, we seek a boon divine;

2 Since Thou tak'st delight in giving,
    We would gladly ask and have;
Gratefully each gift receiving,
    In His name who died to save.

3 We would seek t' obtain His favor,
    Which is better far than gold;
May His gospel prove the savor
    Of a life that's ne'er been told.

4 Passing honors, transient pleasures,
    Boasting joys forever flown;
May we seek to lay up treasures
    Where decay shall ne'er be known.

5 Savior, to assist our weakness,
    Let Thy grace sufficient be;
Bless with wisdom and with meekness,
    Till we full salvation see.

HYMN 50. (C.M.)

1 My God, the spring of all my joys,
    The life of my delights,
The glory of my brightest days,
    And comfort of my nights!

2 In darkest shades, if Thou appear,
    My dawning is begun;
Thou art my soul's bright morning star,
    And Thou my rising sun.

3 The op'ning heavens around me shine
   With beams of sacred bliss,
If Jesus shows His mercy mine,
   And whispers, I am His!

4 My soul would leave this heavy clay
   At that transporting word;
Run up with joy the shining way,
   To see and praise my Lord.

5 Fearless of hell and ghastly death,
   I'll break through every foe;
The wings of love and arms of faith
   Would bear me conq'ror through.

HYMN 51. (L.M.)

1 Great God, indulge my humble claim;
   Thou art my hope, my joy, my rest;
The glories that compose Thy name
   Stand all engaged to make me blest.

2 Thou great and good, Thou just and wise,
   Thou art my Father and my God,
And I am thine by sacred ties,
   Thy son, thy servant, bought with blood.

3 With early feet I love t' appear
    Among Thy Saints, and seek Thy face;
  Oft have I seen Thy glory there,
    And felt the power of sovereign grace.

4 I'll lift my hands, I'll raise my voice,
    While I have breath to pray or praise;
  This work shall make my heart rejoice
    Throughout the remnant of my days.

HYMN 52. (8-7's.)

1 Where the voice of friendship's heard,
  Sounding like a sweet toned bird;
  Where the holy notes inspire
  With devotion's pure desire;
  Where fond actions speak the soul;
  Where true love finds no control :
  Where the sons of God agree,
  There may all the faithful be.

2 Where the weary find a home;
  Where the wild deer fearless roam;
  Where the mellow fruit-tree grows;
  Where the golden harvest flows;
  Where the bee, the grape and kine
  Yield their honey, milk and wine;
  Where the curse from earth shall flee,
  There may all the faithful be.

3 Where the Temple-block is laid;
  Where no foe shall e'er invade;
  Where the Priesthood's power shall claim
  All that heaven and earth can name;
  Where the judge by justice rules;
  Where the couns'lors are not fools;
  Where the poor shall judgment see,
  There may all the faithful be.

4 Where the dew-distilling hills
  Drop their fatness in the rills;
  Where the river, lake and stream
  With their finny myriads teem;
  Where the shade trees round the fold
  Shield from heat and winter's cold;
  Where all nature sings with glee,
  There may all the faithful be.

HYMN 53. (8's, 7's, & 4.)

1 Lo! the mighty God appearing,—
    From on high Jehovah speaks!
  Eastern lands the summons hearing,
    O'er the west His thunder breaks.
      Earth behold Him!
    Universal nature shakes.

2 Zion, all its light unfolding,
   God in glory shall display;
Lo! He comes! nor silence holding,
   Fire and clouds prepare His way;
     Tempests round Him
Hasten on the dreadful day.

3 To the heavens His voice ascending,
   To the earth beneath He cries;
Souls immortal now descending,
   Let the sleeping dust arise!
     Rise to judgment;
Let Thy throne adorn the skies.

4 Gather first my Saints around me,
   Those who to my cov'nant stood—
Those who humbly sought and found me
   Through the dying Savior's blood.
     Blest Redeemer!
Dearest sacrifice to God!

5 Now the heavens on high adore Him,
   And His righteousness declare;
Sinners perish from before Him,
   But His Saints His mercies share.
     Just His judgment:
God, Himself the judge, is there.

HYMN 54. (8's & 7's.)

1 Should you feel inclined to censure
  Faults you may in others view,
Ask your own heart, ere you venture,
  If that has not failings too.

2 Let not friendly vows be broken;
  Rather strive a friend to gain ;
Many a word in anger spoken
  Finds its passage home again.

3 Do not, then, in idle pleasure,
  Trifle with a brother's fame ;
Guard it as a valued treasure,
  Sacred as your own good name.

4 Do not form opinions blindly;
  Hastiness to trouble tends ;
Those of whom we thought unkindly,
  Oft become our warmest friends.

HYMN 55. (6-8's.)

1 I'll praise my Maker while I've breath ;
And when my voice is lost in death,
  Praise shall employ my noblest powers.
My days of praise shall ne'er be past
While life and thought and being last,
  Or immortality endures.

2 Happy the man whose hopes rely
On Israel's God; He made the sky,
And earth, and sea, with all their train.
His truth forever stands secure;
He saves oppressed ones, feeds the poor,
And none shall find His promise vain.

3 The Lord gives eyesight to the blind;
The Lord supports the fainting mind;
He sends the troubled conscience peace.
He helps the stranger in distress,
The widow and the fatherless,
And grants the prisoner sweet release.

4 I'll praise Him while He lends me breath,
And when my voice is lost in death,
Praise shall employ my nobler powers;
My days of praise shall ne'er be past
While life and thought and being last,
Or immortality endures.

HYMN 56. (L.M.)

1 Praise ye the Lord! 'tis good to raise
Your hearts and voices in His praise;
His nature and His works invite
To make this duty our delight.

2 He formed the stars, those heavenly flames,
   He counts their numbers, calls their names;
   His wisdom's vast and knows no bound—
   A deep where all our thoughts are drowned.

3 Sing to the Lord, exalt Him high,
   Who spreads His clouds along the sky;
   There He prepares the fruitful rain,
   Nor lets the drops descend in vain.

4 He makes the grass the hills adorn,
   And clothes the smiling fields with corn;
   The beasts with food His hands supply,
   And the young ravens when they cry.

5 And Saints are lovely in His sight;
   He views His children with delight;
   He sees their hope, he knows their fears,
   And looks and loves His image there.

HYMN 57. (L.M.)

1 Away with our fears! the glad morning appears,
   When an heir of salvation was born!
   From Jehovah I came, for His glory I am,
   And to Him I with singing return.

2 With thanks I rejoice in Thy Fatherly choice,
　　Of my state and condition below;
　If of parents I came who honored Thy name,
　　'Twas Thy wisdom appointed it so.

3 I sing of Thy grace from my earliest days,
　　Ever near to allure and defend;
　Hitherto Thou hast been my preserver from sin,
　　And I trust Thou wilt save to the end.

4 Oh, the infinite cares and temptations and snares,
　　Thy hand hath conducted me through;
　Oh, the blessings bestowed by a bountiful God,
　　And the mercies eternally new.

5 What a mercy is this, what a heaven of bliss,
　　How unspeakably happy am I!
　Gathered into the fold, with Thy people enrolled,
　　With Thy people to live and to die.

6 All honor and praise to the Father of grace,
　　To the Spirit and Son I return;
　The work I'll pursue He hath set me to do
　　And rejoice that I ever was born.

HYMN 58. (P.M.)

1 O Saints, have ye seen o'er yon mountain's
    proud height,   [beaming?
  The day-star of promise so brilliantly
Its rays shall illumine the world with its
    light,   [ing,
  And the ensign of Zion, exultingly stream-
All nations invite to walk in its light,
And join to maintain the proud standard
    of right;
The standard of Zion! O long may it
    wave
O'er the land of the free and the home of the
    brave.

2 Our motto is peace, and the triumph of
    right :   [dawning,
  And we joyfully hail the Millennial
When men can emerge from a long dreary
    night
  And bask in the sunbeams of Zion's bright
    morning,
The white flag so rare, still floating in air,
Proclaims 'mid the mountains that peace is
    now there;
Let the standard of Zion eternally wave
O'er the land of the free and the home of
    the brave.

3 Though earth and its treasures should melt
   in the fire ;
  The planets be riven with the trumpet's
   loud thunder;
The sunlight of heaven wax dim and expire,
  And the vail of eternity parted asunder:
Yet firm and unshaken the truth shall re-
   main,   [shall reign,
And the heirs of the Priesthood for ever
And the standard of Zion eternally wave
O'er the land of the free and the home of
   the brave.

HYMN 59. (P.M.)

1 O, say, what is truth? 'Tis the fairest gem
  That the riches of worlds can produce;
And priceless the value of truth will be, when
The proud monarch's costliest diadem
  Is counted but dross and refuse.

2 Yes, say, what is truth? 'Tis the brightest
   prize
  To which mortals or Gods can aspire :
Go search in the depths where it glittering
   lies,
Or ascend in pursuit to the loftiest skies;
  'Tis an aim for the noblest desire.

3 The sceptre may fall from the despot's grasp,
   When with winds of stern justice he copes,
  But the pillar of truth will endure to the last,
  And its firm-rooted bulwarks outstand the rude blast
  And the wreck of the fell tyrant's hopes.

4 Then, say, what is truth? 'Tis the last and the first,
   For the limits of time it steps o'er :
  Though the heavens depart, and the earth's fountains burst,   [the worst,
  Truth, the sum of existence, will weather
  Eternal, unchanged, evermore.

HYMN 60. (C.M.)

1 Father, how wide Thy glories shine!
   How high Thy wonders rise!   [signs,
  Known through the earth by thousand
   By thousands, through the skies.

2 Those mighty orbs proclaim Thy power,
   Their motions speak Thy skill,
  And on the wings of every hour
   We read Thy patience still.

3 But when we view Thy strange design
   To save rebellious worms,
  Where justice and compassion join
   In their divinest forms;

4 There the whole Deity is known,
   Nor dare a creature guess
 Which of the glories brightest shone,
   The justice or the grace.

5 O may I bear some humble part
   In truth's immortal song!
 Wonder and joy shall tune my heart,
   And love command my tongue.

HYMN 61. (9's & 8's.)

1 Up, awake, ye defenders of Zion!
   The foe's at the door of your homes:
 Let each heart be the heart of a lion,
   Unyielding and proud as he roams.
 Remember the wrongs of Missouri;
   Forget not the fate of Nauvoo;
 When the God-hating foe is before you,
   Stand firm, and be faithful and true.

2 By the mountains our Zion's surrounded;
   Her warriors are noble and brave;
 And their faith on Jehovah is founded,
   Whose power is mighty to save.
 Opposed by a proud, boasting nation,
   Their numbers, compared, may be few;
 But their union is known through creation,
   And they've always been faithful and true.

3 Shall we bear with oppression forever?
　　Shall we tamely submit to the foe,
　While the ties of our kindred they sever?
　　Shall the blood of our Prophets still flow?
　No! the thought sets the heart wildly beating;
　　Our vows at each pulse we renew,
　Ne'er to rest till our foes are retreating,
　　While we remain faithful and true!

4 Though, assisted by legions infernal,
　　The plundering wretches advance,
　With a host from the regions eternal,
　　We'll scatter their troops at a glance.
　Soon "the Kingdom" will be independent;
　　In wonder the nations will view
　The despised ones in glory resplendent;
　　Then let us be faithful and true!

HYMN 62.　(2-8's & 6.)

1 Hail! bright millennial day of rest,
　　When earth's restored and Saints are blest,
　　　Secured from Bab'lon's doom:
　Gathered afar from every clime,
　　To spend that blissful, happy time,
　　　Where vernal pastures bloom.

2 There tyranny no more shall reign,
  Nor famished children beg in vain
    For what their fathers toiled ;
  Nor proud men spurn the poor man's lot—
  Alike they'll share, and envy not
    What selfishness hath spoiled.

3 There equity and truth will shine,
  And all revere God's laws divine,
    Nor fear oppressor's wrong ;
  Each shall possess his dwelling fair,
  And eat the fruits the vineyards bear.
    Rejoicing all day long.

4 O heavenly paradise of joy!
  Where meek ones live without annoy,
    Far, far away from Gentile strife ;
  Where God and angels love to dwell
  With the redeemed, whose anthems swell
    The song of endless life.

5 O God ! may all Thy Saints endure,
  That we Thy blessings may secure
    Within Thy promised rest;
  Then shall our tongues, in ceaseless praise,
  Extol Thy name through endless days
    On earth when it is blest.

HYMN 63. (2-8's & 6.)

1 O happy home! O blest abode!
Where Saints communion hold with God,
  Without a doubt or fear:
When shall I reach thy fertile plains,
Ascend the mount where virtue gains
  A more exalted sphere?

2 In Babylon I loathe to stay;
Dire are the evils day by day
  Within her precincts dark.
Truth's brighter rays expose the night,
Each honest mind receives the light,
  And presses to the mark.

3 No love but heaven's would I receive—
No other doctrines e'er believe,
  Than those by Jesus taught.
I'd trace the path His footsteps trod—
The only way that leads to God;
  All other ways are naught.

4 Come, sacred power, exert thy sway,
To guide in the celestial way,
  Tradition to forsake,
My Savior's footsteps to pursue.
Each selfish principle subdue,
  To righteousness awake.

5 Let friends or kindred, near or dear,
  Exert their power; no servile fear
    Shall e'er my spirit bind,
  Though now affections warmer rise
  In souls enlightened from the skies,
    And blest with Jesus' mind.

6 For he hath said (whose lips divine
  To naught but truth did e'er incline—
    Jesus, our only theme),
  Whoe'er their kindred better love
  Than me, my heart can ne'er approve,
    Nor him will I esteem.

7 But those who in my righteous cause
  Are firm, nor seek the world's applause,
    My glory shall partake.
  Then, brethren, sisters, patient share
  His sufferings; this will us prepare,
    And sinners perfect make.

HYMN 64. (L. M.)

1 Shall I, for fear of feeble man,
  The Spirit's course in me restrain?
  Or, undismayed in deed and word,
  Be a true witness for the Lord?

2 Awed by a mortal's frown, shall I
  Conceal the word of God most high?
  How then before Thee shall I dare
  To stand, or how Thine anger bear?

3 Shall I, to soothe the godless throng,
  Soften Thy truths and smooth my tongue,
  To gain earth's gilded toys, or flee
  The cross, my God, endured by Thee?

4 What, then, is he whose scorn I dread,
  Whose wrath or hate makes me afraid?
  A man—an heir of death—a slave
  To sin—a bubble on the wave.

5 Yea, let men rage, since Thou wilt spread
  Thy shadowing wings around my head,
  Since, in all pain, Thy tender love
  Will still my sure refreshment prove.

6 Savior of men, Thy searching eye
  Doth all my inmost thoughts descry;
  Doth aught on earth my wishes raise,
  Or the world's pleasures, or its praise?

7 The love of Christ doth me constrain
  To seek the wand'ring souls of men;
  With cries, entreaties, tears to save,
  To snatch them from the gaping grave.

8 For this let men revile my name,
  No cross I shun, I fear no shame—
  All hail reproach ! and welcome pain !
  Thy terrors only, Lord, restrain.

9 My life, my blood, I here present,
  If for Thy truth they may be spent;
  Fulfil Thy sovereign counsel, Lord ;
  Thy will be done, Thy name adored.

10 Give of Thy strength, O God of power:
   Then let winds blow, or thunders roar,
   Thy faithful witness will I be:
   'Tis fixed—I can do all through Thee.

HYMN 65. (8's & 7's.)

1 Glorious things are sung of Zion,
    Enoch's city seen of old,
  Where the righteous, being perfect,
    Walked with God in streets of gold.
  Love and virtue, faith and wisdom,
    Grace and gifts were all combined ;
  As himself each loved his neighbor ;
    All were one in heart and mind.

2 There they shunned the power of Satan,
    And observed celestial laws;
For in Adam-ondi-Ahman
    Zion rose where Eden was.
When beyond the power of evil,
    So that none could covet wealth,
One continual feast of blessings
    Crowned their days with peace and health.

3 Then the towers of Zion glittered
    Like the sun in yonder skies,
And the wicked stood and trembled,
    Filled with wonder and surprise:
Then their faith and works were perfect—
    Lo, they followed their great Head;
So the city went to heaven,
    And the world said Zion's fled!

4 When the Lord returns with Zion,
    And we hear the watchman cry,
Then we'll surely be united,
    And we'll all see eye to eye;
Then we'll mingle with the angels,
    And the Lord will bless His own;
Then the earth will be as Eden,
    And we'll know as we are known.

HYMN 66. (C.M.)

1 How are Thy servants blest! O Lord,
    How sure is their defense!
Eternal wisdom is their guide,
    Their help, Omnipotence.

2 In foreign realms and lands remote,
    Supported by Thy care,
Through burning climes they pass unhurt,
    And breathe in tainted air.

3 When by the dreadful tempest borne
    High on the broken wave,
They know Thou art not slow to hear,
    Nor impotent to save.

4 The storm is laid, the winds retire,
    Obedient to Thy will;
The sea that roars at Thy command,
    At Thy command is still.

5 In midst of dangers, fear and death,
    Thy goodness we'll adore;
We'll praise Thee for Thy mercies past,
    And humbly hope for more.

HYMN 67. (2-8's & 7.)

1 Before all lands in east or west,
   We love the land of Zion best!
     With God's choice gifts 'tis teeming.
   There Seers and Prophets as of old,
   The mysteries of heaven unfold,
     Through holy Priesthood streaming.

2 'Mong Zion's homesteads joys abound,
   True souls of worth are gather'd round
     Their Prophet and their leader;
   No tyrant there shall dare to reign;
   For God will Zion's rights maintain
     And on to glory speed her.

3 Before all people, east or west,
   We love the Saints of God the best—
     A race of noble spirits:
   Then let us with God's laws comply,
   That when His Saints are raised on high,
     Their joys we may inherit.

4 We'll gladly join with heart and hand,
   A chosen, true, devoted band,
     To conquer Satan's powers:
   To endless life we'll onward press,
   For God will all our wrongs redress,
     And victory is ours.

HYMN 68. (P.M.)

1 What, though the Gentiles wildly rage
    And over us black war clouds lower?
'Tis with our God they madly wage
    A war, and seek to break His power;
Like surges dashing 'gainst the rock
In wild confusion--vain the shock:
    Satan, thy reign is o'er!

2 While in its infancy, in vain
    They sought to crush the germ of truth;
And shall they now their purpose 'gain
    When in the vigor of its youth?
No, brethren, no! Though hosts combine
In dread array, God's arm divine
    Will shield us from their wrath!

3 Though few we seem, yet, glorious thought
    With God and angels we are one.
In the same cause for which they fought,
    Undaunted, we are battling on:
Assured of triumph in the end—
That soon our foes shall humbly bend,
    And victory be won!

4 Then let us still on God depend,
    And on His promises rely—
That Zion's cause He will defend,
    Our hopes confirm, our foes destroy;

With truth within and God o'erhead,
We know no fear, we feel no dread—
 The reign of peace is nigh!

HYMN 69. (4-6's & 2-8's.

1 O Lord, our sovereign King,
   Our infant charge now bless;
 Him to Thee now we bring,
   O grant him now Thy grace.
 And to us, Lord, may grace be given
 To train this gift of Thine for heaven.

2 A gift of richest worth,
   On us Thou hast bestowed,
 O may he, from his birth,
   Follow the Lord his God;
 Sustained by grace divine, may he
 Be taught, O Lord, our God, by Thee.

3 Thou art his Father, Lord;
   His spirit pure and free,
 Obedient to Thy word,
   Rejoiced in heaven with Thee.
 O may the spirit Thou hast given,
 Return unsullied back to heaven.

HYMN 70. (8's & 7's,.)

1 We have met, dear friends and brethren,
    Our respects to pay to one
Who has left this world of sorrow,
    And to glory now has gone.

2 Since our friend has gone to glory,
    Though we mourn, yet we'll rejoice:
For he sought the way to heaven,
    And made Jesus Christ his choice.

3 To all those who sleep in Jesus,
    Death is sweet and has no sting;
But to haughty, stubborn sinners,
    Death, of terrors is the king.

4 Then, poor sinner, stop and ponder
    Well your steps as you pass on,
Lest you end your days in sorrow
    When your fancied joys are gone.

HYMN 71. (C.M.D.)

1 The Gospel standard high is raised
    On Zion's sacred shore;
Rejoice, ye Saints, our God be praised.
    Satan's long reign is o'er;
The bright Millennium dawns at last,
    The faithful shall be free,
Christ will reward their trials past
    With immortality.

2 Earth, to proud loveliness restored,
   Shall echo back the strains
From thousand heavenly choirs poured,
   When Christ in triumph reigns:
Refulgent in the beams of love,
   The Savior's presence given,
The Saints on earth, with Saints above,
   Shall share the rest of heaven.

HYMN 72. (S.M.)

1 Lord, make Thy mercy known
   To all who here reside;
Let heaven's blessing rest upon
   And with them all abide.

2 My Master and my God
   Has sent me forth to bless
And preach to all His holy word,
   And dwell with sons of peace.

3 A son of peace dwells here,
   Thy grace to him be given,
On earth may he Thy law revere,
   And dwell with Thee in heaven.

HYMN 73. (6-8's.)

1 Captain of Israel's host, and guide
   Of all who seek the land above,
Beneath the shadow we abide—
   The cloud of Thy protecting love.

Our strength, Thy grace, our rule, Thy word,
Our end, the glory of the Lord.

2 By Thy unerring Spirit led,
   We shall not in the desert stray;
We shall no other guidance need,
   Nor miss our providential way;
As far from danger as from fear,
While love, almighty love, is near.

HYMN 74. (6-8's.)

1 When quiet in my house I sit,
   Thy book be my companion still;
My joy, Thy sayings to repeat,
   Talk o'er the records of Thy will,
And search the oracles divine,
Till every heart-felt word be mine.

2 O may Thy gracious word divine
   Subject of all our converse be;
So will the Lord His foll'wer join,
   And walk and talk, Himself, with me;
So shall my heart His presence prove,
And burn with everlasting love.

3 Oft as I lay me down to rest,
   O may the reconciling word
Sweetly compose my weary breast,
   While on the bosom of my Lord
I sink in blissful dreams away
And visions of eternal day.

4 Rising to sing my Savior's praise,
    Thee may I publish all day long
And let Thy precious word of grace
    Flow from my heart and fill my tongue;
Fill all my life with purest love,
And join me to the Church above.

HYMN 75. (8's & 7's.)

1 Go, ye messengers of heaven,
    Chosen by divine command;
Go and publish free salvation
    To a dark, benighted land.

2 Go to island, vale and mountain,
    To fulfil the great command;
Gather out the sons of Jacob,
    To possess the promised land.

3 When your thousands all are gathered,
    And their prayers for you ascend,
And the Lord has crowned with blessings
    All the labors of your hand,

4 Then the song of joy and transport
    Will from every land resound;
Then the heathen, long in darkness,
    By their Savior will be crowned.

HYMN 76. (L.M.)

From all that dwell below the skies
Let the Creator's praise arise:
Let the Redeemer's name be sung
Through every land, by every tongue.

Eternal are Thy mercies, Lord,
Eternal truth attends Thy word;
Thy praise shall sound from shore to shore,
Till suns shall rise and set no more.

HYMN 77. (P.M.)

Israel, awake from thy long, silent slumber,
  Shake off the fetters that bound thee so long;
Chains of oppression! we'll break them asunder,
  And join with the ransomed in victory's song!

    Rise! for the time has come,
    Israel must gather home;
High on the mountains the ensign we see;
    Fallen is Gentile power,
    Soon will their reign be o'er,
    Tyrants shall rule no more,
Israel is free!

2 Tremble, ye nations of Gentiles, for yonder
　Hosts of the despot, in battle array;
Engines of war shake the earth with their
　　thunder,
　　The bright sword is drawn and the sheath
　　thrown away.

　　Sound the alarm of war
　　Through nations near and far,
Sending its tones over land, over sea.
　　Zion shall dwell in peace,
　　Israel will still increase,
　　Liberty ne'er shall cease,
Israel is free!

3 Come to the land of the mountain and
　　prairie,
　　Gather in strength to our home in the west:
Free are her sons as the breeze round the
　　aerie—
　　Birth-place of prophets and home of the
　　blest.

　　Come, let us haste away,
　　Here we'll no longer stay;
Zion, thy beauties we're yearning to see.
　　Saints, raise the heavenly song,
　　Join with the ransomed throng,
　　Angels the notes prolong,
Israel is free!

HYMN 78. (C.M.D.)

O Lord, do Thou Thy gifts bestow
  On these adopted ones;
And let Thy Spirit largely flow,
  And own them as Thy sons;
E'en as Thy promise was of old,
  One Spirit they should have,
That all things past it should unfold,
  With present light to save.

In dreams and visions of the night,
  Revealing things to come,
Unfolding wisdom's purest light,
  Of Zion's happy home;
New tongues declaring heavenly power,
  Interpretations plain,
That Saints may know in this dread hour,
  Thy gifts are come again.

Give faith to realize the same,
  With truth Thy Saints inspire,
And own Thy people's faith to claim
  All else their hearts desire.
Let wisdom, knowledge, truth and love
  Lead them in Thy commands,
That they may prove Thy gifts divine,
  By laying on of hands.

HYMN 79. (P.M.)

1 For the strength of the hills we bless Thee
   Our God, our fathers' God ;
Thou hast made Thy children mighty,
   By the touch of the mountain sod ;
Thou hast led Thy chosen Israel
   To freedom's last abode—
For the strength of the hills we bless Thee,
   Our God, our fathers' God.

2 At the hands of foul oppressors,
   We've borne and suffered long ;
Thou hast been our help in weakness,
   And Thy power hath made us strong ;
Amid ruthless foes, outnumbered,
   In weariness we trod ;
For the strength of the hills we bless Thee,
   Our God, our fathers' God.

3 Thou hast led us here in safety,
   Where mountain bulwark stands,
As the guardian of the loved ones
   Thou hast brought from many lands:
For the rock and for the river,
   The valley's fertile sod;
For the strength of the hills we bless Thee,
   Our God, our fathers' God.

Here the wild bird swiftly darts on
   His quarry from the heights,
And the red untutored Indian
   Seeketh here his rude delights;
But the Saints for Thy communion
   Have sought the mountain sod :
For the strength of the hills we bless Thee,
   Our God, our fathers' God.

We are watchers of a beacon
   Whose light must never die ;
We are guardians of an altar
   'Midst the silence of the sky :
Here the rocks yield founts of courage,
   Struck forth as by Thy rod :
For the strength of the hills we bless Thee,
   Our God, our fathers' God.

For the shadow of Thy presence,
   Around our camp o'erspread ;
For the cañon's ragged defiles,
   And the beetling crags o'erhead ;
For the snows and for the torrents,
   And for our burial sod ;
For the strength of the hills we bless Thee
   Our God, our fathers' God.

HYMN 80. (8's.)

1 This God is the God we adore,
   Our faithful, unchangeable friend,
   Whose love is as large as His power,
   And knows not beginning nor end.

2 'Tis Jesus, the first and the last,
   Whose Spirit shall guide us safe home
   We'll praise Him for all that is past,
   And trust Him for all that's to come.

HYMN 81. (8's, 7's & 4,)

1 Men of God! go, take your stations:
   Darkness reigns throughout the earth
   Go, proclaim among all nations
   Joyful news of heavenly birth:
     Bear the tidings
   Angels brought again to earth.

2 Of the Gospel not ashamed,
   As the power of God to save;
   Go, and let it be proclaimed
   To the free-born and the slave—
     Blessed freedom,
   Such as Zion's children have.

3 When exposed to fears and dangers,
   Jesus will His own defend:
   Borne afar 'midst foes and strangers,
   Jesus will appear your friend,
     And His presence
   Shall be with you to the end.

HYMN 82. (8's, 7's & 4.)

1 O'er the gloomy hills of darkness,
    Look, my soul, be still and gaze;
All the promises do travail
    With the glorious day of grace;
        Blessed Jubilee!
Let thy glorious morning dawn.

2 Let the Indian and the negro,
    Let the rude barbarian see
That divine and glorious conquest
    Once obtained on Calvary;
        Let the Gospel
Soon resound from pole to pole.

3 Kingdoms wide that sit in darkness,
    Grant them, Lord, the glorious light;
And from eastern coast to western,
    May the morning chase the night—
        Chase the darkness
From their long benighted eyes.

4 Fly abroad, thou mighty Gospel,
    Win and conquer, never cease;
So Immanuel's fair dominions
    Shall extend and still increase,
        Till the kingdoms
Of the world are all His own.

HYMN 83. (L.M.)

1 Come hither, all ye weary souls;
   Ye heavy-laden sinners, come;
I'll give you rest from all your toils,
   And raise you to My heavenly home.

2 They shall find rest that learn of Me—
   I am of meek and lowly mind;
But passion raises like the sea,
   And pride is restless as the wind.

3 Blest is the man whose shoulders take
   My yoke, and bear it with delight:
My yoke is easy to his neck,
   My grace shall make the burden light.

4 Then, Lord, we humbly venture near,
   By unbelief and guilt oppressed
Henceforth, Thine easy yoke we'll bear,
   And seek in Thee the promised rest.

HYMN 84. (C.M.D.)

1 When sickness clouds the soul with grief,
   And wastes this mortal frame,
Thine ord'nance brings our woes relief,
   Through faith in Thy great name.

Anointed with the holy oil,
  And by Thy servants blest,
We wait upon Thy promised aid
  In all that we request.

2 If sin has brought Thy scourging rod
  May we Thy chast'ning prove,
And learn, from all we suffer here,
  Thy precepts more to love.
But should the enemy of man
  Distracting cares intrude,
Give faith to overcome the ill,
  And triumph in the good.

3 When darkness and temptations come,
  And worldly cares arise,
And sickness, poverty and death
  Our fondest hope surprise,
O let Thy Spirit's light impart
  Renewing strength divine,
That we may rise above them all,
  And know that we are Thine.

HYMN 85. (L.M.)

1 Before Jehovah's glorious throne,
  Ye nations bow with sacred joy:
Know that the Lord is God alone,
  He can create, and He destroy.

2 His sovereign power, without our aid,
    Made us of clay and formed us men ;
And when like wand'ring sheep we strayed,
    He brought us to His fold again.

3 We'll crowd Thy gates with thankful songs,
    High as the heavens our voices raise;
And earth, with her ten thousand tongues,
    Shall fill Thy courts with sounding praise.

4 Wide as the world is Thy command,
    Vast as eternity Thy love ;
Firm as a rock Thy truth shall stand,
    When rolling years shall cease to move.

HYMN 86. (L.M.)

1 Dark is the human mind, when bound
    In unbelief's degrading thrall ;
Debased the soul that scorns the sound
    Of truth's ennobling, saving call.

2 Lord, give us faith, that we may rend
    The monster's clutch from every breast—
A faith by which we may ascend
    From truth to truth to reach Thy rest.

3 Faith that shall pierce doubt's thickest gloom
    And see Thy glory shining clear;
Faith that through life, and 'yond the tomb,
    Shall find Thy promised blessings near.

HYMN 87. (8's & 7's, 6 lines.)

1 Satan's empire long has flourished,
   Satan's power has mighty grown,
Nations bend beneath his sceptre,
   Princes bow before his throne:
Sons of Zion, up! arouse you!
   Satan's might must be o erthrown.

2 Buckle on Jehovah's armor:
   Truth, the weapon; faith, the shield;
Endless lives await the victors;
   God is with us; sin must yield:
On, and fear not! earth's redemption
   Waits the issue of the field.

HYMN 88. (P, M.)

1   Go! ye Gospel heralds, go!
   To the lands of darkness go,
   And to every clime proclaim:
   Christ will come on earth to reign—
And then we'll go, we'll go to Zion's land.

2   In a gallant ship we ride,
   Sent to spread the Gospel wide,
   And its glorious tidings roll
   O'er the earth from pole to pole—
And then we'll go, we'll go to Zion's land.

3 Come, ye faithful Saints, and sing
   Sacred songs to Zion's King:
   Take the crown so freely given
   By the mighty Lord of heaven;
And then sit down, sit down with Christ
   the Lamb.

HYMN 89. (7's.)

1 Lord, we come before Thee now,
   At Thy feet we humbly bow;
   Do not Thou our suit disdain;
   Shall we seek Thee, Lord, in vain?

2 In Thine own appointed way,
   Now we seek Thee; here we stay:
   Lord, from hence we would not go,
   Till a blessing Thou bestow.

3 Send some message from Thy word,
   That may joy and peace afford;
   Comfort those who weep and mourn,
   Let "the time of love" return.

4 Grant, we all may seek and find
   Thee, our gracious God and kind;
   Heal the sick, the captive free,
   Let us all rejoice in Thee.

HYMN 90. (L.M.)

1 Come, dearest Lord, descend and dwell,
   By faith and love, in every breast;
Then shall we know and taste and feel
   The joys that cannot be expressed.

2 Come, fill our hearts with inward strength;
   Make our enlarging souls possess
And learn the height and breadth and length
   And depth of Thine unmeasured grace.

3 Now to the God whose power can do
   More than our thoughts or wishes know,
Be everlasting honor done,
   By all the Church, through Christ, His Son.

HYMN 91. (C.M.)

1 Come, Thou desire of all Thy Saints,
   Our humble strains attend,
While with our praises and complaints,
   Low at Thy feet we bend.

2 When we Thy wondrous glories hear,
   And all Thy sufferings trace,
What sweetly awful scenes appear!
   What rich, unbounded grace!

3 How should our songs, like those above,
   With warm devotion rise!
How should our soul, with wings of love,
   Mount upward to the skies!

4 But ah! the song, how cold it flows!
   How languid our desire!
How faint the sacred passion glows,
   Till Thou the heart inspire!

5 Come, Lord, Thy love alone can raise
   In us the heavenly flame!
Then shall our lips resound Thy praise,
   Our hearts adore Thy name.

HYMN 92. (8's & 7's.)

1 Lo! the Gentile chain is broken;
   Freedom's banner waves on high;
List, ye nations! by this token
   Know that our redemption's nigh.

2 See, on yonder distant mountain,
   Zion's standard wide unfurled;
Far above Missouri's fountain,
   Lo, it waves for all the world.

3 Freedom, peace and full salvation
   Are the blessings guaranteed—
Liberty to every nation,
   Every tongue, and every creed.

4 Come, ye Christian sects, and pagan,
    Pope and Protestant and priest;
Worshipers of God, or Dagon,
    Come to freedom's glorious feast.

5 Come, ye sons of doubt and wonder,
    Indian, Moslem, Greek or Jew;
All your shackles burst asunder;
    Freedom's banner waves for you.

6 Cease to persecute each other,
    Join the covenant of peace;
Be to all a friend, a brother;
    This will bring the world release.

7 Lo! the King, whom we desire,
    Prince of Peace, shall come to reign;
Sound again, ye heavenly choir,
    Peace on earth, good will to men.

HYMN 93. (8's & 7's.)

1 As the dew, from heaven distilling,
    Gently on the grass descends,
And revives it, thus fulfiling
    What Thy providence intends,

2 Let Thy doctrine, Lord, so gracious,
    Thus descending from above,
Blest by Thee, prove efficacious
    To fulfil Thy work of love.

3 Lord, behold this congregation;
    Precious promises fulfil;
  From Thy holy habitation
    Let the dews of life distill.

4 Let our cry come up before Thee;
    Thy sweet Spirit shed around:
  So the people shall adore Thee,
    And confess the joyful sound.

HYMN 94. (L.M.)

1 O Thou, at whose almighty word
    The glorious night from darkness sprung,
  Thy quick'ning influence afford,
    And clothe with power the preacher's tongue.

2 As when of old the waters flowed
    Forth from the rock at Thy command,
  In vain had Moses waved his rod
    Without Thy wonder-working hand.

3 As when the walls of Jericho
    Down to the earth at once were cast,
  It was Thy power that brought them low,
    And not the trumpet's feeble blast.

4 Thus we would in the means be found,
   And thus on Thee alone depend:
O make the Gospel's joyful sound
   Effectual to the promised end.

HYMN 95. (C.M.)

1 Once more we come before our God—
   Once more His blessing ask:
O may not duty seem a load,
   Nor worship prove a task!

2 May we receive the word we hear,
   Each in an honest heart;
And keep the sacred treasure there,
   Nor ever with it part.

3 Awake, O heavenly wind, awake!
   Refreshing breezes, blow;
Let every plant Thy power partake,
   And all the garden grow.

4 Revive the parched with soft'ning showers,
   The cold with warmth divine;
The benefit shall all be ours,
   And all the glory Thine.

HYMN 96. (C.M.)

1 With joy we own Thy servants, Lord,
    Thy ministers below,
Ordained to spread Thy truth abroad,
    That all Thy name may know.

2 O may they now, and ever, keep
    Their eyes intent on Thee!
Do Thou, Great Shepherd of the sheep,
    Their bright example be.

3 With plenteous grace their hearts prepare,
    To execute Thy will;
And give them patience, love, and care,
    And faithfulness and skill.

4 Inspire their minds with ardent zeal,
    Thy flock to feed and teach;
And may they live, and may they feel
    The truths they're called to preach.

5 As showers refresh the thirsty plain,
    So let their labors prove:
By them extend Thy righteous reign—
    The reign of truth and love.

HYMN 97. (7's.)

1 Hark! the song of jubilee,
   Loud as mighty thunders roar;
Or the fulness of the sea,
   When it breaks upon the shore.

2 See! Jehovah's banner's furled,
   Sheathed His sword, He speaks, 'tis done!
Now the kingdoms of this world
   Are the kingdoms of His Son.

3 He shall reign from pole to pole,
   With supreme unbounded sway;
He shall reign when, like a scroll,
   Yonder heavens have passed away.

4 Hallelujah! for the Lord,
   God omnipotent, shall reign;
Hallelujah! let the word
   Echo round the earth and main.

HYMN 98. (8's, 7's, 4.)

1 Lord, dismiss us with Thy blessing;
   Fill our hearts with joy and peace;
Let us each, Thy love possessing,
   Triumph in redeeming grace.
      O refresh us,
Traveling through this wilderness.

2 Thanks we give, and adoration,
   For the Gospel's joyful sound;
May the fruits of Thy salvation
   In our hearts and lives abound.
      Ever faithful
To the truth may we be found.

HYMN 99. (C.M.)

1 May we, who know the joyful sound,
   Still practice what we know—
The hearers of the word be found,
   And doers of it, too.

2 By acts of mercy let us show
   We have not heard in vain,
But kindly feel another's woe,
   And long to ease his pain.

3 The widow's heart shall share our joy;
   The orphan and oppressed
Shall see we love the sweet employ
   To succor the distressed.

4 We'll teach the ignorant the way
   True happiness to know,
And how the vilest sinners may
   Escape eternal woe.

5 Thankful that we the Gospel hear,
   And love the joyful sound,
 O may the sacred fruits appear,
   And in our lives abound.

HYMN 100. (L.M.)

1 Though now the nations sit beneath
  The darkness of o'erspreading death,
  God will arise with light divine,
  On Zion's holy towers to shine.

2 That light shall glance on distant lands;
  And heathen tribes, in joyful bands,
  Come with exulting haste to prove
  The power and greatness of His love.

3 Lord, spread the triumphs of Thy grace;
  Let truth and righteousness and peace,
  In mild and lovely forms, display
  The glories of the latter day.

HYMN 101. (L.M.)

1 The rising sun has chased the night
  And brought again the cheering light;
  This mercy multiplies our days
  And calls us to renew our praise.

2 We laid us down and sweetly slept;
  The Lord our souls in safety kept;
  We wake, His goodness to proclaim
  And sing new honors to His name.

3 We know not what His will ordains;
  But 'tis our joy that Jesus reigns;
  Though dangers, snares and foes abound,
  Protecting arms will us surround.

4 Teach us to walk with Thee to-day,
  And ever keep Thy holy way;
  Ourselves to Thee we would resign,
  Content to know that we are Thine.

HYMN 102. (7's & 6's D.)

1 We'll sing the songs of Zion,
    Though now in distant lands;
  Our harps shall not be lying
    Untouched by skilful hands.
  The winds in flitting breezes
    Will sweep the sounding string,
  And tune its lofty praises,
    If Saints neglect to sing.

2 O Zion! long predicted
    By Seers and Saints of old,
  The blessings they depicted
    And beauties we behold;

Thy walls are sure salvation,
   And all Thy gates are praise,
A peaceful habitation
   In these the latter days.

When Zion reached the mountains,
   They gave their golden store,
And all the limpid fountains
   Did healing virtues pour.
Where reigned but gloomy sadness
   And earth seemed in repose,
Resounds the song of gladness,
   And blossoms forth the rose.

4 From Zion's favored valley,
   Shines Gospel light and grace,
And millions soon will rally
   Around her gath'ring place,
Where every law of heaven,
   Its councils do design
To save us, will be given
   Within her sacred shrine.

5 The wealth and scenes of splendor
   That worldly minds may prize
Are nothing to the grandeur
   Of Zion, in our eyes.
Adorned with all the graces
   Of Him who called thee forth,

We love thy chosen places
  Alone of all the earth.

6 Yes! Zion's theme and spirit
  Our bosoms will inspire,
Until we shall inherit
  The land that we desire;
Where Saints from every nation
  Will swell the strain anew,
Ascribe the great salvation
  To Him who brought us through.

HYMN 103. (C.M.)

1 O God, Thou great, Thou good, Thou wise,
  Eternal is Thy name;
Thy power hath reared the lofty skies,
  And built creation's frame.

2 The universe Thy praise declares;
  Through all its vast design,
Thy glorious handiwork appears,
  Thy power and wisdom shine.

3 And ere creation had its birth,
  Thou didst devise a plan,
Amidst Thy glorious works on earth,
  To form Thy creature, man.

4 Thou mad'st him monarch of the world,
    And didst his kindred own,
Until by sin down he was hurled,
    And forfeited his throne.

5 Then Satan seized the power of state,
    And did his sceptre sway;
Brought down the strong, the wise, the great,
    To mingle with the clay.

6 Thus did the foe his malice glut,
    And all the world enslave,
The spirit in the prison shut—
    The body in the grave.

Second Part.

1 But hark! how sweet the joyful sound!
    How grateful to the ear!
A ransom for the lost is found;
    A Savior doth appear.

2 He meets Apollyon, lays him low
    In every deadly strife,
Becomes victorious o'er his foe,
    And reigns the Prince of Life.

3 The power of death and hell He shakes,
    His power and love to show;
The prison door asunder breaks,
    And lets the captive go.

4 Then, for this cause the body bends
    Beneath the liquid wave,
In favor of our kindred friends
    Who slumber in the grave;

5 That, through the law our God doth give,
    All who obedient prove
Together on the earth may live,
    When all is peace and love.

6 Thus, for the dead we do baptize,
    That when Christ comes again,
All Zion from beneath may rise,
    And in His kingdom reign.

7 The Saints below and Saints above
    And Saints on earth agree
To praise, in unison and love,
    Our God eternally.

HYMN 104. (8's & 7's.)

1 See, the mighty angel flying!
    See, he speeds his way to earth
To proclaim the blessed Gospel,
    And restore the ancient faith.

2 Hear, O men, the proclamation!
    Cease from vanity and strife;

Hasten to receive the Gospel,
   And obey the words of life.

3 Soon the earth will hear the warning;
   Then the judgments will descend!
Oh! before the days of sorrow,
   Make the Lord of Hosts your friend.

4 Then, when dangers are around you,
   And the wicked are distressed;
You, with all the Saints in Zion,
   Shall enjoy eternal rest.

HYMN 105.   (8's, 7's & 4.)

1 On the mountain's top appearing,
   Lo! the sacred herald stands!
Welcome news to Zion bearing,
   Zion, long in hostile lands.
      Mourning captive!
   God Himself shall loose thy bands.

2 Lo! thy sun is risen in glory!
   God Himself appears thy Friend;
All thy foes shall flee before thee;
   Here their boasted triumphs end.
      Great deliverance
   Zion's King vouchsafes to send.

3 Enemies no more shall trouble;
   All thy wrongs shall be redressed;
For thy shame thou shalt have double,
   In thy Maker's favor blest.
     All thy conflicts
End in an eternal rest.

HYMN 106. (S.M.)

1 And are we yet alive,
   And see each other's face?
Glory and praise to Jesus give
   For his redeeming grace.

2 Preserved by power divine,
   To full salvation here;
Again in Jesus' praise we join,
   And in His sight appear.

3 What troubles have we seen,
   What conflicts have we passed;
What strifes without and fears within,
   Since we assembled last!

4 But out of all, the Lord
   Hath brought us by His love,
And still He doth His help afford,
   And hides our life above.

5 Then let us make our boast
    Of His redeeming power,
Which saves us to the uttermost,
    Till we can sin no more.

6 Let us take up the cross,
    Till we the crown obtain;
And gladly reckon all things loss,
    So we may Jesus gain.

HYMN 107. (C.M.)

1 All praise to our redeeming Lord,
    Who joins us by His grace,
And bids us, each to each restored,
    Together seek His face.

2 He bids us build each other up;
    And, gathered into one,
To our high calling's glorious hope
    We hand in hand go on.

3 The gift which he on one bestows,
    We all delight to prove;
The grace through every vessel flows
    In purest streams of love.

4 E'en now we think and speak the same,
    And cordially agree,
United all, through Jesus' name,
    In perfect harmony.

5 We all partake the joy of one,
    The common peace we feel—
A peace to sensual minds unknown,
    A joy unspeakable.

6 And if our fellowship below
    In Jesus be so sweet,
What heights of rapture shall we know
    When round His throne we meet.

HYMN 108. (S.M.)

1 How beauteous are their feet
    Who stand on Zion's hill!
Who bring salvation on their tongues,
    And words of peace reveal!

2 How charming is their voice!
    How sweet their tidings are:
"Zion, behold thy Savior King,
    He reigns triumphant here!"

3. How blessed are our ears
    That hear this joyful sound,
Which kings and prophets waited for,
    And sought, but never found!

4 How blessed are our eyes
    That see this heavenly light,

So long desired by seers and kings,
Who died without the sight.

5 The watchmen join their voice,
And tuneful notes employ;
Jerusalem breaks forth in songs,
And deserts learn the joy.

6 The Lord makes bare His arm
Through all the earth abroad:
Let every nation now behold
Their Savior and their God.

HYMN 109. (L.M.)

1 Praise ye the Lord! my heart shall join
In work so pleasant, so divine,
Now, while the flesh is my abode,
And when my soul ascends to God.

2 Praise shall employ my noblest powers
While immortality endures;
My days of praise shall ne'er be past,
While life and thought and being last.

3 Why should I make a man my trust?
Princes must die and turn to dust;
Their breath departs, their pomp and power
And thoughts, all vanish in an hour.

4 Happy the man whose hopes rely
On Israel's God! He made the sky
And earth and seas, with all their train;
And none shall find His promise vain.

5 His truth forever stands secure;
He saves th' oppressed, He feeds the poor;
He sends the troubled conscience peace,
And grants the captive sweet release.

6 The Lord hath eyes to give the blind;
The Lord supports the sinking mind;
He helps the stranger in distress,
The widow and the fatherless.

7 He loves the Saints, He knows them well,
But turns the wicked down to hell:
Thy God, O Zion, ever reigns—
Praise Him in everlasting strains.

HYMN 110. (L.M.)

1 Salvation! sacred word of love,
  Of joy and peace, of truth and light,
First heard in holy courts above,
  Far from this fallen sphere of night.

2 Salvation! thrilling, sweetest sound
  That can intelligences greet!
Anthem of heaven, from thence it found
  Its way through space to man's retreat.

3 Salvation! precious, priceless boon,
   Gift of the Gods by God, the Son!
 Creation, shout! for know that soon
   The heavens and earth will join in one.

4 Salvation, like a stream of life,
   Is rushing round our favored earth:
 The meek, illumed, emerged from strife,
   Are joyous in the heavenly birth.

5 Salvation! let the echo ring
   To every people, kindred, tongue,
 For Christ shall reign, of kings a King:
   The "Golden Age" has then begun.

6 Salvation brings a jubilee;
   Anon the Saints shall toil no more;
 Rejoice! in triumph bend the knee,
   The crown put on, the Lord adore.

HYMN 111. (C.M.D.)

1 To Thee, O God, we do approach
    With gratitude and praise,
  To know Thy character is such
    As 'twas in former days;
  That Thou hast made us in Thy form,
    Though now we fallen be,
  Yet still in fashion though a worm,
    We'll rise to life with Thee.

2 Thou dwellest in the purest light,
    Where truth and glory shine;
The brightest of perfected power
    And majesty are Thine.
But man, alas! how prone to sin,
    How subject to disease;
Deformed and fallen, touched by death,
    He bends to every breeze.

3 Yet thanks be to Thy holy name
    For truth restored to earth;
That man, though lost, can now regain
    A pure celestial birth;
And be restored to Thy bright form
    Through constancy and love,
To see Thy face, and live with Thee
    On earth and heaven above.

4 What honor, glory, and renown
    Await the pure in heart,
When they, transformed to be like Thee,
    Shall all Thy light impart,
And have eternal lives to give,
    Kingdoms and worlds to sway,
And neither pain nor sorrow feel
    Through all eternity.

HYMN 112. (L.M.)

Lord, Thou hast searched and seen me thro';
Thine eye commands with piercing view

My rising and my resting hours,
My heart and flesh, with all their powers.

2 My thoughts before they are my own,
Are to my God distinctly known;
He knows the words I mean to speak,
Ere from my opening lips they break.

3 Within Thy circling powers I stand;
On every side I find Thy hand;
Awake, asleep, at home, abroad,
I am surrounded still with God.

4 Amazing knowledge, vast and great!
What large extent, what lofty height!
My soul, with all the powers I boast,
Is in the boundless prospect lost.

5 O may these thoughts possess my breast,
Where'er I rove, where'er I rest;
Nor let my weaker passions dare
Consent to sin, for God is there.

HYMN 113. (2-8's & 6.)

1 Come, let us purpose with one heart
To follow virtue, and impart
　　The bliss of life below,
That we industriously may live,
And by our labor have to give,
　　As Gospel precepts show.

2 With diligence we'll still pursue
  Those acts of grace and mercy due
    To toil-worn, lab'ring man!
  We'll aid the helpless and secure
  The means of life to bless the poor,
    And help them all we can.

3 Neat in our dress, not sumptuous clad,
  Nor vain, nor sombre, looking sad;
    In all our garments clean.
  Fresh in our bodies, whole our clothes,
  And free from all the Spirit loathes;
    Nor proud, nor lowly mean.

4 Still working with our heads or hands,
  We may lay up for just demands,
    And honestly provide
  For heavenly light and earthly things,
  That we may have the joy that brings
    A heaven to each fireside.

HYMN 114. (L.M.)

1 With all the powers of heart and tongue,
  I'll praise my Maker in my song;
  Angels shall hear the notes I'll raise,
  Approve the song, and join the praise.

2 I'll sing Thy truth and mercy, Lord,
I'll sing the wonders of Thy word;
Not all Thy works and names below
So much Thy power and glory show.

3 To God I cried when troubles rose;
He heard me and subdued my foes;
He did my rising fears control,
And strength diffused through all my soul.

4 Amidst a thousand snares I stand,
Upheld and guided by Thy hand:
Thy words my fainting soul revive,
And keep my dying faith alive.

HYMN 115. (L.M.)

1 How sweet communion is on earth
With those who've realized the birth
Of water—who the Spirit's power
Receive, in genial quick'ning shower.

2 To such these sacred emblems prove
Blest source of purity and love;
They onward to perfection press,
Observing laws of righteousness.

3 Each evil they are taught to shun,
Remembering God's incarnate Son,
Who suffered death on Calvary,
To set the contrite sinner free.

4 Who e'er His sacred laws obey,
And are baptized without delay—
To such the promise still is given:
This is the door that opens heaven.

5 May we who thus have humbly fled
To Jesus as our living head,
This day our solemn vows record,
And ever live to serve the Lord,

6 Till we around the sacred board,
The marriage supper of our Lord,
Behold Him crowned, our vict'ries bring
And own Him as our sovereign King.

HYMN 116. (C.M.)

1 Ye sons of men, a feeble race,
   Exposed to every snare,
Come, make the Lord your dwelling-place,
   And try and trust His care.

2 No ill shall enter where you dwell;
   Or, if the plague comes nigh
And sweeps the wicked down to hell,
   'Twill raise the Saints on high.

3 He'll give His angels charge to keep
   Your feet in all your ways;
To watch your pillows while you sleep,
   And guard your happy days.

4 Their hands shall bear you, lest you fall
   And dash against the stones :
Are they not servants at His call,
   And sent to aid His sons?

5 Because on Me they set their love,
   I'll save them, saith the Lord ;
I'll bear the joyful souls above
   Destruction and the sword.

6 My grace shall answer when they call,
   In trouble I'll be nigh ;
My power shall help them when they fall,
   And raise them when they die.

HYMN 117. (P.M.)

1 Up! arouse thee, O beautiful Zion,
   Wake, awake, hear the warder's deep cry,
For the season of slumber hath ended,
   And the spoiler is watchful and nigh.
With courage elate, and heart to be great,
   All deadly incumbrance cast down,
Gird on for the fight, your armor so bright,
   For the prize is a glorious crown.

2 Up! arouse thee, O beautiful Zion,
   Give the mammon care-clouds to the wind;
When the bugle's shrill summons is—Rally!
   They are cowards that linger behind.

You've foes to o'ercome in each heart and
    home,
  Then fixed be your purpose, and high,
With God at your head, O feel not dismayed,
  But go forward to conquer, or die.

3 Who would shrink from the glorious battle,
    With so dazzling a guerdon in view?
  If so base as to herd with the traitor,
    It is, dastard! not sparkling for you.
With nerve strong as steel, and soul that
    can feel,
  Stand firm for the pure and the brave;
Be foremost in right, and trust in God's
    might—
  'Tis such heroes that heaven will save.

4 Lo! destruction hangs over the nations,
    Though not seen by the unholy throng;
  But there soon will be death in the echoes
    Of the gathering, ominous storm!
Then arouse Thee, O beautiful Zion,
    Wake, awake, 'tis the warder's deep cry,
For the season of slumber hath ended,
  And the spoiler is watchful and nigh.

HYMN 118. (L.M.)

1 When God's own people stand in need,
    His goodness will provide supplies;
  Thus when Elijah faints for bread,
    A raven to his succor flies.

2 At God's command, with speedy wings,
    The hungry bird resigns its prey,
  And to the holy Prophet brings
    The needful portion day by day.

3 This method may be counted strange,
    But happy was Elijah's lot;
  For nature's course shall sooner change
    Than God's dear children be forgot.

4 This wonder has been oft renewed,
    And Saints by sweet experience find
  Their evils overruled for good,
    Their foes to friendly deeds inclined.

5 Who shall distrust that mighty hand
    That rules with universal sway;
  Which nature's laws can countermand
    And feed us by the birds of prey?

HYMN 119. (L.M.)

1 O Lord, do Thou in heaven seal
    The solemn pledge these two have made;
  And may they still be blest to feel
    The obligations on them laid!

2 O may their constancy of heart
    Be like the Master whom they serve;
  Nor aught in life ill thoughts impart,
    To cause them from this bond to swerve.

3 Give them intelligence and light
    To build their future bliss upon,
  And may Thy laws, by day and night,
    Unite their hearts, in Thee, as one!

4 And may this solemn rite inspire
    The flame of pure connubial love,
  And virtue prompt each pure desire
    In all the scenes of life to move.

5 As many streams unite in one,
    And, flowing deep, their channels wear;
  May they in love glide smoothly on,
    Still gathering as they onward bear.

6 And, like each tributary stream,
    Their loving offspring still increase,
  Till generations countless, seem
    An ocean full of love and peace.

7 Give him the power to guard and shield
    This helpmate of his future life;
  May she by softer passions yield
    The solace of a virtuous wife.

8 And when their mortal course is run,
    May still this bond of love endure,
  Till they, celestial honors won,
    Live with the loving and the pure.

HYMN 120. (L.M.)

How great the joy, that promised day,
When the disciples met to pray;
Through the whole house the Spirit came,
And crowned their heads like tongues of flame.

The gifts dispensed that happy hour,
Attended with convincing power,
And every soul assembled there
In his own tongue the truth did hear.

Endowed thus with the power of God,
The Savior's words they spread abroad:
Go and declare the glorious scheme;
My Gospel shall mankind redeem.

He that believes what you proclaim,
And is baptized in Jesus' name,
My pard'ning ordinance shall have,
And feel the Gospel's power to save.

The honest soul, though learned, or rude,
Shall by these tidings be subdued,
And shall receive the Comforter,
That by your hands I will confer.

6 Satan shall tremble at his loss,
 And man, enraged, defend his cause ;
 But ye shall win your widening way,
 Till nations shall the truth obey.

HYMN 121. (L.M.)

1 Sweet is the work, my God, my King,
 To praise Thy name, give thanks and sing,
 To show Thy love by morning light,
 And talk of all Thy truths at night.

2 Sweet is the day of sacred rest,
 No mortal care shall seize my breast;
 O may my heart in tune be found,
 Like David's harp of solemn sound.

3 My heart shall triumph in my Lord,
 And bless His works, and bless His word;
 Thy works of grace, how bright they shine,
 How deep Thy councils, how divine !

4 But oh ! what triumph shall I raise
 To Thy dear name, through endless days,
 When in the realms of joy I see
 Thy face in full felicity.

5 Sin, my worst enemy before,
 Shall vex my eyes and ears no more;
 My inward foes shall all be slain,
 Nor Satan break my peace again.

6 Then shall I see and hear and know
All I desired and wished below,
And every power find sweet employ
In that eternal world of joy.

HYMN 122. (8's & 7's.)

1 O awake! my slumbering minstrel,
Let my harp forget its spell;
Say, O say, in sweetest accents,
Zion prospers, all is well.

2 Strike a chord unknown to sadness,
Strike, and let its numbers tell,
In celestial tones of gladness,
Zion prospers, all is well.

3 Zion's welfare is my portion,
And I feel my bosom swell
With a warm, divine emotion,
When she prospers, all is well.

4 Zion, lo! thy day is dawning.
Though the darksome shadows swell,
Faith and hope prelude the morning,
Thou art prospering, all is well.

5 Thy swift messengers are treading
Thy high courts where princes dwell,
And thy glorious light is spreading;
Zion prospers, all is well.

HYMN 123. (4-6's & 2-8's.)

1 High on the mountain top
   A banner is unfurled,
 Ye nations now look up,
   It waves to all the world
In Deseret's sweet, peaceful land;
On Zion's mount behold it stand!

2 For God remembers still
   His promise made of old,
 That he on Zion's hill
   Truth's standard would unfold!
Her light should there attract the gaze
Of all the world in latter days.

3 His house shall there be reared,
   His glory to display;
 And people shall be heard
   In distant lands to say,
We'll now go up and serve the Lord,
Obey His truth, and learn His word.

4 For there we shall be taught
   The law that will go forth,
 With truth and wisdom fraught,
   To govern all the earth;
Forever there His ways we'll tread,
And save ourselves with all our dead.

5 Then hail to Deseret,
    A refuge for the good,
And safety for the great,
    If they but understood
That God with plagues will shake the world
Till all its thrones shall down be hurled.

6 In Deseret doth truth
    Rear up its royal head ;
Though nations may oppose,
    Still wider it shall spread ;
Yes, truth and justice, love and grace,
In Deseret find ample place.

HYMN 124 (L.M.)

1 Oh, fear not, brother, years of peace,
    Of joy celestial thine shall be ;
Thy grievous trials then will cease,
    And thou shalt rest contentedly.

2 Oh, care not, brother, let the day
    Of fierce, contentious struggle come ;
'Twill serve to hasten thee away
    To Zion's consecrated home.

3 Hope ! hope on, brother, happier times
    Await but now thine own command
In Zion's pure and peaceful climes,
    In Ephraim's fair and goodly land,

4 Oh, weep not, sister, dry thy tears!
    Thy Savior bids them cease to flow;
Forego thy griefs, forget thy fears,
    And hope far brighter days to know.

5 Cheer! cheer thee, sister, heavenly joy
    Shall fill thy soul, shall swell thy heart;
Thy peace shall be without alloy;
    This is indeed the better part.

6 See, see! my brother, see! it breaks—
    The dawn of earth's Sabbatic day;
It's genial light prophetic speaks:
    "Thy toils will soon have passed away."

7 Look! look thou, sister, see the Sun
    Of Zion's glory shines for thee;
Hark! hear His voice—the Holy One:
    "Come all ye faithful, reign with me."

HYMN 125. (2-8's & 6's.)

1 Except the Lord conduct the plan,
  The best concerted schemes are vain
    And never can succeed;
We spend our wretched strength for naught,
But if our works in Thee are wrought,
    They shall be blest indeed.

2 Lord, if Thou didst, Thyself, inspire
Our souls with this intense desire
   Thy goodness to proclaim,
Thy glory—if we now intend,
O let our deeds begin and end
   Complete in Jesus' name.

3 In Jesus' name, behold we meet,
Far from an evil world retreat,
   And all its frantic ways;
One thing alone resolved to know,
To square our useful lives below
   By reason and by grace.

4 Not in the tombs we pine to dwell,
Nor in the dark monastic cell,
   By vows and grates confined;
Freely to all ourselves we give,
Constrained by Jesus' love to live
   The servants of mankind.

5 Now, Jesus, now Thy love impart,
To govern each devoted heart,
   And fit us for Thy will;
Deep founded in the truth of grace,
Build up the rising Church, and place
   The city on the hill.

6 O may our love and faith abound,
  And may our lives to all around
    With purest lustre shine,
  That all around our works may see,
  And give the glory, Lord, to Thee,
    The heavenly light divine.

HYMN 126. (3-8's & 7's.)

1 The trials of the present day
  Require the Saints to watch and pray,
  That they may keep the narrow way
    To the celestial glory.

2 For even Saints may turn aside,
  For fear of ills that may betide,
  Or else induced by worldly pride,
    And lose celestial glory.

3 O'er rugged cliffs and mountains high,
  Through sunless vales the path my lie,
  Our faith and confidence to try
    In the celestial glory.

4 Why should we fear, though cowards say
  Old Anak's hosts in ambush lay,
  Or there's a lion in the way,
    To the celestial glory.

5 Fear not, though life should be at stake,
  But think how Jesus for our sake
  Endured, that we might yet partake
    Of the celestial glory.

6 We here may sometimes suffer wrong,
  But when we join with Enoch's throng,
  We'll loudly echo victory's song
    In the celestial glory.

7 What though, by some who seem devout,
  Our names as evil are cast out,
  If honor clothe us round about
    In the celestial glory.

8 Be steadfast, and with courage hold
  The key of God's eternal mould,
  That will the mysteries unfold
    Of the celestial glory.

9 O let your hearts and hands be pure,
  And faithful to the end endure,
  That you the blessings may secure
    Of the celestial glory.

10 With patience cultivate within
   Those principles averse to sin,
   And be prepared to enter in
     To the celestial glory

1 Then let the times and seasons fly,
  And bring the glorious period nigh
  When Zion will be raised on high
    In the celestial glory.

HYMN 127. (C.M.)

1 God of all consolation, take
    The glory of Thy grace;
  Thy gifts to Thee we render back
    In ceaseless songs of praise.

2 Through Thee we here together came,
    In singleness of heart;
  We meet, O Jesus, in Thy name,
    And in Thy name we part.

3 We part in body, not in mind;
    Our minds continue one,
  And, each to each in Jesus joined,
    We hand in hand go on.

4 Our souls are in Thy mighty hand,
    Lord, keep us faithful still!
  That we with all Thy Saints may stand
    On Zion's holy hill.

HYMN 128. (8's & 6's.)

1 "Now," is the voice that nature breathes
   To those her book can read;
The changeful cloud, the fleeting beam,
The fading rose, the restless stream
   Confirm her warning creed.

2 "Now," is the word that wisdom writes
   On palace, hall and bower;
The buried past from hope is free,
The future, what is that to thee?
   Improve the present hour.

3 "Now," saith the Spirit from on high,
   "Now," saith the page sublime;
To-morrow hath its load of cares,
To-morrow's hand no promise bears
   Of the "accepted time."

4 Now, though another morn may rise
   In purple and in gold,
Thine eye made dim by failing breath
And shrouded in the dust of death,
   May not its light behold.

5 Now, not to-morrow, oh, my soul,
   Obey thy Maker's call,
Lest darkly on the scroll of fate
Stand forth the fearful doom—too late
   And thou, bereft of all.

HYMN 129. (C.M.)

1 Sing to the great Jehovah's praise,
    All praise to him belongs;
  Who kindly lengthens out our days
    Demands our choicest songs.

2 His providence has brought us through
    Another various year;
  We all, with vows and anthems new,
    Before our God appear.

3 Father, thy mercies past we own,
    Thy still continued care;
  To Thee presenting, through Thy Son,
    Whate'er we have or are.

4 Our lips and lives shall gladly show
    The wonders of thy love,
  While on in Jesus' steps we go
    To seek Thy face above.

5 Our residue of days or hours,
    Thine, wholly Thine shall be:
  And all our consecrated powers
    A sacrifice to Thee.

6 Till Jesus in the clouds appears
    To Saints on earth, forgiven.
  And brings the grand Sabbatic years,
    The Jubilee of heaven.

HYMN 130. (8's & 7's.)

1 O my Father, Thou that dwellest
    In the high and glorious place!
When shall I regain Thy presence,
    And again behold Thy face?
In Thy holy habitation,
    Did my spirit once reside?
In my first primeval childhood,
    Was I nurtured near Thy side?

2 For a wise and glorious purpose
    Thou hast placed me here on earth,
And withheld the recollection
    Of my former friends and birth.
Yet ofttimes a secret something
    Whispered, "You're a stranger here;"
And I felt that I had wandered
    From a more exalted sphere.

3 I had learned to call Thee Father,
    Through Thy Spirit from on high;
But, until the Key of Knowledge
    Was restored, I knew not why.
In the heavens, are parents single?
    No; the thought makes reason stare!
Truth is reason; truth eternal
    Tells me, I've a mother there.

4 When I leave this frail existence,
   When I lay this mortal by,
 Father, Mother, may I meet you
   In your royal courts on high?
 Then, at length, when I've completed
   All you sent me forth to do,
 With your mutual approbation
   Let me come and dwell with you.

HYMN 131. (C.M.)

1 Weep not for him that's dead and gone,
   Nor to despair be driven;
 Your child is saved through Jesus Christ;
   He now has gone to heaven.

2 Gone far away from wicked men,
   To mingle with the good, [white
 Who washed their robes and made them
   In Christ's atoning blood.

3 'Tis true the trial was severe
   That tore him from your breast;
 But oh! do not desire him now,
   For he has gone to rest.

4 When lying suff'ring on your knee,
   Your heart did almost break,
 And oft you sighed and wept aloud,
   Oh! could my child but speak!

5 And still you mourn his absence now,
    And think you are bereaved;
Sister, look up, thy God is good!
    Woman, thy child is saved!

6 Shed not for him the bitter tear,
    Nor yield to sore regret;
'Tis but the casket that lies here,
    The gem is sparkling yet.

HYMN 132. (8's & 7's.)

1 The night is wearing fast away,
    A stream of light is dawning,
Sweet harbinger of that bright day,
    The fair Millennial morning.

2 Gloomy and dark the night has been,
    And long the way and dreary;
And sad the weeping Saints are seen,
    And faint, and worn, and weary.

3 Ye mournful pilgrims, cease your tears
    And hush each sigh of sorrow;
The light of that bright morn appears,
    The long Sabbatic morrow.

4 Lift up your heads! behold from far
    A flood of splendor streaming!
It is the bright and Morning Star,
    In living lustre beaming.

5 And see that star-like host around
   Of angel bands, attending;
Hark! hark! the trumpet's joyful sound,
   'Mid shouts of triumph blending.

6 He comes, the Bridegroom promised long;
   Go forth with joy to meet him,
And raise the new and nuptial song,
   In cheerful strains, to greet Him.

7 Adorn thyself, the feast prepare,
   While bridal strains are swelling;
He comes, with thee all joys to share
   And make this earth His dwelling.

HYMN 133. (L.M.)

1 Great God, attend while Zion sings
The joy that from Thy presence springs;
To spend one day with Thee on earth
Exceeds a thousand days of mirth.

2 Might I enjoy the meanest place
Within Thy house, O God of grace;
Not tents of ease, nor thrones of power
Should tempt my feet to leave Thy door.

3 God is our sun—He makes our day;
  God is our shield—He guards our way
  From all assaults of hell and sin,
  From foes without and fears within.

4 All needful grace will God bestow,
  And crown that grace with glory too;
  He gives us all things, and withholds
  No blessings due to upright souls.

5 Our God, our King, whose sovereign sway
  The glorious hosts of heaven obey,
  (And devils at Thy presence flee)
  Blest is the man that trusts in Thee.

HYMN 134. (C.M.)

1 O God! our help in ages past,
    Our hope for years to come,
  Our shelter from the stormy blast,
    And our eternal home.

  Under the shadow of Thy throne,
    Still may we dwell secure!
  Sufficient is Thine arm alone,
    And our defense is sure.

3 Before the hills in order stood,
    Or earth received her frame,
  From everlasting Thou art God,
    To endless years, the same.

4 A thousand ages in Thy sight
    Are like an evening gone,
  Short as the watch that ends the night
    Before the rising sun.

5 The busy tribes of flesh and blood,
    With all their cares and fears,
  Are hurried downward by the flood,
    And lost in following years.

6 Time, like an ever-rolling stream,
    Bears all his sons away;
  Thy fly, forgotten, as a dream
    Dies at the opening day.

7 O God! our help in ages past,
    Our hope for years to come,
  Be Thou our guide while life shall last,
    And our perpetual home.

HYMN 135. (8's & 7's.)

1 May the grace of Christ our Savior,
    And the Father's boundless love,
  With the Holy Spirit's favor,
    Rest upon us from above.

2 Thus may we abide in union
    With each other and the Lord,
    And possess, in sweet communion,
    Joys which earth can not afford.

HYMN 136. (L.M.)

Praise God, from whom all blessings flow;
Praise Him, all creatures here below;
Praise Him above, ye heavenly host;
Praise Father, Son and Holy Ghost.

HYMN 137. (2-6's 4 & 3-6's 4.)

1 Glory to God on high;
    Let heaven and earth reply,
        Praise ye His name.
    His love and grace adore,
    Who all our sorrows bore;
    Sing loudly evermore,
        Worthy the Lamb!

2 Jesus, our Lord and God,
    Bore sin's tremendous load;
        Praise ye His name!

Tell what His arm has done,
What spoils from death He won;
Sing His great name alone;
  Worthy the Lamb!

3 Let all the hosts above
Join in one song of love,
  Praising His name.
To Him ascribed may be
Honor and majesty,
Through all eternity;
  Worthy the Lamb!

HYMN 138. (C.M.)

To Father, Son and Holy Ghost,
  The God whom we adore,
Be glory, as it was, is now,
  And shall be evermore.

HYMN 139. (P.M.)

1 Your sweet little rose-bud has left you
  To bloom in a holier sphere;
He that gave it, in wisdom bereft you;
  Then why should you cherish a tear?

2 Your babe in the grave is not sleeping,
  She joined her dear sisters above;
The bright beings now have them in keeping,
  In mansions of beauty and love.

3 They're treasures you've laid up in heaven;
   They're only removed from your sight;
 To your bosom again they'll be given,
   With fulness of joy and delight.

4 They've gone where life's ills cannot find them;
   They're safe from each danger and snare;
 O how cruel the love that would bind them
   To years of affliction and care.

5 Look up and you'll find consolation
   Which God by His Spirit will give;
 And through faith, the rich manifestation:
   Those gems, your sweet children, yet live.

HYMN 140. (L.M.)

1 'Twas on that dark, that solemn night,
   When powers of earth and hell arose
 Against the Son, e'en God's delight,
   And friends betrayed Him to His foes.

2 Before the mournful scene began,
   He took the bread, and blessed, and broke;
 What love through all His actions ran!
   What wondrous words of grace He spoke:

3 "This is My body slain for sin ;
　　Receive and eat the living food ;"
　Then took the cup and blessed the wine:
　　" 'Tis the new covenant of my blood."

4 For us His precious blood was spilt,
　　To purchase pardon for our guilt ;
　When for our sins He suff'ring dies,
　And gives His life a sacrifice,

5 "Do this," He cries, "Till time shall end,
　Remembering your dying Friend ;
　Meet at My table and record
　The love of your departed Lord."

6 Jesus, Thy feast we celebrate,
　　We show Thy death, we sing Thy name,
　Till Thou return, and we shall eat
　　The marriage supper of the Lamb.

HYMN 141. (4-6's & 2-8's.)

1 Arise, my soul, arise,
　　Shake off thy guilty fears ;
　The bleeding sacrifice
　　In my behalf appears ;
　Before the throne my surety stands,
　My name is written on His hands.

2 He ever lives above,
    For me to intercede,
His all-redeeming love,
    His precious blood to plead ;
His blood atoned for all our race,
And sprinkles now the throne of grace.

3 Five bleeding wounds He bears,
    Received on Calvary ;
They pour effectual prayers,
    They strongly speak for me ;
"Forgive him, oh! forgive!" they cry,
"Nor let the ransomed sinner die!"

4 The Father hears Him pray,
    His dear Anointed One ;
He cannot turn away
    From His beloved Son ;
His Spirit answers to the blood,
And tells me I am born of God.

5 To God I'm reconciled,
    His pard'ning voice I hear ;
He owns me for His child,
    I can no longer fear ;
With confidence I now draw nigh,
And "Father, Abba, Father," cry.

HYMN 142.   (8's, 7's & 4.)

1 Israel, Israel, God is calling ;
    Calling thee from lands of woe ;
  Babylon the great is falling,
    God shall all her towers o'erthrow.
      Come to Zion
    Ere His floods of anger flow.

2 Israel, Israel, God is speaking ;
    Hear your great Deliv'rer's voice !
  Now a glorious morn is breaking
    For the people of His choice.
      Come to Zion,
    And within her walls rejoice.

3 Israel, angels are descending
    From celestial worlds on high,
  And to man their powers extending,
    That the Saints may homeward fly.
      Come to Zion,
    For your coming Lord is nigh.

4 Israel, Israel, canst thou linger
    Still in error's gloomy ways ?
  Mark how judgment's pointing finger
    Justifies no vain delays !
      Come to Zion,
    Zion's walls shall ring with praise.

HYMN 143. (L.M.)

1 He died! the Great Redeemer died,
    And Israel's daughters wept around;
A solemn darkness veiled the sky,
    A sudden trembling shook the ground.

2 Come, Saints, and drop a tear or two
    For Him who groaned beneath your load;
He shed a thousand drops for you,
    A thousand drops of precious blood.

3 Here's love and grief beyond degree;
    The Lord of glory died for men;
But lo! what sudden joys were heard!
    Jesus, though dead, revived again.

4 The rising Lord forsook the tomb,
    In vain the tomb forbade Him rise:
Cherubic legions guard Him home,
    And shout Him welcome to the skies.

5 Wipe off your tears, ye Saints, and tell
    How high your great Deliv'rer reigns;
Sing how He triumphed over hell,
    And how He'll bind your foe in chains.

6 Say, live forever, wondrous King,
    Born to redeem, and strong to save!
Then ask the monster, Where's thy sting?
    And where's thy vict'ry, boasting grave?

HYMN 144. (7's & 6's D.)

1 O God, th' Eternal Father,
    Who dwells amid the sky !
In Jesus' name we ask Thee
    To bless and sanctify,
If we are pure before Thee,
    This bread and cup of wine,
That we may all remember
    That offering divine.

2 That sacred, holy off'ring,
    By man least understood,
To have our sins remitted,
    And take His flesh and blood;
That we may ever witness
    The suff'rings of Thy Son,
And always have His Spirit,
    To make our hearts as one.

3 When Jesus, the Anointed,
    Descended from above,
And gave Himself a ransom
    To win our souls with love,
With no apparent beauty,
    That men should Him desire,
He was the promised Savior,
    To purify with fire.

4 How infinite that wisdom,
    The plan of holiness,
That made salvation perfect,
    And veiled the Lord in flesh,
To walk upon His footstool,
    And be like man, almost,
In His exalted station,
    And die, or all was lost!

5 'Twas done; all nature trembled;
    Yet, by the power of faith,
He rose as God triumphant,
    And broke the bands of death,
And rising conqu'ror, "captive
    He led captivity,"
And sat down with the Father
    To all eternity.

6 He is the true Messiah
    That died and lives again;
We look not for another,
    He is the Lamb once slain;
He is the stone and shepherd
    Of Israel scattered far,
The glorious branch from Jesse,
    The bright and morning star.

7 Again, He is that Prophet
   That Moses said should come,
Raised up among His brethren,
   To call the righteous home;
And all that will not hear Him,
   Shall feel His chast'ning rod,
Till wickedness is ended,
   As saith the Lord, our God.

8 He comes! He comes in glory,
   The veil has vanished too,
With angels, yea, our fathers,
   To drink this cup anew,
And sing the songs of Zion,
   And shout, "'Tis done,'tis done!"
While every son and daughter
   Rejoices: We are one.

HYMN 145. (L.M.)

1 I know that my Redeemer lives;
What comfort this sweet sentence gives!
He lives, He lives, who once was dead,
He lives, my ever-living head.

2 He lives to bless me with His love,
He lives to plead for me above,

He lives, my hungry soul to feed,
He lives to bless in time of need.

3 He lives to grant me rich supply,
He lives to guide me with His eye,
He lives to comfort me when faint,
He lives to hear my soul's complaint.

4 He lives to silence all my fears,
He lives to wipe away my tears,
He lives to calm my troubled heart,
He lives, all blessings to impart.

5 He lives, my kind, wise, heavenly friend,
He lives and loves me to the end,
He lives, and while He lives I'll sing,
He lives, my Prophet, Priest and King.

6 He lives, and grants me daily breath,
He lives, and I shall conquer death,
He lives, my mansion to prepare,
He lives to bring me safely there.

7 He lives, all glory to His name!
He lives, my Jesus, still the same;
O, the sweet joy this sentence gives,
"I know that my Redeemer lives!"

HYMN 146. (4-7's & 4.)

1 Gently raise the sacred strain,
  For the Sabbath come again,
    That man may rest,
  And return his thanks to God,
    For His blessings to the blest.

2 Holy day, devoid of strife;
  Let us seek eternal life,
    That great reward,
  And partake the Sacrament
    In remembrance of our Lord.

3 Sweetly swells the solemn sound,
  While we bring our gifts around
    Of broken hearts,
  As a willing sacrifice,
    Showing what His grace imparts.

4 Happy type of things to come,
  When the Saints are gathered home
    To praise the Lord,
  In eternity of bliss,
    All as one with one accord.

5 Holy, holy is the Lord,
   Precious, precious is His word;
      Repent and live;
   Though your sins be crimson red,
      Oh! repent, and He'll forgive.

6 Softly sing the joyful lay,
   For the Saints to fast and pray,
      As God ordains,
   For His goodness and His love,
      While the Sabbath day remains.

HYMN 147. (S.M.)

1 Ye children of our God,
      Ye Saints of latter days,
   Surround the table of the Lord,
      And join to sing His praise.

2 He gives His flesh and blood,
      Our souls to purify,
   And blesses us with every good,
      And thus He brings us nigh.

3 We do remember Him,
      His sorrow, pain and death,
   And how with power He rose again,
      Triumphant from the earth.

4 He triumphed o'er the grave,
    And then ascended high,
Where, throned in power, He sits to save
    And bring the sinner nigh.

5 He soon will come again,
    And with His people taste
The marriage supper of the Lamb,
    With His own presence blest.

6 Arrayed in spotless white,
    We'll then each other greet,
And see Messiah throned in might,
    And worship at His feet.

HYMN 148. (C.M.)

1 Behold Thy sons and daughters, Lord,
    On whom we lay our hands;
They have fulfilled the Gospel word,
    And bowed at Thy commands.

2 O now send down the heavenly Dove,
    And overwhelm their souls
With peace and joy and perfect love,
    As lambs within Thy fold.

3 Seal them by Thine own Spirit's power,
    Which purifies from sin,
And may they find from this good hour,
    They are adopted in.

4 Increase their faith, confirm their hope,
    And guide them in the way;
With comfort bear their spirits up,
    Unto the perfect day.

HYMN 149. (8's & 7's.)

1 Jesus, mighty King in Zion,
    Thou alone our guide shalt be;
Thy commission we rely on,
    We will follow none but Thee.

2 As an emblem of Thy passion,
    And Thy victory o'er the grave,
We, who know Thy great salvation,
    Are baptized beneath the wave.

3 Fearless of the world's despising,
    We the ancient path pursue,
Buried with the Lord, and rising
    To a life divinely new.

HYMN 150. (6-8's.)

1 In Jordan's tide the Prophet stands,
    Immersing the repentant Jews;
The Son of God the rite demands,
    Nor dares the holy man refuse.
The Savior sinks beneath the wave,
The emblem of His future grave.

2 Wonder, ye heavens! your Maker lies
    In deeps concealed from human view;
Ye men, behold Him sink and rise,
    A fit example, this, for you.
The sacred record, while you read,
Calls you to imitate the deed.

3 But lo! from yonder parting skies,
    What beams of dazzling glory spread!
Dove-like the Holy Spirit flies
    And lights on the Redeemer's head.
Amazed, they see the power divine
Around the Savior's temples shine.

4 But hark, my soul, hark and adore!
    What sounds are those that roll along,
Not like loud Sinai's awful roar,
    But soft and sweet as Gabriel's song:
"This is My well-beloved Son;
I see, well pleased, what He hath done?"

5 Thus the Eternal Father spoke,
   Who shakes creation with a nod;
Through parting skies the accents broke,
   And bid us hear the Son of God.
Oh! hear the Gospel word to-day;
Hear, all ye nations, and obey.

HYMN 151. (P.M.)

1 Do what is right; the day-dawn is breaking,
   Hailing a future of freedom and light;
Angels above us are silent notes taking
   Of every action; do what is right!

CHORUS:

Do what is right; let the consequence follow;
   Battle for freedom in spirit and might.
And with stout hearts look ye forth till tomorrow;
   God will protect you, do what is right!

2 Do what is right; the shackles are falling;
   Chains of the bondsmen no longer are bright;
Lighted by hope, soon they'll cease to be galling;
   Truth goeth onward, do what is right!

3 Do what is right; be faithful and fearless;
    Onward, press onward, the goal is in sight;
Eyes that are wet now, ere long will be tearless,
    Blessings await you; do what is right.

HYMN 152. (P.M.)

1 We thank Thee, O God, for a Prophet,
    To guide us in these latter days;
We thank Thee for sending the Gospel
    To lighten our minds with its rays;
We thank Thee for every blessing
    Bestowed by thy bounteous hand;
We feel it a pleasure to serve Thee,
    And love to obey Thy commands.

2 When dark clouds of trouble hang o'er us,
    And threaten our peace to destroy,
There's hope smiling brightly before us,
    We know that deliverance is nigh;
We doubt not the Lord, nor His goodness,
    We've proved Him in days that are past;
The wicked who fight against Zion
    Will surely be smitten at last.

3 We'll sing of His goodness and mercy,
    We'll praise Him by day and by night,
Rejoice in His glorious Gospel,
    And bask in its life-giving light;

Thus on to eternal perfection
  The honest and faithful will go,
While they who reject this glad message
  Shall never such happiness know.

HYMN 153. (L.M.)

1 O Lord, our Father, let Thy grace,
  Shed its glad beams on Jacob's race,
  Restore the long-lost scattered band,
  And call them to their native land.

2 Their bruises let Thy mercy heal,
  Their trespass hide, their pardon seal;
  O God of Israel, hear our prayer,
  And grant that they Thy love may share.

3 How long shall Jacob's offspring prove
  The sad suspension of Thy love?
  And shall Thy wrath forever burn?
  And wilt Thou ne'er to them return?

4 Thy quick'ning Spirit now impart;
  Awake to joy each grateful heart,
  While Israel's rescued tribes in Thee
  Their life and full salvation see.

HYMN 154.　(L. M.)

1 Do we not know that solemn word,
　That we are buried with the Lord,
　Baptized into His death, and then
　Put off the body of our sin?

2 Our souls receive diviner breath,
　Raised from corruption, guilt and death;
　So from the grave did Christ arise,
　And lives to God above the skies.

3 No more let sin or Satan reign
　Within our ransomed souls again;
　The hateful lusts we served before,
　Shall have dominion never more.

HYMN 155.　(8's, 7's & 4.)

1 Zion stands with hills surrounded—
　　Zion, kept by power divine;
　All her foes shall be confounded,
　　Though the world in arms combine;
　　　Happy Zion,
　What a favored lot is thine!

2 Every human tie may perish,
    Friend to friend unfaithful prove,
Mothers cease their own to cherish,
    Heaven and earth at last remove;
        But no changes
Can attend Jehovah's love.

3 In the furnace God may prove thee,
    Thence to bring thee forth more bright,
But can never cease to love thee—
    Thou art precious in His sight;
        God is with thee;
Thou shalt triumph in His might.

HYMN 156. (8's & 7's.)

1 Now he's gone, we'd not recall him
    From a paradise of bliss,
Where no evil can befall him,
    To a changing world like this.

2 His loved name will never perish,
    Nor his mem'ry crown the dust;
For the Saints of God will cherish
    The remembrance of the just.

HYMN 157. (8's & 7's.)

1 Hark! ten thousand thousand voices
    Sing the song of jubilee!
Earth, through all her tribes, rejoices—
    Broke her long captivity.
Hail, Emanuel! Great Deliverer!
    Hail, Emanuel! praise to Thee!
Now the theme, in pealing thunders,
    Through the universe is rung;
Now, in gentler tones, the wonders
    Of redeeming grace are sung.

2 Wider now, and louder rising,
    Swells and soars the lofty strain,
Earth's unnumbered tongues comprising;
    Hark! the Conqueror's praise again.
Hail, Emanuel! Great Deliverer!
    Stones shall speak if we refrain;
Thus, while heart and pulse are beating,
    To His name let praise arise,
Till from earth the soul, retreating,
    Joins the chorus of the skies.

3 Then in loftier, sweeter numbers,
    We shall sing Emanuel's praise;
Free from all that now encumbers,
    Nobler songs our voices raise.

Hail, Emanuel! Great Deliverer!
  Live forever in our lays.
While our crowns of glory casting
  At His feet, in rapture lost,
We, in anthems everlasting,
  Join with the angelic host.

4 But, till that great consummation,
  That bright Sabbath of mankind;
Till each distant tribe and nation
  Tastes the bliss by God designed,
Speed the Gospel! Let its tidings
  Gladden every human mind;
Be its silver trumpets sounded,
  Let the joyous echoes roll,
Till a sea of bliss unbounded
  Spreads on earth from pole to pole!

5 Then shall come the great Messiah,
  In Millennial glory crowned;
"Israel's hope," and "earth's desire,"
  Now triumphant and renowned.
Hail, Messiah! Reign forever!
  Heaven to earth reflects the sound.
Heaven and earth with all their regions,
  At His footstool prostrate fall;
Heaven and earth, with all their legions,
  Crown Emanuel, Lord of all!

HYMN 158. (L.M.)

1 All you that love Immanuel's name,
Whose spirits burn, with ardent flame,
To see His glory, learn His praise,
And follow Him in all His ways;

2 'Tis you, ye children of the light,
The Spirit and the Bride invite;
Come, come, ye subjects of His grace,
Where He reveals His smiling face.

3 Come to His Church, pass through His gates;
For you His gracious presence waits;
Here peace and pardon are bestowed—
Great gifts, and worthy of a God.

HYMN 159. (C.M.)

1 Mourn not for those who peaceful lay
   Their wearied bodies down,
Who leave the frail and mortal clay
   To seek a fadeless crown.

2 Dry up the unavailing tear,
   Repress the selfish sigh;
Know that the spirit ransomed here
   Yet lives, and ne'er shall die.

3 When winter spreads her shroud of snow
 O'er nature's silent face,
Upon the landscape hid below
 No signs of life we trace.

4 Above, around, peals Heaven's praise
 From many a varied form;
The hard and crusted earth betrays
 Not e'en a living worm.

5 Yet spring upon it gently breathes;
 And changing form and hue,
With it a thousand garlands wreathes,
 Replete with life anew.

6 So death is but the wintry snow
 Which veils the spirit's bloom,
That soon with radiant life shall glow,
 Enfranchised from the tomb.

7 As from that snowy shroud there springs
 A brighter, lovelier earth,
So vanquished death his trophies brings
 To grace a nobler birth.

8 Then why the sorrowing lip and eye,
 The aching heart and head?
Remember, He who cannot lie
 Hath said, "Mourn not the dead."

HYMN 160. (4-6s & 2-8's.)

1 Behold the Lamb of God,
   In His divine array,
Go down into the flood,
   His Father to obey—
In Jordan's stream to be baptized,
Though by a carnal world despised.

2 Can we pretend to know
   More fully God's design?
Can we pretend to show
   A conduct more divine?
Can we neglect this ordinance
Without an insult to our Prince?

3 Jesus, we will obey
   Thy practice and command:
Behold us here to-day!
   We in thy presence stand,
Devoted to Thy blessed will,
Thy pleasure ready to fulfil.

4 We sink beneath the wave;
   The water we go through—
The emblems of thy grave
   And resurrection too;
We die, are buried, rise again,
In hopes with Thee to live and reign.

5 Great Father, cast Thine eye
   On us, dispel our fear,
Our every want supply,
   Give grace to persevere;
And then rejoicing we will go
To do our Father's will below.

HYMN 161. (L.M.)

1 'Twas the commission of our Lord,
   "Go, teach the nations, and baptize!"
The nations have received the word,
   Since He ascended to the skies.

2 He sits on the eternal hills,
   With grace and pardon in His hands,
And sends His covenant with the seals,
   To bless the distant heathen lands.

3 "Repent and be baptized," He saith,
   "For the remission of your sins:"
And thus our sense assists our faith,
   And shows us what the Gospel means.

4 Our souls He washes in His blood,
   As water makes the body clean;
And the good Spirit from our God
   Descends like purifying rain.

5 Thus we engage ourselves to Thee,
   And seal our cov'nant with Thee, Lord;
Oh, may the great, Eternal Three,
   In heaven our solemn vows record!

HYMN 162.   (L.M.)

1 In ancient times a man of God
   Came preaching in the wilderness;
He did baptize in Jordan's flood,
   Requiring fruits of righteousness.

2 He said, Repent, the time's fulfilled,
   The Son of God will soon appear;
Make straight His paths and do His will,
   For lo! His kingdom now is near.

3 With water I baptize you now
   For the remission of your sin;
Bu He, the Spirit shall bestow,
   To witness to your souls within.

4 Thus was Messiah's way prepared,
   When first He came unto His own;
And by this means, when He appeared,
   To His disciples He was known.

5 E'en so, in this the latter-day,
    Before He comes on earth to reign,
His servants must prepare His way,
    And all His paths make straight again.

6 Come, then, ye erring ones who stray,
    Arise, return unto your fold;
Come, be baptized without delay,
    And thus pursue the path of old.

HYMN 163. (C.M.)

1 Father in heaven, we do believe
    The promise Thou hast made;
The word with meekness we receive,
    Just as Thy Saints have said.

2 We now repent of all our sins,
    And come with broken heart,
And to Thy covenant enter in,
    And choose the better part.

3 We will be buried in the stream,
    In Jesus' blessed name,
And rise, while light shall on us beam—
    The Spirit's heavenly flame.

4 O Lord, accept us while we pray,
    And all our sins forgive;
New life impart in us this day,
    And bid the sinners live.

5 Baptize us with the Holy Ghost,
   And seal us as Thine own,
That in Thy kingdom we may stand,
   And with Thy Saints be one.

HYMN 164. (L.M.)

1 How foolish to the carnal mind,
   God's ordinances do appear!
Men count them as a puff of wind,
   And gaze with a contemptuous sneer.

2 What! buried now beneath the flood,
   To wash away our guilt and sin?
Are not some other means as good,
   Nay, better! Why appear so mean?

3 Thus they despise the proffered grace,
   And die and perish in their sin;
So the Assyrian leper thought—
   What! wash in Jordan and be clean?

4 Nay, in a rage he turned away,
   And would remain a leper still:
But lo! his humble servant's sway
   Prevailed at last, and turned his will.

5 He washed in Jordan's rolling flood,
   And found the foul disease removed;

The virtue of the word of God,
Thus by experience Naaman proved.

6 Poor sinners now would fain perform
Some great and meritorious deed;
Bow to the systems mortals form,
That from their sins they may be freed.

7 But why not yield to simple means?
The Gospel is the power of God;
'Twill save the vilest from their sins,
Who yield obedience to His word.

HYMN 165. (C.M.)

1 Lo! on the water's brink we stand,
To do the Father's will;
To be baptized by His command,
And thus the word fulfil.

2 Lord, we have sinned, but we repent,
And put our sins away;
With joy receive the message sent
In this the latter day.

3 Thou wilt accept our humble prayer,
And all our sins forgive;
For Jesus is the sinners' friend;
He died that we might live.

4 We lay our sinful bodies now
   Beneath the parting wave;
Then rise to life divinely new,
   As from the bursting grave.

5 So when the trump of God shall blow,
   The Saints shall burst the tomb,
Eternal beauty crown their brow,
   With an immortal bloom.

HYMN 166. (P.M.)

1 Come all ye sons of God, who have received the Priesthood,
   Go spread the Gospel wide, and gather in His people;
The latter-day work has begun, to gather scattered Israel in,
   And bring them back to Zion to praise the Lamb.

2 Come all ye scattered sheep, and listen to your Shepherd;
   While you the blessings reap, which long have been predicted;
By Prophets it has been foretold, He'll gather you into His fold;
   And bring you home to Zion, to praise the Lamb.

3 Repent and be baptized and have your sins remitted,
  And get the Spirit's seal; O then you'll be united;
  Go cast upon Him all your care, He will regard your humble prayer,
  And bring you home to Zion, to praise the Lamb.

4 And when your grief is o'er and ended your affliction,
  Your spirits then will soar until the resurrection;
  And then His presence you'll enjoy, in heavenly bliss your time employ,
  A thousand years in Zion, to praise the Lamb.

HYMN 167. (4-6's & 2-8's.)

1 Repent ye Gentiles all,
  And come and be baptized;
  It is the Savior's call;
  Appearing in the skies,
  He sent the message we declare,
  His second coming to prepare.

2 Be buried with our Lord,
  And rise, divinely new—
  'Tis His eternal word;
  The ancient path pursue,

The promised blessing now secure,
The Spirit's seal, forever sure,

3 Ye souls with sins distressed,
   Who fain would find relief,
Come, on His promise rest,
   He will assuage your grief;
He'll send His Spirit from on high,
When with the Gospel you comply.

4 Come, be adopted in,
   With Israel's chosen race,
And, cleansed from every sin,
   Enjoy the promised grace;
The covenant stands forever sure,
To all who to the end endure.

HYMN 168. (C.M.)

1 Let those who would be Saints indeed
   Fear not what others do,
But each unto himself take heed,
   And righteousness pursue.

2 What though the storm-clouds gather dark,
   Look up and trust in God;
And keep your eye upon the mark—
   Hold fast the "iron rod."

3 Fear not the darkness of the night
    But move with careful tread,
  Till morning break, and azure light
    The canopy o'erspread.

4 Sell not your birthright for a mess
    Of pottage, nor betray
  Your holy covenants for a kiss;
    'Tis now a proving day.

5 The wheat has cleared the threshing floor,
    The sieve is shaking now;
  And when the sifting time is o'er
    Will glory wreathe your brow.

6 And Zion's furnace, too, will burn,
    That when the chaff shall fly,
  The dross will be consumed in turn,
    The gold to purify.

7 In His own time God will remove
    Whatever now offends.
  When he chastises, 'tis in love,
    To all who prove His friends.

8 Maintain the freedom you have won—
    Virtue is liberty;
  Take not the yoke of bondage on;
    The pure in heart are free.

HYMN 169. (8's & 7's.)

1 Sister, thou wast mild and lovely,
   Gentle as the summer breeze,
Pleasant as the air of evening
   When it floats among the trees.

2 Peaceful be thy silent slumber,
   Peaceful in the grave so low;
Thou no more wilt join our number,
   Thou no more our songs shalt know.

3 Dearest sister, thou hast left us,
   Here thy loss we deeply feel;
But 'tis God that hath bereft us,
   He can all our sorrows heal.

4 Yet again we hope to meet thee,
   When death's gloomy night has fled;
Then on earth with joy to greet thee,
   Where no bitter tears are shed.

HYMN 170. (C.M.)

1 Think gently of the erring one!
   O, let us not forget,
However darkly stained by sin,
   He is our brother yet!

2 Heir of the same inheritance,
   Child of the self-same God,
 He hath but stumbled in the path
   We have in weakness trod.

3 Speak gently to the erring ones!
   We yet may lead them back,
 With holy words, and tones of love,
   From misery's thorny track.

4 Forget not, brother, thou hast sinned,
   And sinful yet mayst be;
 Deal gently with the erring heart,
   As God hath dealt with thee.

HYMN 171. (L.M.)

1 Creation speaks with awful voice;
   Hark! 'tis a universal groan
     Re-echoes through the vast extent
   Of worlds unnumbered, called to mourn.

2 For sickness, sorrow, pain and death,
   With awful tyranny have reigned:
 While all eternity has shed
     Her tears of sorrow o'er the slain.

3 But hark! again a voice is heard
   Resounding through the solemn gloom;
   A mighty conqu'ror has appeared,
   In triumph rising from the tomb.

4 No longer let creation mourn;
   Ye sons of sorrow, dry your tears;
   Life! life! eternal life is ours!
   Dismiss your doubts, dispel your fears.

5 The King shall soon in clouds descend,
   With all the heavenly host above;
   The dead shall rise and hail their friends,
   And always dwell with those they love.

6 No tear, no sorrow, death, or pain,
   Shall e'er be known to enter there;
   But perfect peace, immortal bloom,
   Shall reign triumphant everywhere!

HYMN 172. (L.M.)

1 The morning flowers display their sweets,
   And gay their silken leaves unfold,
   As careless of the noontide heats,
   As fearless of the evening cold.

2 Nipped by the wind's unkindly blast,
    Parched by the sun's directer ray,
The momentary glories waste,
    The short-lived beauties die away.

3 So blooms the human face divine,
    When youth its pride of beauty shows;
Fairer than spring in colors shine,
    And sweeter than the virgin rose.

4 Or worn by slowly rolling years,
    Or broke by sickness in a day,
The fading glory disappears,
    The short-lived beauties die away.

5 Yet these, new-rising from the tomb,
    With lustre brighter far shall shine;
Revive with everlasting bloom,
    Safe from diseases and decline.

6 Let sickness blast, let death devour,
    If heaven but recompense our pains;
Perish the grass and fade the flower,
    If firm the word of God remains.

HYMN 173. (L.M.)

1 Let earth's inhabitants rejoice,
   And gladly hail the glorious hour;
Again is heard a Prophet's voice,
   And all may feel the Gospel's power.

2 Soon will the blissful time arrive
   Which holy men of old foretold,
When man no more with man will strive,
   But all in each a friend behold.

3 Oppression will no more be found,
   Nor tyrant hold relentless sway;
But love to God and man abound
   Throughout a long Millennial day.

HYMN 174. (L.M.)

1 Ye differing, jarring sects attend,
   The voice of inspiration hear;
Now may your doubtings have an end,
   And unity and peace appear.

2 Break off your chains of slavish dread,
   Let chilling unbelief give way;
For Gospel light begins to spread
   And usher in eternal day. .

3 Soon will mankind behold aright
   The perfect "Law of liberty;"
And every nation, with delight,
   Share in a glorious jubilee.

HYMN 175. (7's.)

1 Now we'll sing with one accord,
   For a Prophet of the Lord,
Bringing forth His precious word,
   Cheers the Saints as anciently.

2 When the world in darkness lay,
   Lo! he sought the better way,
And he heard the Savior say,
   "Go and prune my vineyard, son!"

3 And an angel, surely then,
   For a blessing unto men,
Brought the Priesthood back again,
   In its ancient purity.

4 Even Joseph he inspired,
   Yea, his heart he truly fired
With the light that he desired,
   For the work of righteousness.

5 And the Book of Mormon, true,
   With its Covenant, ever new,

For the Gentile and the Jew,
   He translated sacredly.

6 God's commandments to mankind,
  For believing Saints designed,
  And to bless the seeking mind,
     Came through him from Jesus Christ.

7 Precious are the years to come,
  While the righteous gather home
  For the great Millennium,
     When they'll rest in blessedness.

8 Prudent in this world of woes,
  They will triumph o er their foes,
  While the realm of Zion grows
     Purer for eternity.

HYMN 176. (12's & 11's.)

1 Awake! O ye people, the Savior is coming;
   He'll suddenly come to His temple, we hear;
  Repentance is needed of all that are living,
   To gain them a lot of inheritance near.

2 To-day will soon pass and that unknown to-morrow
   May leave many souls in a more dreadfu state

Than came by the flood, or that fell on Gomorrah—
Yea, weeping and wailing and gnashing of teeth.

Be ready, O islands, the Savior is coming;
He'll bring again Zion, the Prophets declare;
Repent of your sins, and have faith in redemption,
To gain you a lot of inheritance there.

A voice to the nations in season is given,
The glories of Eden to show them again,
To call the elect from the four winds of Heaven;
For Jesus is coming, on earth He shall reign.

HYMN 177. (P.M.)

From regions of glory an angel descended,
And told the strange news how the babe was attended.
Go, shepherds, and visit this heavenly stranger;
Beneath that bright star, there's your Lord in a manger!

Hallelujah to the Lamb,
  Whom your souls may rely on;
We shall see Him on earth,
  When He brings again Zion.

2 Glad tidings I bring unto you and each nation,
  Glad tidings of joy, now behold your salvation;
  Arise, all ye pilgrims, and lift up your voices,
  And shout, the Redeemer, while heaven rejoices.
    Hallelujah to the Lamb, etc.

3 Let glory to God in the highest be given,
  And glory to God be re-echoed in heaven;
  Around the whole world let us tell the glad story,
  And sing of His love, His salvation and glory
    Hallelujah to the Lamb, etc.

4 The kingdom is yours by the will of the Father,
  Whose word has gone forth that the righteous He'll gather;
  Before all the wicked will perish by fire,
  The heavens shall shine with the coming Messiah.
    Hallelujah to the Lamb, etc.

HYMN 178. (2-8's & 6's.)

1 Hark! from afar, a funeral knell
 Moves on the breeze—its echoes swell
  The chorus for the dead!
 A consort's moans are in the sound,
 And sobs of children weeping round
  A parent's dying bed

2 He's gone! his work on earth is done,
 His battle's fought, his race is run;
  Blest is the path he trod.
 For he espoused the glorious cause,
 In prompt obedience to the laws
  Of the eternal God.

3 He sleeps; his troubles here are o'er;
 He sleeps where earthly ills no more
  Will break the slumb'rer's rest.
 His dust is laid beneath the sod,
 His spirit has returned to God,
  To mingle with the blest.

4 Death sunders every tender tie;
 Pierced by his shaft, life's prospects lie
  Like masts by tempests cleft.

But hope points forward to a scene
Where sorrow will not intervene,
  Nor friends, of friends bereft.

5 The Savior conquered death; although
It slays our friends, and lays them low,
  They in immortal bloom,
When Jesus Christ shall come to reign,
Shall burst their icy bands in twain,
  And triumph o'er the tomb.

HYMN 179. (6's, & 7's D.)

1 Let us pray, gladly pray,
  In the house of Jehovah,
Till the righteous can say,
  "O, our warfare is over!"
Then we'll dry up our tears,
  Sweetly praising together,
Through the great thousand years,
  Face to face with the Savior.

2 What a joy will be there,
  At that great resurrection,
As the Saints in the air,
  Meet in robes of perfection;
Then the Lamb, then the Lamb,
  With a God's mandatory,
As I AM THAT I AM
  Fills the world with His glory.

3 We can then live in peace,
    And inhabit the mountains,
Spread abroad and increase,
    Like the streams from the fountains;
And the world will be blest
    With a light to rely on,
From the east to the west,
    Through the glory of Zion.

HYMN 180. (C.M.D.)

Let Zion in her beauty rise,
    Her light begins to shine;
Ere long her King will rend the skies,
    Majestic and divine.
The Gospel's spreading through the land,
    A people to prepare,
To meet the Lord and Enoch's band,
    Triumphant in the air.

Ye heralds, sound the Gospel trump
    To earth's remotest bound;
Go, spread the news from pole to pole,
    In all the nations round,
That Jesus in the clouds above,
    With hosts of angels too,
Will soon appear, His Saints to save,
    His enemies subdue.

3 But ere that great and solemn day,
    The stars from heaven shall fall,
The moon be turned into blood,
    The waters into gall;
The sun with blackness will be clothed,
    All nature look afright,
While men, rebellious, wicked men,
    Gaze heedless on the sight.

4 The earth shall reel, the heavens shake,
    The sea move to the north,
The earth shall roll up like a scroll,
    When God's command goes forth;
The mountains sink, the valleys rise,
    And all become a plain;
The islands and the continents
    Will then unite again.

5 Alas! the day will soon arrive
    When rebels to God's grace
Will call for rocks to fall on them
    And hide them from His face.
Not so with those who keep His law;
    They'll joy to meet the Lord
In clouds above, with those who slept
    In Christ, their sure reward.

6 That glorious rest will then commence,
    Which prophets did foretell,
When Christ will reign with Saints on earth,
    And in their presence dwell
A thousand years; O, glorious day!
    Dear Lord, prepare my heart
To stand with Thee on Zion's mount,
    And never more to part.

7 Then when the thousand years are past,
    And Satan is unbound,
The wicked hosts will be destroyed
    By fire from heaven sent down;
And when the great, last change shall come
    To end death's mighty sway,
Then we in the celestial world
    Will spend eternal day.

HYMN 181. (L.M.)

1 My soul is full of peace and love;
I soon shall see Christ from above,
And angels too, the hallowed throng,
Shall join with me in holy song.

2 The Spirit's power has sealed my peace,
And filled my soul with heavenly grace;
Transported, I, with peace and love,
Am waiting for the throne above.

3 Prepare my heart, prepare my tongue,
To join this glorious, heavenly throng,
To hail the Bridegroom from above,
And join the band in songs of love.

4 Let all my powers of soul combine
To hail my Savior all divine,
To hear His voice, attend His call,
And crown Him King and Lord of all.

HYMN 182. (12's & 11's, D.)

1 Now let us rejoice in the day of salvation;
No longer as strangers on earth need we roam,
Good tidings are sounding to us and each nation, . [come.
And shortly the hour of redemption will
When all that was promised the Saints will be given, [even,
And none will molest them from morn until
And earth will appear as the garden of Eden,
And Jesus will say to all Israel, Come home.

2 We'll love one another, and never dissemble,
But cease to do evil, and ever be one;

And when the ungodly are fearing, and
    remble,   will come
We'll watch for the day when the Savior
When all that was promised the Saints will
    be given,   [even,
And none will molest them from morn until
And earth will appear as the garden of Eden,
    And Jesus will say to all Irsael, Come
    home.

3 In faith we'll rely on the arm of Jehovah
    To guide through these last days of
        trouble and gloom,
And, after the scourges and harvest are over,
    We'll rise with the just when the Savior
        doth come.
Then all that was promised the Saints will
    be given,   [heaven,
And they will be crowned as the angels of
And earth will appear as the garden of Eden,
    And Christ and His people will ever be one.

HYMN 183. (C.M.)

1 The glorious day is rolling on—
    All glory to the Lord—
When, fair as at creation's dawn,
    The earth will be restored.

2 A perfect harvest then will crown
    The renovated soil,
And rich abundance drop around
    Without corroding toil.

3 For, in its own primeval bloom
    Will nature smile again,
And blossoms, fragrant with perfume,
    Adorn the verdant plain.

4 The Saints will then, with pure delight,
    Possess the holy land,
And walk with Jesus Christ in white,
    And in His presence stand.

5 What glorious prospects! Can we claim
    These hopes, and call them ours?
Yes, if, through faith in Jesus' name,
    We conquer Satan's powers;

6 If we, like Jesus, bear the cross,
    Like Him despise the shame,
And count all earthly things but dross,
    For His most holy name.

7 Then, when the powers of darkness rage,
    With glory in our view,
In Jesus' strength let us engage,
    To press to Zion too.

8 For Zion will like Eden bloom,
   And Jesus come to reign;
  The Saints, immortal from the tomb,
   With angels meet again.

HYMN 184. (L.M.)

1 Behold, the great Redeemer comes
To bring His ransomed people home,
He comes to save His scattered sheep,
He comes to comfort those who weep.

2 He comes, all blessings to impart
Unto the meek and contrite heart,
He comes, He comes, His Saints admire;
He comes to burn the proud by fire.

3 He comes to bless the humble poor,
He comes, creation to restore,
He comes, the earth to purify,
He comes, but not again to die.

4 He comes, He comes unto His own,
He comes to reign on David's throne,
He comes to stand on Zion's hill,
He comes the Scriptures to fulfil.

5 He comes to tread the wicked down,
He comes, the martyrs soon to crown,

He comes to dry the mourners' tears,
He comes to reign a thousand years.

6 He comes, on Olive's Mount to stand,
He comes, all Israel to defend,
He comes to lay the sinner low,
He comes that Judah may Him know.

7 He comes to show His hands and side,
He comes to wed His ready bride,
He comes to reign as King of kings,
He comes, and all creation sings.

HYMN 185. (S.M.)

1 Behold, the Savior comes!
   Ye Saints, your hearts prepare;
In Zion gather, to your homes,
   For soon you'll meet Him there.

2 The signs which He foretold
   Already do appear;
Blood, smoke and fire, we oft behold,
   And these bespeak Him near.

3 Then let us lift our heads
   With joy, and sing His praise;
The fig tree putting forth its buds
   Bespeaks the latter days.

HYMN 186. (L.M.)

1 Earth is the place where Christ will reign
   With all His Saints a thousand years;
   He'll end their sorrows and their pain,
   Dismiss their woes, and dry their tears.

2 He'll burst the portals of the tomb,
   And bring their sleeping dust to light;
   He'll clothe them with immortal bloom,
   Arrayed in garments clean and white.

3 He'll cleanse the earth from wicked men,
   And bind old Satan with a chain;
   He'll raise the meek and humble, then,
   To thrones of power, and bid them reign.

4 Hosanna to the Son of God,
   Who soon will come to earth again,
   To smite the wicked with His rod,
   And o'er the earth exalted reign !

HYMN 187. (L.M.)

1 Behold the Mount of Olives rend! ·
   And on its top Messiah stand,
   His chosen Israel to defend,
   And save them with a mighty hand.

2 The mountains sink, the valleys rise,
    And all the land becomes a plain;
He brings deliv'rance to the Jews,
    While all their enemies are slain.

3 But lo! what pen can paint the scene!
    His wounded hands and side they see,
Where once the nails and spear have been;
    This our Messiah! Can it be?

4 Whence, then, these wounds? Ah! who has pierced
    Our great Deliv'rer's heart and hands?
"These are the wounds I once received
    Amid my kindred and my friends."

5 Thus the Messiah stands revealed,
    And they their blest Deliv'rer own;
They're humbled when at last they find
    Jesus, Messiah, both are one.

6 Like Joseph's brethren, now they mourn,
    And humbly own a Savior slain;
They crown Him King on David's throne,
    That o'er the nations He may reign.

HYMN 188. (L.M.)

1 Hosanna to the Great Messiah,
    The long expected Savior King,

He'll come and cleanse the earth by fire,
    And gather scattered Israel in.

2 On Zion's mount His throne shall be,
    His sanctuary stand secure,
His sceptre o'er the nations sway,
    And all creation Him adore.

3 He'll judge with justice for the poor,
    He will with equity reprove,
He'll smite the wicked with His power,
    Oppression from the earth remove.

4 Then princes, kings, and dukes and lords,
    And mighty men of great renown,
Shall pray, though not unto the Lord,
    But to the rocks and hills bow down!

5 Ye rocks and mountains, on us fall.
    To hide us from the great Messiah,
For lo! the day of wrath has come,
    The Lord's great day of dreadful ire.

6 The poor and meek shall then rejoice,
    The Saints in peace possess the land,
The sheep shall hear the Shepherd's voice,
    And with him on Mount Zion stand.

HYMN 189. (7's.)

1 Jesus, once of humble birth,
Now in glory comes to earth;
Once he suffered grief and pain,
Now he comes on earth to reign.

2 Once a meek and lowly Lamb,
Now the Lord, the great I AM;
Once upon the cross He bowed,
Now His chariot is the cloud.

3 Once he groaned in blood and tears,
Now in glory he appears;
Once rejected by His own,
Now their King He shall be known.

4 Once forsaken, left alone,
Now exalted to a throne;
Once all things He meekly bore,
But he now will bear no more.

HYMN 190. (P.M.)

1 This earth shall be a blessed place,
  To Saints celestial given,
Where Christ again shall show His face.
With the redeemed of Adam's race,
  In clouds descend from heaven.

2 Yes, when He comes on earth again,
　The vile shall burn as stubble;
His enemies shall all be slain,
And o'er the nations He shall reign,
　And end the scenes of trouble.

3 The trump of war will sound no more,
　But strife shall all be ended,
When Jesus all things shall restore
To order, as they were before,
　And peace be wide extended.

4 Sing, O ye heavens! let earth rejoice,
　While Saints shall flow to Zion,
And rear the temple of His choice,
And in its courts unite their voice,
　In praise to Judah's Lion.

5 Hosanna to the reign of peace,
　The day so long expected,
When earth shall find a full release,
The groanings of creation cease,
　The righteous be protected.

6 Come, sound His praise in joyful strains,
　Who dwell beneath His banner;
He'll bind old Satan fast in chains,
While wide o'er earth's extended plains
　The nations shout Hosanna.

HYMN 191. (7's & 6's.)

1 At first, the babe of Bethlehem,
   Of meek and humble mien;
But next, the Lord from heaven,
   In glory shall be seen.

2 The first, so meek and lowly,
   Upon an ass He rode;
The second, crowned with glory,
   Returned to His abode.

3 The first was persecuted,
   And into Egypt fled,
A pilgrim and a stranger,
   Not where to lay His head.

4 The second, in His temple
   All suddenly appears,
And all His Saints come with Him,
   To reign a thousand years.

5 The first, a man of sorrows,
   Rejected by His own,
And Israel left in blindness
   To wander forth forlorn;

6 The second brings deliv'rance,
   They crown Him as their King,

They own Him as their Savior,
  And join His praise to sing.

7 The first was all compassion,
    And healing His employ;
  The second, clothed in vengeance,
    The wicked shall destroy.

8 The first claimed no proud kingdom
    Of this wide, wicked world;
  The last, all kings shall own Him,
    Or from their thrones be hurled.

9 Let Jews and Gentiles mingle,
    Messiah, Jesus, own;
  His first and second coming
    Will show that both are one.

HYMN 192. (4-6's & 2-8's.)

1 Come, O Thou King of kings—
     We've waited long for Thee—
   With healing in Thy wings,
     To set Thy people free.
   Come, Thou desire of nations, come,
   Let Israel now be gathered home.

2 Come, make an end of sin,
     And cleanse the earth by fire,

And righteousness bring in,
   That Saints may tune the lyre,
With songs of joy, a happier strain,
To welcome in Thy peaceful reign.

3 Hosannas now shall sound
     From all the ransomed throng,
  And glory echo round,
     A new triumphal song;
The wide expanse of heaven fill
With anthems sweet from Zion's hill.

4 Hail! Prince of Life and Peace!
     Thrice welcome to Thy throne!
  While all the chosen race
     Their Lord and Savior own,
The heathen nations bow the knee,
And every tongue sounds praise to Thee.

HYMN 193. (7's & 6's, D.)

1 Farewell, all earthly honors,
     I bid you all adieu;
  Farewell, all sinful pleasures,
     I want no more of you.
  I want my habitation
     On that eternal soil,
  Beyond the powers of Satan,
     Where sin can not defile.

2 I want my name engraven
    Among the righteous ones,
  Who worship God, the Father,
    And wear a righteous crown.
  For such eternal riches,
    I'm willing to pass through
  All needful tribulations,
    And count them my just due.

3 I'm willing to be chastened,
    And bear my daily cross;
  I'm willing to be cleansed
    From every kind of dross.
  I see a fiery furnace,
    I feel its piercing flame;
  The fruits of it are holy,
    The gold will still remain.

4 All earthly tribulations
    Are but a moment here;
  Then, oh! if we prove faithful,
    A righteous crown we'll wear.
  We shall be counted holy,
    And feed on angels' food,
  Rejoicing in bright glory,
    Before the throne of God.

5 There Christ Himself has promised
    A mansion to prepare,

And all who serve Him truly,
   The victor's wreath shall wear.
Bright crowns shall then be given
   To all the ransomed throng,
And glory! glory! glory!
   Shall be the conq'ror's song.

HYMN 194. (P.M.)

1 Redeemer of Israel,
     Our only delight,
On whom for a blessing we call;
   Our shadow by day,
     And our pillar by night,
Our King, our Deliv'rer, our all!

2 We know He is coming
     To gather His sheep,
And lead them to Zion in love;
   For why in the valley
     Of death should they weep,
Or in the lone wilderness rove!

3 How long we have wandered
     As strangers in sin,
And cried in the desert for Thee!
   Our foes have rejoiced
     When our sorrows they've seen,
But Israel will shortly be free.

4   As children of Zion,
      Good tidings for us,
  The tokens already appear;
      Fear not, and be just,
      For the kingdom is ours;
  The hour of redemption is near.

HYMN 195.   (L.M.)

1 What wondrous things we now behold,
  By prophets seen in days of old,
  In visions with th' Almighty Lord
  Confirmed by His unchanging word.

2 The second time He sets His hand,
  To gather Israel to their land,
  Fulfil the covenants He has made,
  And pour His blessings on their head.

3 Then Ephraim's sons, a warlike race,
  Shall seek their rest and dwell in peace,
  And earth's remotest parts abound
  With joys of everlasting sound.

4 Yes, Abram's children then shall be
  Like sands in number by the sea,
  While kindred, tongues and nations all,
  Combine to make their numbers full.

5 The dawning of that day has come,
See! Abram's sons are gath'ring home;
And daughters too, with joyful lays,
Are hast'ning here to join in praise.

6 O God, our Father and our King,
Inspire the theme our voices sing;
Let all our powers of soul combine,
To sing Thy praise in songs divine.

HYMN 196. (7's.)

1 In the sun, and moon and stars,
   Signs and wonders there shall be;
Earth shall quake with inward wars,
   Nations with perplexity.

2 Soon shall ocean's hoary deep,
   Tossed with stronger tempest rise,
Wilder storms the mountains sweep,
   Louder thunders shake the skies.

3 Dread alarms shall shake the proud,
   Pale amazement, restless fear;
Joy, ye Saints, in yonder cloud
   See you Savior King appear!

HYMN 197. (4-6s & 2-8's.)

1 Ye ransomed of our God,
  To Zion now return,
And seek a safe abode,
  Before the wicked burn ;
The year of Jubilee draws near,
Soon Jesus will on earth appear.

2 Let Israel now return
  Unto their ancient home,
Possess the Holy Land,
  And build Jerusalem,
And there await the Jubilee ;
They shall the King of Glory see.

3 Let Gentiles throng the way
  To Zion's happy land ;
Those who the truth obey
  Shall in His presence stand ;
Shall sparkle with celestial light,
And walk with Jesus Christ in white.

4 Let Joseph's remnants come
  To Zion's sacred hill,
And throng the house of God,
  And learn to do His will,
That Zion may arise and shine
With light celestial and divine.

5 Let Saints in every clime,
    Their waiting hearts prepare,
From every tribe and tongue,
    To Zion's mount repair;
The marriage of the Lamb is near,
For soon the Bridegroom will appear.

HYMN 198. (L.M.)

1 A holy angel from on high,
    The joyful message has made known,
Which brings our longing spirits nigh,
    To bow and worship near the throne.

2 Together truth and mercy meet,
    And joy and peace, with fond embrace,
The earth and heaven with gladness greet
    Their offspring, truth and righteousness.

3 Lo! from the heavens comes righteousness,
    And truth from earth exulting springs;
These, joined in one, shall Israel bless,
    Borne, as it were, on eagles' wings.

4 Wide round the earth the echo flies,
    From their long sleep the nations wake,
The righteous shout with glad surprise,
    While the ungodly fear and quake.

5 Thus truth shall spread through every clime,
  And Israel's tribes be gathered home,
And watch for the appointed time
  To see the great Messiah come.

HYMN 199. (L.M.)

1 What wondrous scenes mine eyes behold!
  What glories burst upon my view!
When Ephraim's records I unfold,
  All things appear divinely new.

2 Good news to earth have angels borne,
  Which fills our souls with joy and peace ;
Good news to comfort those who mourn,
  And bring the captive full release.

3 Now, Israel, long oppressed and grieved
  In every land, in every clime,
Shall hear the word of God and live;
  This is the time, the chosen time.

4 The scattered sheep, who once were sold
  In darkness o'er the mountains far,
Shall now return unto their fold,
  And there their waiting hearts prepare.

5 When lo ! their Shepherd shall descend,
  With all the glorious, heavenly throng,

Destroy the wolves, the sheep defend,
From every woe, from every wrong.

To God give glory! tune the lyre,
  Shout loud hosannas to His name;
Let Jews and Gentiles, join the choir,
  And round the earth the news proclaim.

HYMN 200. (4-6's & 2-8's.)

1 An angel from on high,
    The long, long silence broke;
  Descending from the sky,
    These gracious words he spoke:
Lo ! in Cumorah's lonely hill,
A sacred record lies concealed.

2 Sealed by Moroni's hand,
    It has for ages lain,
  To wait the Lord's command,
    From dust to speak again.
It shall again to light come forth,
To usher in Christ's reign on earth.

3 It speaks of Joseph's seed,
    And makes the remnant known
  Of nations long since dead,
    Who once had dwelt alone.

The fulness of the Gospel, too,
Its pages will reveal to view.

4   The time is now fulfilled,
       The long expected day;
    Let earth obedience yield,
       And darkness flee away;
    Open the seals, be wide unfurled
    Its light and glory to the world.

5   Lo, Israel filled with joy,
       Shall now be gathered home.
    Their wealth and means employ
       To build Jerusalem ;
    While Zion shall arise and shine,
    And fill the earth with truth divine.

HYMN 201. (C.M.)

1 Behold, the mountain of the Lord
    In latter days shall rise,
  On mountain tops, above the hills,
    And draw the wond'ring eyes.

2 To this the joyful nations round,
    All tribes and tongues, shall flow;
  "Up to the hill of God," they'll say,
    "And to His house, we'll go."

3 The rays that shine from Zion's hill
    Shall lighten every land;
  The King who reigns in Salem's towers
    Shall all the world command.

4 Among the nations He shall judge,
    His judgments truth shall guide,
  His sceptre shall protect the just,
    And quell the sinner's pride.

5 No strife shall rage, nor hostile feuds
    Disturb those peaceful years;
  To plowshares men shall beat their swords
    To pruning-hooks their spears.

6 No longer host, encount'ring host,
    Shall crowds of slain deplore;
  They'll hang the trumpet in the hall,
    And study war no more.

7 Come then, O house of Jacob, come,
    To worship at His shrine,
  And, walking in the light of God,
    With holy beauties shine.

HYMN 202. (L.M.)

1 Unveil thy bosom, faithful tomb,
    Take this new treasure to thy trust!

  And give these sacred relics room
   To slumber in the silent dust.

2 Nor pain, nor grief, nor anxious fear,
  Invade thy bounds; no mortal woes
Can reach the peaceful sleeper here,
  While angels watch the soft repose.

3 So Jesus slept; God's dying Son
  Passed through the grave and blessed the bed;
Rest here, blest Saints, till from His throne
  The morning breaks to pierce the shade.

4 Break from His throne, illustrious morn!
  Attend, O earth, His sovereign word!
Restore Thy trust; a glorious form
  Shall then arise to meet the Lord.

HYMN 203. (C.M.)

1 Lord, when iniquities abound,
  And blasphemy grows bold,
When faith is hardly to be found,
  And love is waxing cold,

2 Is not Thy chariot hastening on?
  Hast Thou not made the sign?

May we not trust and live upon
     A promise so divine?

3 "Yes," saith the Lord, "now will I rise,
     And make oppressors flee;
   I will appear to their surprise,
     And set my servants free."

4 Thy word, like silver seven times tried,
     Through ages shall endure;
   The men that in Thy truth confide
     Shall find the promise sure.

HYMN 204.   (L.P.M.)

1 Judges, who rule the world by laws,
   Will ye despise the righteous cause
     When the oppressed before you stand?
   Dare ye condemn the righteous poor,
     And let rich sinners go secure,
       While gold and greatness bribe your hand?

2 Have ye forgot, or never knew,
   That God will judge the judges, too?
     High in the heavens His justice reigns,
   Yet you invade the rights of God,
   And send your bold decrees abroad,
     To bind the conscience in your chains!

3 The Lord God thunders from the sky,
　Their grandeur melts, their titles die,
　　They perish like dissolving frost;
　As empty chaff, when whirlwinds rise,
　Before the sweeping tempest flies,
　　So shall their hopes and names be lost.

4 Thus shall the vengeance of the Lord
　Safety and joy to Saints afford;
　　And all that hear shall join and say,
　"Sure, there's a God that rules on high,
　A God that hears His children cry,
　　And will their sufferings well repay."

HYMN 205. (L.M.)

1 This child we dedicate to Thee,
　O God of grace and purity!
　Shield him from sin and threatening wrong
　And let Thy love his life prolong.

　O may Thy Spirit gently draw
　His willing soul to keep Thy law;
　May virtue, piety and truth,
　Dawn even with his dawning youth.

3 Give him a pure and steadfast heart,
　That from the truth will not depart,
　But every law obey, that's given;
　O! may he share the joys of heaven.

HYMN 206. (C.M.)

1 Lord, let Thy Holy Spirit now
  Shine forth in every heart,
That, as to worship Thee we've met,
  We may rejoicing part.

2 Speak through Thy servants, Lord, and may
  Thy truth each bosom swell,
While every lip and every heart
  Unite Thy love to tell.

HYMN 207. (C.M.)

1 Once more, my soul, the rising day
  Salutes thy waking eyes;
Now let my heart its tribute pay
  To Him who rules the skies.

2 Night unto night His name repeats,
  And day renews the sound;
Wide as the heavens on which He sits,
  To turn the seasons round.

3 'Tis He supports my mortal frame;
  My tongue shall sing His praise,
And I will glory in His name,
  While He extends my days.

4 And when my mortal course is done,
　　And I must yield my breath,
　O may my soul, bright as the sun,
　　Shine o'er the night of death.

HYMN 208.　(S.M.)

1 See how the morning sun
　　Pursues his shining way,
　And wide proclaims his Maker's praise
　　With every bright'ning ray.

2 Thus would my rising soul
　　Of heaven's parent sing,
　And spread the truth from pole to pole,
　　Of Jesus, my great King.

3 In faith I laid me down
　　Beneath His guardian care,
　I slept, and I awoke and found
　　That He was just as near.

4 O Lord, I want to live
　　So humbly unto Thee,
　That in Thy presence I may spend
　　A blest eternity.

5 Give me Thy Spirit, then,
   To guide me through this day,
That I may just and upright be,
   And always watch and pray.

HYMN 209. (L.M.)

1 Waked from my bed of slumber sweet,
   Refreshed in body and in mind,
The morning light with joy I greet,
   Aud offer up a song divine.

2 Thy praise, O God, shall be my theme,
   While day and night their course pursue,
Till time shall end its transient dream,
   Through endless day the theme renew.

3 Thy mercy has preserved my soul,
   Through toils and dangers, griefs and fears
And still upon this earthly ball
   It multiplies my days and years.

4 O, grant me, then, Thy Spirit's power,
   To guide my feet in ways of peace;
Preserve me Thine each day and hour,
   Till from a world of sin released.

5 Then when my mortal life is closed,
    Eternal glory mine shall be,
And, all arrayed in spotless white,
    I shall the King of Glory see.

HYMN 210. (C.M.)

1 Come, let us sing and evening hymn,
    To calm our minds for rest,
And each one try, with single eye,
    To praise the Savior best.

2 Yea, let us sing a sacred song,
    To close the passing day,
With one accord call on the Lord,
    And ever watch and pray.

3 O, thank the Lord for grace and gifts
    Renewed in latter days,
For truth and light to guide us right
    In wisdom's pleasant ways.

4 For every line we have received,
    To turn our hearts above,
For every word and every good
    That fill our souls with love.

5 O, let us raise a holier strain,
   For blessings great as ours,
And be prepared, while angels guard
   Us through our slumb'ring hours.

6 O, may we sleep and wake in joy,
   While life with us remains,
And then go home beyond the tomb,
   Where peace forever reigns.

HYMN 211. (L.M.)

1 Glory to Thee, my God, this night,
For all the blessings of the light;
Keep me, O keep me, King of kings,
Beneath the shadow of Thy wings.

2 Forgive me, Lord, for Thy dear Son,
The sins that I this day have done,
That with the world, myself and Thee,
I, ere I sleep, at peace may be.

3 Teach me to live that I may dread
The grave as little as my bed;
Teach me to die, that so I may
Triumphant rise to endless day.

4 Oh! may my soul on Thee repose,
   And may sweet sleep mine eyelids close—
   Sleep, that shall me more able make,
   To serve my God, when I awake.

5 If in the night I sleepless lie,
   My soul with heavenly thoughts supply;
   Let no ill dreams disturb my rest,
   Nor powers of darkness me molest.

6 Let my blest guardian, while I sleep,
   His watchful station near me keep;
   My heart with love celestial fill,
   And guard me from approach of ill.

7 May he celestial joys rehearse,
   And thought in thought with me converse,
   Or, in my stead, the whole night long,
   Sing to my God a grateful song.

8 Lord, let my soul forever share
   The bliss of Thy paternal care;
   'Tis heaven on earth, 'tis heaven above
   To see Thy face and sing Thy love.

9 O when shall I, in endless day,
   Forever chase dark sleep away,
   And hymns divine with angels sing,
   Glory to Thee, Eternal King!

HYMN 212. (L.M.)

1 Haste, glorious day when Christ shall come
   To reign supreme o'er land and sea,
When Saints shall all be gathered home
   And earth be ruled with equity.

HYMN 213. (L.M.)

Great God, to Thee my evening song
   With humble gratitude I raise;
O let Thy mercy tune my tongue,
   And fill my heart with lively praise.

2 My days, unclouded as they pass,
   And every onward rolling hour
Are monuments of wondrous grace,
   And witness to Thy love and power.

3 And yet this thoughtless, wretched heart,
   Too oft regardless of Thy love,
Ungrateful, can from Thee depart
   And from the path of duty rove.

4 Seal my forgiveness in the blood
   Of Christ, my Lord; His name alone
I plead for pardon, gracious God,
   And kind acceptance at Thy throne.

5 With hope in Him mine eyelids close,
    With sleep refresh my feeble frame,
And in Thy care may I repose,
    And wake with praises to Thy name.

HYMN 214. C.M.)

1 Lord, Thou wilt hear me when I pray,
    I am forever Thine!
I fear before Thee all the day;
    O may I never sin.

2 And while I rest my weary head,
    From cares and business free,
'Tis sweet conversing on my bed
    With my own heart and Thee.

3 I pay this evening sacrifice,
    And when my work is done,
Great God, my faith, my hope relies
    Upon Thy grace alone.

4 Thus, with my thoughts composed to peace,
    I'll give mine eyes to sleep;
Thy hand in safety keeps my days,
    And will my slumbers keep.

HYMN 215. (S.M.)

1 The day is past and gone,
    The evening shades appear;
O may we all remember well
    The night of death draws near.

2 We lay our garments by,
    While we retire to rest;
So death will soon disrobe us all
    Of what is here possessed.

    Lord, keep us safe this night
        Secure from all our fears,
    May angels guard us while we sleep
        Till morning light appears.

4 And when we early rise,
    And view the brilliant sun,
May we set out to win the prize,
    And after glory run.

5 And when our days are past,
    And we from time remove,
O may we in Thy kingdom rest,
    Where all is peace and love.

HYMN 216. (8's.)

1 Adieu, my dear brethren, adieu;
   Reluctant we give you the hand,
No more to assemble with you,
   Till we on Mount Zion shall stand.

2 Your acts of benevolence past,
   Your gentle compassionate love,
Henceforth in our mem'ry shall last,
   Though far from your sight we remove.

3 Our hearts swell with tender regret,
   And sigh at each parting embrace,
While heaven our course must direct,
   And others succeed in our place.

4 When trav'ling the Gospel to preach,
   Our course among strangers we steer;
Repentance and faith we will teach
   To all that are willing to hear.

5 O Shepherd of Israel, draw near,
   Thy glorious presence display,
Our parting reflections to cheer,
   And help us, Thy voice to obey.

6 Help us to refrain from each ill,
  Press forward for glory and peace,
 Our sacred engagements fulfil,
  Till Thou shalt command our release.

7 Then may we to Zion repair,
  And wait our blest Master to see,
 To spend the Millennium there,
  From sin and from sorrow set free.

8 How cheerful the thoughts of that rest,
  With Jesus our Savior to reign,
 Till we shall be changed with the blest,
  And glory celestial obtain.

HYMN 217.   (7's & 6's.)

1 Farewell, our friends and brethren,
  Here take the parting hand;
 We go to preach the Gospel
  In every foreign land.

2 Farewell our wives and children,
  Who render life so sweet,
 Dry up your tears, be faithful
  Till we again shall meet.

3 Farewell, ye scenes of childhood
  And fancies of our youth;
  We go to combat error
  With everlasting truth.

4 Farewell, all carnal pleasures,
    Which gild the scenes of mirth,
  Your days are surely numbered,
    To trouble man on earth.

5 Farewell, farewell our country;
    Our home is now abroad,
  To labor in the vineyard,
    In righteousness for God.

6 The gallant ships are ready
    To bear us o'er the sea,
  To gather up the blessed,
    That Zion may be free.

HYMN 218. (7's & 6's, D.)

1 From Greenland's icy mountains,
    From India's coral strand,
  Where Afric's sunny fountains,
    Roll down their golden sand,
  From many an ancient river,
    From many a palmy plain,

They call us to deliver
  Their land from error's chain.

2 What, though the spicy breezes
  Blow soft o'er Ceylon's isle;
Though every prospect pleases,
  And only man is vile;
In vain with lavish kindness
  The gifts of God are strewn,
The heathen in his blindness
  Bows down to wood and stone.

3 Shall we whose souls are lighted
  With wisdom from on high—
Shall we, to men benighted,
  The lamp of life deny?
Salvation! O salvation!
  The joyful sound proclaim,
Till earth's remotest nation
  Has learnt Messiah's name.

4 Waft, waft, ye winds, His story,
  And you, ye waters, roll,
Till, like a sea of glory,
  It spreads from pole to pole;
Till o'er our ransomed nature,
  The Lamb for sinners slain,
Redeemer, King, Creator,
  In bliss returns to reign.

HYMN 219. (11's.)

1 How often in sweet meditation my mind,
Where solitude reigned, and aside from mankind,
Has dwelt on the hour when the Savior did deign
To call me, His servant, to publish His name.

2 To lift up my voice and proclaim the glad news,
First unto the Gentiles, and then to the Jews,
That Jesus, Messiah, in clouds will descend,
Destroy the ungodly, the righteous defend.

3 How rich is the treasure, ye Priests of the Lord,
Entrusted to us, as made known by His word,
The plan of salvation, the Gospel of grace,
To publish abroad unto Adam's lost race.

4 O gladly we'll go to the isles and proclaim,
And nations unknown then shall hear of His fame;

Yea, kingdoms and countries, both Gentiles and Jews,
Shall see us and hear us proclaim the glad news.

5 And millions shall turn to the Lord, and rejoice
That they have made Jesus, the Savior, their choice;
From north and the south, from the east and the west,
We'll bring home our thousands in Zion to rest.

6 As clouds they shall fly to their glorious home,
As doves, to their windows, in flocks they shall come,
While empires shall tremble, and kingdoms decay,
As the visions of Daniel in plainness portray.

7 And Israel shall flourish and spread far abroad,
Till earth shall be full of the knowledge of God;
And thus shall the stone of the mountain roll forth,
Extend its dominion, and fill the whole earth.

HYMN 220. (C.M.D.)

1 The gallant ship is under way
    To bear me off to sea,
And yonder floats the streamer gay
    That says she waits for me.
The seamen dip the ready oar,
    As rippled waves oft tell,
They bear me swiftly from the shore;
    My native land, farewell!

2 I go, but not to plough the main,
    To ease a restless mind;
Nor yet to toil on battle's plain,
    The victor's wreath to find.
'Tis not for treasures that are hid
    In mountain or in dell,
'Tis not for joys like these I bid
    My native land, farewell!

3 I go to break the fowler's snare,
    To gather Israel home;
I go, the name of Christ to bear
    To lands and isles unknown.
And soon my pilgrim feet shall tread
    On land where errors dwell,
Whence light and truth have long since fled;
    My native land, farewell!

4 I go, an erring child of dust,
    Ten thousand foes among,
  Yet on his mighty arm I trust,
    Who makes the feeble strong.
  My sun, my shield, forever nigh,
    He will my fears dispel,
  This hope supports me when I sigh,
    My native land, farewell!

5 I go, devoted to His cause
    And to His will resigned;
  His presence will supply the loss
    Of all I leave behind.
  His promise cheers the sinking heart
    And lights the darkest cell,
  To exiled pilgrims grace imparts;
    My native land, farewell!

6 I go, it is my Master's call,
    He's made my duty plain;
  No danger can the heart appall
    When Jesus stoops to reign.
  And now the vessel's side we've made,
    The sails their bosoms swell,
  Thy beauties in the distance fade;
    My native land farewell!

HYMN 221. (8's, 7's & 4.)

Yes, my native land I love thee,
   All thy scenes, I love them well;
Friends, connections, happy country,
   Can I bid you all farewell?
     Can I leave thee,
Far in distant lands to dwell?

2 Home! thy joys are passing lovely,
   Joys no stranger heart can tell;
Happy home! 'tis sure I love thee,
   Can I, can I say farewell?
     Can I leave thee,
Far in distant lands to dwell?

3 Holy scenes of joy and gladness
   Every fond emotion swell;
Can I banish heartfelt sadness,
   While I bid my home farewell?
     Can I leave thee,
Far in distant lands to dwell?

4 Yes, I hasten from you gladly,
   From the scenes I love so well,
Far away, ye billows, bear me,
   Lovely, native land, farewell!
     Pleased I leave thee,
Far in distant lands to dwell.

5 In the deserts let me labor,
   On the mountains let me tell
How He died, the blessed Savior,
   To redeem a world from hell.
     Let me hasten,
Far in distant lands to dwell.

6 Bear me on, thou restless ocean,
   Let the winds my canvass swell;
Heaves my heart with warm emotion,
   While I go far hence to dwell.
     Glad I bid thee,
Native land, farewell, farewell!

HYMN 222. (L.M.)

1 Farewell, my kind and faithful friend,
   The partner of my early youth,
While from my home my steps I bend,
   To warn mankind and teach the truth.

2 How oft, in silent evening mild,
   I to some lovely place repair,
Thy love and kindness call to mind,
   And lift my voice in humble prayer.

3 O Lord, extend Thine arms of love
   Around the partner of my heart,
For Thou hast spoken from above,
   And called me from my all to part.

Preserve her soul in perfect peace,
  From sickness, sorrow, grief and pain,
Until our pilgrimage shall cease,
  And we on Zion's hill shall reign.

How gladly would my soul retire,
  With thee to spend a peaceful life
In some sequestered, humble vale,
  Far from the scenes of noise and strife.

Where men should grieve our souls no more,
  Nor rage of sin disturb our peace;
Our troubles, toils and sorrows o'er
  Their lies and persecution cease.

HYMN 223. (L.M.)

1 Behold! the harvest wide extends,
   The fields are white o'er all the plain,
The tares in bundles must be bound,
   While we with care secure the grain.

Shall we repine when Jesus calls,
  Or count it sacrifice we make,
To spend our lives as pilgrims here,
  Or lose them for the Gospel sake

3 When Jesus Christ has done the same,
    Without a place to lay His head;
A pilgrim on the earth He came,
    Until for us His blood was shed.

4 Shall we behold the nations doomed
    To sword and famine, blood and fire,
Yet not the least exertion make,
    But from the scene in peace retire?

5 No; while His love for me extends,
    The pattern makes my duty plain;
I'll sound to earth's remotest ends,
    His Gospel to the sons of men.

6 Farewell, my kind and faithful friend,
    Until we meet on earth again,
For soon our pilgrimage shall end,
    And the Messiah come to reign.

HYMN 224. (12's & 11's.)

1 Adieu to the city where long I have wandered
    To tell them of judgments and warn them to flee;
    How often in sorrow their woes I have pondered!
    Perhaps in affliction they'll think upon me.

2 With tears of compassion, in silence retir-
        ing,   [expiring,
    The last ray of hope for your safety
  A feeling of pity this bosom inspiring,
    Sing this lamentation, and think upon me.

  How often at evening your halls have re-
        sounded
    With th' pure testimony of Jesus so free,
  While the meek were rejoicing, the proud
        were confounded,   [upon me.
    The poor had the Gospel; they'll think

4 When empires shall tremble at Israel's re-
        turning,
    And earth shall be cleansed by the spirit
        of burning,
  When proud men shall perish, and priests
        with their learning,
    Sing this lamentation, and think upon me.

5 When th' Union is severed, and liberty's
        blessings,   [free,
    Withheld from the sons of Columbia, once
  When bloodshed and war and famine dis-
        tress them,   [me.
    Remember the warning, and think upon

6 When this mighty city shall crumble to ruin,
    And sink as a millstone, the merchants
        undoing,

The ransomed the highway of Zion pursuing,
Sing this lamentation, and think upon me.

HYMN 225. (8's, 7's & 4.)

1 Come, thou glorious day of promise,
   Come and spread thy cheerful ray,
When the scattered sheep of Israel
   Shall no longer go astray;
     When hosannas,
   With united voice they'll cry.

2 Lord, how long wilt Thou be angry?
   Shall Thy wrath forever burn?
Rise, redeem Thine ancient people,
   Their transgressions from them turn.
     King of Israel,
   Come and set Thy people free.

3 O, that soon Thou wouldst to Jacob
   Thy enlivening Spirit send!
Of their unbelief and mis'ry
   Make, O Lord, a speedy end.
     Lord, Messiah!
   Prince of Peace o'er Israel reign.

HYMN 226. (L.M.)

1 Farewell, ye servants of the Lord,
To whom we oft have preached the word,

May you improve the wisdom given,
And lead ten thousand souls to heaven.

2 Farewell, ye Saints of Latter days,
With whom we've met in prayer and praise,
And in whose hearts the truth has shone,
By which we've gathered all in one.

3 Farewell, kind friends, whose hearts are true,
We can no longer stay with you;
Arise, the voice of truth obey,
O come and wash your sins away.

4 Farewell to all whose stubborn will
Binds them in chains of darkness still;
Our voice no longer your shall hear,
Till Jesus shall in clouds appear.

5 Then you shall see and hear and know
What you rejected here below;
Though you may sink in endless pain,
Yet truth eternal will remain.

HYMN 227. (6-7's.)

1 When shall we all meet again?
When shall we our rest obtain?
When, our pilgrimage be o'er,
Parting sighs be known no more?

When Mount Zion we regain,
There we all may meet again.

2 We to foreign climes repair,
Truth's the message which we bear,
Truth which angels oft have borne,
Truth to comfort those who mourn;
Truth eternal will remain,
On its rock we'll meet again.

3 Now the bright and morning star
Spreads its glorious light afar,
Kindles up the rising dawn
Of that bright Millennial morn;
When the Saints shall rise and reign,
In the clouds we'll meet again.

4 When the sons of Israel come,
When they build Jerusalem,
When the house of God is reared,
And Messiah's way prepared;
When from heaven He comes to reign,
Then we all may meet again.

5 When the earth is cleansed by fire,
When the wicked's hopes expire,
When in cold oblivion's shade,
Proud oppressors all are laid,
Long will Zion's mount remain,
There we all may meet again.

HYMN 228. (11's.)

1 To leave my dear friends and from neighbors to part,
And go from my home, gives me sorrow of heart,
With thoughts of absenting myself far away
From that house of God where I've chosen to pray.

2 But Jesus now calls me, a message to bear
To kingdoms and countries and islands afar;
His presence will bless me and be with me there,
His Spirit inspire me, in answer to prayer.

3 Then why should I linger with fondest desire
O'er home, and the raptures its comforts inspire?
For sweeter, O sweeter, the message I bear,
To comfort the mourner, in answer to prayer.

4 Dear friends, I must leave you and bid you adieu,
And pay my devotion in parts to me new,
And still I remember in pilgrimage there,
The joys that we tasted in answer to prayer.

5 And oft when the day's busy bustle will close,
As nature lies sleeping in silent repose,
To some lone retreat I will fondly repair,
Remember my kindred and pray for them there.

HYMN 229. (4-6's & 2-8's.)

1 When time shall be no more,
    It joys and sorrows fled,
When all its cares are o'er,
    And numbered with the dead,
Unveiled, eternal truth shall shine,
In its own image, all divine.

2 The Saints in robes of light
    Shall walk the golden street,
Rejoice in Jesus' sight
    And worship at His feet;
Shall rule on thrones eternally
Endowed with might and majesty.

3 O, sinner, wouldst thou stand
    In that blest company?
Obey the Lord's command,
    And from thy sins be free.
I shall be there and look for thee;
Farewell! till then, remember me.

HYMN 230. (P.M.)

1 An angel came down from the mansions of
   glory,
  And told that a record was hid in Cumorah,
  Containing our Savior's glorious Gospel,
  And also the cov'nant to gather His people.
   O Israel! O Israel! in all your abidings,
    Prepare for your Lord, when you hear
     these glad tidings.

2 A heavenly treasure, a book full of merit,
  It speaks from the dust by the power of the
   Spirit;
  A voice from the Savior that Saints can
   rely on,
  To watch for the day when he brings again
   Zion.

   O Israel! O Israel! etc.

3 O listen, ye isles, and give ear every nation,
  For great things await you in this gener-
   ation,
  The kingdom of Jesus in Zion shall flourish,
  The righteous will gather, the wicked must
   perish.
   O Israel! O Israel! etc.

HYMN 231. (7's & 6's.)

1 If you could hie to Kolob,
    In th' twinkling of an eye,
And then continue onward,
    With that same speed to fly,

2 D'ye think that you could ever,
    Through all eternity,
Find out the generation
    Where Gods began to be?

3 Or see the grand beginning,
    Where space did not extend?
Or view the last creation,
    Where Gods and matter end?

4 Methinks the Spirit whispers,
    "No man has found 'pure space,'
Nor vacuum yet discovered
    Where nothing has a place.

5 The works of Gods continue,
    And world's and lives abound;
Improvement and progression
    Have one eternal round.

6 There is no end to matter,
　　There is no end to space,
　There is no end to spirit,
　　There is no end to race.

7 There is no end to virtue,
　　There is no end to might,
　There is no end to wisdom,
　　There is no end to light.

8 There is no end to union,
　　There is no end to youth,
　There is no end to priesthood
　　There is no end to truth.

　There is no end to glory,
　　There is no end to love,
　There is no end to being,
　　There is no death above."

HYMN 232.　(C.M.)

1 To Him who rules on high,
　　Whom heavenly hosts adore,
　The sovereign Lord of earth and sky,
　　Be glory evermore.

2 Let Saints their voices raise,
   His wond'rous love to sing,
  Conspire with one accord to praise
   Their Father and their King.

3 Extol the wisdom great
   That framed salvation's scheme,
  Which not alone could man create,
   But fallen man redeem.

4 Sing of the glorious time
   When all will own His sway,
  And sing His praise in song sublime,
   In realms of endless day.

HYMN 233. (8's.)

1 A poor wayfaring man of grief
   Hath often crossed me on the way,
  Who sued so humbly for relief
   That I could never answer, Nay.

2 I had not power to ask His name,
   Whereto He went or whence He came,
  Yet there was something in His eye
   That won my love, I knew not why.

3 Once, when my scanty meal was spread,
    He entered, not a word He spake;
Just perishing for want of bread,
    I gave Him all, He blessed it, brake,

4 And ate, but gave me part again;
Mine was an angel's portion then,
For while I fed with eager haste,
The crust was manna to my taste.

5 I spied him where a fountain burst
    Clear from the rock; his strength was gone,
The heedless water mocked his thirst,
    He heard it, saw it hurrying on.

6 I ran and raised the suff'rer up;
Thrice from the stream he drained my cup,
Dipped, and returned it running o'er;
I drank and never thirsted more.

7 'Twas night; the floods were out; it blew
    A winter-hurricane aloof;
I heard His voice abroad, and flew
    To bid Him welcome to my roof.

8 I warmed and clothed and cheered my guest,
And laid Him on my couch to rest,
Then made the earth my bed, and seemed
In Eden's garden while I dreamed.

9 Stript, wounded, beaten nigh to death,
　　I found Him by the highway side;
　I roused His pulse, brought back His breath,
　　Revived His spirit, and supplied

10 Wine, oil, refreshment—He was healed;
　　I had myself a wound concealed,
　　But from that hour forgot the smart,
　　And peace bound up my broken heart.

11 In prison I saw Him next, condemned
　　To meet a traitor's doom at morn;
　　The tide of lying tongues I stemmed,
　　And honored Him 'mid shame and scorn.

12 My friendship's utmost zeal to try,
　　He asked if I for Him would die;
　　The flesh was weak, my blood ran chill,
　　But the free spirit cried, "I will!"

13 Then in a moment to my view,
　　The stranger darted from disguise;
　　The tokens in His hands I knew,
　　The Savior stood before mine eyes.

14 He spake, and my poor name He named,
　　"Of Me thou hast not been ashamed;
　　These deeds shall thy memorial be,
　　Fear not, thou didst them unto Me."

HYMN 234. (6's & 7's, D.)

1 Come, all ye sons of Zion,
    And let us praise the Lord;
His ransomed are returning,
    According to His word;
In sacred songs and gladness
    They walk the narrow way,
And thank the Lord who brought them
    To see the latter day.

2 Come, ye dispersed of Judah,
    Join in the theme and sing,
With harmony unceasing,
    The praises of our King,
Whose arm is now extended,
    On which the world may gaze,
To gather up the righteous
    In these the latter days.

3 Rejoice, rejoice, O Israel,
    And let your joys abound!
The voice of God shall reach you
    Wherever you are found,
And call you back from bondage,
    That you may sing His praise
In Zion's peaceful valleys,
    In these the latter days.

4 Then gather up for Zion,
   Ye Saints throughout the land,
And clear the way before you,
   As God shall give command.
Though wicked men and devils
   Exert their power, 'tis vain,
Since He who is eternal
   Has said you shall obtain.

HYMN 235. (6-7's.)

Earth, with her ten thousand flowers,
Air, with all its beams and showers,
Heaven's infinite expanse,
Sea's resplendent countenance,
All around and all above
Bear this record, God is love.

2 Sounds among the vales and hills,
   In the woods and by the rills,
Of the breeze and of the bird,
By the gentle murmur stirred,
Sacred songs, beneath, above,
Have one chorus, God is love.

3 All the hopes that sweetly start
From the fountain of the heart,
All the bliss that ever comes
To our earthly human homes,
All the voices from above
Sweetly whisper, God is love.

HYMN 236. (8's, 7's & 4.)

1 Guide us, O Thou great Jehovah,
   Guide us to the promised land.
We are weak, but Thou art able—
   Hold us with Thy powerful hand.
      Holy Spirit,
Feed us till the Savior comes.

2 Open, Jesus, Zion's fountains,
   Let her richest blessings come,
Let the fiery, cloudy pillar
   Guard us to this holy home.
      Great Redeemer,
Bring, O, bring the welcome day!

3 When the earth begins to tremble,
   Bid our fearful thoughts be still;
When Thy judgments spread destruction,
   Keep us safe on Zion's hill,
      Singing anthems,
Songs of glory unto Thee.

HYMN 237. (11's.)

1 How firm a foundation, ye Saints of the Lord,
Is laid for your faith in His excellent word!
What more can He say than to you He hath said,
You who unto Jesus for refuge have fled?

2 In every condition, in sickness, in health,
In poverty's vale or abounding in wealth,
At home or abroad, on the land or the sea,
As thy days demand it, thy succor shall be.

3 Fear not, I am with thee, O, be not dismayed, [aid;
For I am Thy God, and will still give thee
I'll strengthen thee, help thee, and cause thee to stand,
Upheld by my righteous, omnipotent hand.

4 When through the deep waters I call thee to go,
The rivers of sorrow shall not thee o'erflow,
For I will be with thee, thy troubles to bless,
And sanctify to thee thy deepest distress.

5 When through fiery trials thy pathway
    shall lie,
My grace, all sufficient, shall be thy supply
The flame shall not hurt thee, I only design
Thy dross to consume and thy gold to refine.

6 E'en down to old age, all my people shall
    prove
My sov'reign, eternal, unchangeable love;
And then, when gray hairs shall their
    temples adorn,
Like lambs shall they still in my bosom be
    borne.

7 The soul that on Jesus hath leaned for
    repose
I will not, I cannot desert to His foes;
That soul, though all hell should endeavor
    to shake,
I'll never, no never, no never forsake!

HYMN 238. (6, 6, 8, D.)

1 How pleasant 'tis to see
   Kindred and friends agree;
Each in his proper station move,
   And each fulfil his part,
   With sympathizing heart,
In all the cares of life and love.

2 'Tis like the ointment shed
   On Aaron's sacred head:
Divinely rich, divinely sweet,
   The oil through all the room
   Diffused a choice perfume,
Ran through his robes and blest his feet.

3 Like fruitful showers of rain
   That water all the plain,
Descending from surrounding hills,
   Such streams of pleasure roll
   Through every friendly soul,
Where love like heavenly dew distils.

HYMN 239. (6, 6, 8, D.)

1 How pleased and blest was I
   To hear the people cry,
"Come, let us seek our God to-day;"
   Yes, with a cheerful zeal,
   We'll haste to Zion's hill,
And there our vows and honors pay.

2 Zion, thrice happy place,
   Adorned with wondrous grace,
High walls of strength embrace thee round
   In thee our tribes appear,
   To praise and pray and hear
The sacred Gospel's joyful sound.

3 There, David's greater Son
   Has fixed His royal throne;
He sits for grace and judgment there,
   He bids the Saints be glad,
   He makes the sinners sad,
And humble souls rejoice with fear.

4 May peace attend thy gates,
   While joy within thee waits,
To bless the soul of every guest!
   The man that seeks thy peace,
   And wishes thine increase,
A thousand blessings on him rest.

5 My tongue repeats her vows,
   "Peace to this sacred house!
For here my friends and kindred dwell;"
   And since my glorious God
   Makes thee His blest abode,
My soul shall ever love thee well.

HYMN 240. (L.M.)

1 Know this, that every soul is free
To choose his life and what he'll be,
For this eternal truth is given;
That God will force no man to heaven.

2 He'll call, persuade, direct aright,
And bless with wisdom, love and light;
In nameless ways, be good and kind,
But never force the human mind.

3 Freedom and reason make us men,
Take these away, what are we then?
Mere animals, and just as well
The beasts may think of heaven or hell.

4 May we no more our powers abuse,
But ways of truth and goodness choose;
Our God is pleased when we improve
His grace, and seek His perfect love.

5 It is my free will to believe,
'Tis God's free will me to receive,
To stubborn willers this I'll tell,
'Tis all free grace and all free will.

6 Those who despise grow harder still,
If they adhere He turns their will,
And thus despisers sink to hell,
While those who heed in glory dwell.

7 But if we take the downward road,
And make in hell our last abode,
Our God is clear, and we shall know
We plunged ourselves in endless woe.

HYMN 241. (L.M.)

1 The great and glorious Gospel light
Has ushered forth into my sight,
Which in my soul I have received,
From bondage and from death relieved.

2 With Saints below and Saints above
I'll join to praise the God I love,
Like Enoch, too, I will proclaim
A loud hosanna to His name.

3 Hosanna! let the echo fly
From pole to pole, from sky to sky,
And Saints and angels join to sing,
Till all eternity shall ring.

4 Hosanna! let the voice extend,
Till time shall cease and have an end,
Till all the throngs of heaven above
Shall join the Saints in songs of love.

5 Hosanna! let the trump of God
Proclaim His wonders far abroad,
And earth and air and skies and seas
Conspire to sound aloud His praise.

HYMN 242. (L.M.)

1 The happy day has rolled on,
The truth restored is now made known,
The promised angel's come again
To introduce Messiah's reign.

2 The Gospel trump again is heard,
The truth from darkness has appeared,
The lands which long benighted lay,
Have now beheld a glorious day.

3 The day by Prophets long foretold,
The day which Abram did behold,
The day that Saints desired so long,
When God His strange work would perform·

4 The day when Saints again shall hear
The voice of Jesus in their ear,
And angels, who above do reign,
Come down to converse hold with men.

HYMN 243. (C.M.)

1 Come, listen to a Prophet's voice,
And hear the word of God,
And in the way of truth rejoice,
And sing for joy aloud.

CHORUS.

We've found the way the Prophets went,
  Who lived in days of yore;
Another Prophet now is sent,
  This knowledge to restore.

2 The gloom of sullen darkness, spread
  Through earth's extended space,
Is banished by our living Head,
  And God has shown His face.

3 Through erring schemes in days now past,
  The world has gone astray;
Yet Saints of God have found at last
  The straight and narrow way.

4 'Tis not in man they put their trust,
  Or on his arm rely,
Full well assured, all are accursed,
  Who Jesus Christ deny.

5 The Savior to His people saith,
  Let all my words obey,
And signs shall follow living faith,
  Down to the latest day.

6 The sick on whom the oil is poured,
  And hands in meekness laid,
Are by the power of God restored,
  Through faith, as Jesus said.

7 No more in slavish fear we mourn,
　　Nor yoke of bondage wear;
　No more beneath delusion groan,
　　Nor superstitious fear.

8 Of every dispensation past,
　　Of every promise made,
　The first be last, the last be first,
　　The living and the dead.

9 To Zion's mount shall saviors come,
　　Their thousands bring to rest,
　Who through the great Millennium,
　　Shall be among the blest.

HYMN 244.　(11's & 12's.)

1 The Spirit of God like a fire is burning!
　　The latter-day glory begins to come forth,
　The visions and blessings of old are return-
　　　ing,
　　And angels are coming to visit the earth.
　We'll sing and we'll shout with the armies
　　　of heaven,
　　Hosanna, hosanna to God and the Lamb!
　Let glory to them in the highest be given,
　　Henceforth and forever; Amen and Amen!

2 The Lord is extending the Saints' under-
    standing,
  Restoring their judges and all as at first,
  The knowledge and power of God are ex-
    panding,
  The vail o'er the earth is beginning to burst.
        We'll sing and we'll shout, etc.

3 We'll call in our solemn assemblies in spirit,
  To spread forth the kingdom of heaven
    abroad,
  That we through our faith may begin to in-
    herit
  The visions and blessings and glories of God.
        We'll sing and we'll shout, etc.

4 We'll wash and be washed, and with oil be
    anointed,
  Withal not omitting the washing of feet,
  For he that receiveth his penny appointed
  Must suerly be clean at the harvest of wheat.
        We ll sing and we'll shout, etc.

5 Old Israel, that fled from the world for his
    freedom,   [amain,
  Must come with the cloud and the pillar
  A Moses and Aaron and Joshua lead him,
  And feed him on manna from heaven again.
        We'll sing and we'll shout, etc.

6 How blessed the day when the lamb and the lion
Shall lie down together without any ire,
And Ephraim be crowned with his blessing in Zion,
As Jesus decends with His chariots of fire!

We'll sing and we'll shout with the armies of heaven,
Hosanna, hosanna to God and the Lamb!
Let glory to them in the highest be given,
Henceforth and forever; Amen, and Amen!

HYMN 245. (11's.)

1 The sun that declines in the far western sky
Has rolled o'er our heads till the summer's gone by,
And hushed are the notes of the warbles of spring,
That in the green bower did exultingly sing.

2 The changes for autumn already appear,
A harvest of plenty has crowned the glad year,

While soft smiling zephyrs from orchards and bowers,
Bring odors of joy from the fruit and the flowers.

3 The summer of youth passes swiftly away,
The locks of our temples are silvered with gray;
And so the fair landscape and flowery lawn,
Though loosing their beauty, their glory put on.

4 O, when the sweet summer of life shall have fled,
Her joys and her sorrows entombed with the dead,
Then may we, by faith, like good Enoch, arise,
Be crowned with the just in the midst of the skies;

5 Descend with the Savior in glory profound,
And reign in perfection when Satan is bound,
While love and sweet union together shall blend,
And peace, gentle peace, like a river extend,

HYMN 246. (L.M.)

1 The towers of Zion soon shall rise
 Their lofty spires toward the skies,
 Attract the gaze and wond'ring eyes
  Of all that worship, gloriously.

2 The Saints shall see their cities stand
 Upon the consecrated land,
 And Israel, numerous as the sand,
  Inherit them eternally.

3 O that the day would hasten on,
 When wickedness shall all be gone,
 And Saints and angels join in one,
  To praise the Man of Holiness!

4 Then will the vail of heaven rend,
 The Son Ah-Man in power descend,
 A vast eternity to spend
  In perfect peace and righteousness.

5 Exalt the name of Zion's God,
 Praise ye His name in songs aloud,
 Proclaim His majesty abroad,
  Ye banner-bearing messengers.

6 Cry to the nations far and near,
 To come and in the glory share
 Which on Mount Zion will appear,
  When earth shall rest from wickedness.

HYMN 247. (12's, 11's & 10's.)

1 There is now a feast for the righteous preparing,
The good of this world all the Saints shall be sharing;
The harvest is ripe, and the reapers have learned
To gather the wheat that the tares may be burned.
Come to the supper, come to the supper,
Come to the supper of the great Bridegroom.

2 Go forth, all ye servants, go visit each nation,
And lift up your voices and make proclamation,
To cease from all evil and leave off all mirth
The Savior is coming to reign on the earth.
Come to the supper, etc.

3 Go, set forth the judgments to come, and the sorrow,
For after to-day, O! there cometh to-morrow,

When sinners, ungodly, rebellious and proud,
Shall burn like the stubble, O! cry it aloud.
    Come to the supper, etc.

4 Go, pass throughout Europe and Asia's dark regions,
To China's far shores, and to Africa's legions;
Proclaim to all people, as you're passing by,
The fig trees are leafing, the summer is nigh.
    Come to the supper, etc.

5 Go, call on the great men of fame and of power,
The king on his throne and the brave in his tower;
Inform them all kingdoms must fall but the one
As clear as the moon and as fair as the sun.
    Come to the supper, etc.

6 Go, preach on the continents, then on the islands,
To Jews and to Gentiles, in valleys and highlands;

Exclaim to old Israel in every land,
Repent ye! the kingdom of God is at hand.
   Come to the supper, etc.

7 Go, carry glad tidings, that none need doubt whether
The lamb and the lion shall lie down together;
The venom will cease when the devil is bound, [round.
And peace, like a river, extend the world
   Come to the supper, etc.

8 Go, publish the Gospel, the truth of the Savior; [find favor
The poor and the meek may begin to
And joy in their coming Redeemer and Friend,
For lo! He is with you henceforth to the end.
   Come to the supper, etc.

9 O go and invite them, regardless of trouble,
The rich and the learned, the wise and the noble,
That they may be ready when Jesus shall come,
To welcome forever the holy Bridegroom.
   Come to the supper, etc.

10 Go, gather the willing, and push them together,
  Yes, push them to Zion, (the Saints' rest forever,)
  Where all that the heavens and earth can afford
  Will grace the first marriage and feast of the Lord.
      Come to the supper, etc.

11 Go, welcome His people, let nothing preclude you,
  Come, Joseph and Simeon, Reuben and Judah,
  Come, Napthali, Issachar, Levi and Dan,
  Gad, Zebulon, Asher, and come Benjamin.
      Come to the supper, etc.

12 Be faithful and just to the end of your calling
  Till Babel the great and the proud shall be fallen!
  Return then and take the just servant's reward;
  Sit down to the feast of the house of the Lord,
  Come to the supper, come to the supper,
  Come to the supper with the great Bridegroom.

HYMN 248. (P.M.)

1 This earth was once a garden place,
 With all her glories common,
And men did live a holy race,
And worship Jesus face to face,
 In Adam-ondi-Ahman.

2 We read that Enoch walked with God,
 Above the power of mammon,
And Zion spread herself abroad,
And Saints and angels sang aloud,
 In Adam-ondi-Ahman.

3 Her land was good and greatly blest,
 Beyond old Israel's Canaan,
Her fame was known from east to west,
Her peace was great, and pure the rest
 Of Adam-ondi-Ahman.

4 Hosanna to such days to come,
 The Savior's second coming,
When all the earth in glorious bloom
Affords the Saints a holy home,
 Like Adam-ondi-Ahman.

HYMN 249. (L.M. or 6-8's.)

1 Though in the outward Church below
 The wheat and tares together grow,

Ere long will Jesus weed the crop,
And pluck the tares in anger up.
  For soon the reaping time will come,
  And angels shout the harvest home.

2 Will it relieve their horror there
To recollect their stations here—
How much they heard, how much they knew,
How much among the wheat they grew?

3 No; this will aggravate their case,
They perish under means of grace,
To them the word of life and faith
Became an instrument of death.

4 We seem alike when here we meet,
Strangers may think we all are wheat,
But to the Lord's all searching eyes,
Each heart appears without disguise.

5 The tares are spared for various ends,
Some for the sake of praying friends,
Others, the Lord, against their will,
Employ, His counsels to fulfil.

6 But though they grow so tall and strong,
His plan will not require them long;
In harvest, when He saves His own,
The tares shall into hell be thrown.

7 O! awful thought, and is it so?
Must all mankind the harvest know?
Is ev'ry man a wheat or tare?
Me for that harvest, Lord, prepare.

HYMN 250. (12's & 11's D.)

1 What fair one is this, from the wilderness trav'ling,
And looking for Christ, the beloved of her heart?
O, this is the Church, the fair bride of the Savior,
Who with every idol is willing to part;
While men in contention are constantly howling,
And Babylon's bells are continually tolling,
From now all the craft of her merchants is failing,
And Jesus is coming to reign on the earth.

2 There is a sweet sound in the Gospel of heaven, [stand;
And people are joyful when they under-
The Saints on their way home to glory are even
Determined by goodness to reach the blest land.
Old formal professors are crying "delusion,"
And high-minded hypocrites say, "'tis confusion,"

While grace is poured out in a blessed effusion,
: And Saints are rejoicing that priestcraft must fall.

3 A blessing! a blessing! the Savior is coming,
: As prophets and pilgrims of old have declared,
And Israel, the favored of God, is beginning
: To come to the feast for the righteous prepared.
The desert has fountains continually spring-[ing,
The heavenly music of Zion is ringing,
The Saints all their tithes and their off'rings are bringing,
: They thus prove the Lord and His blessings receive.

4 The name of Jehovah is worthy of praising,
: And so is the Savior an excellent theme;
The Elders of Israel a standard are raising,
: And calling all nations to come to the same.
These Elders go forth and the good news are telling,
Their words find a place in the hearts of the willing,
And thus is the vision of Daniel fulfilling,
: The stone of the mountain will soon fill the earth.

HYMN 251. (8's.)

1 When Joseph his brethren beheld
   Afflicted and trembling with fear,
His heart with compassion was filled,
   From weeping he could not forbear.

2 Awhile his behavior was rough,
   To bring their past sins to their mind;
But when they were humbled enough,
   He hastened to show himself kind.

3 How little they thought it was he,
   Whom they had ill-treated and sold!
How great their confusion must be,
   As soon as his name he had told!

4 "I'm Joseph, your brother," he said,
   "And still to my heart you are dear,
You sold me and thought I was dead,
   But God, for your sake, sent me here."

5 Though greatly distressed before,
   When charged with concealing the cup,
They now are confounded much more,
   Not one of them dared to look up.

6 "Can Joseph, whom we would have slain,
   Forgive us the evil we did?
And will he our households maintain?
   O, this is a brother indeed!"

HYMN 252. (L.M.)

1 When restless on my bed I lie,
  Still courting sleep, which still will fly,
  Then shall reflection's brighter power
  Illume the lonely midnight hour.

2 If hushed the breeze and calm the tide,
  Soft will the stream of mem'ry glide,
  And all the past, a gentle train,
  Waked by remembrance, live again.

3 If loud the wind, the tempest high
  And darkness wraps the sullen sky,
  I muse on life's tempestuous sea,
  And sigh, O Lord, to come to Thee.

4 Tossed on the deep and swelling wave,
  O, mark my trembling soul and save!
  Give to my view that harbor near,
  Where Thou wilt chase each grief and fear.

HYMN 253. (C.M.)

1 Hark! listen to the trumpeters!
 They sound for volunteers,
On Zion's bright and flowery mount
 Behold the officers.

2 Their horses white, their armor bright,
 With courage bold they stand,
Enlisting soldiers for their King,
 To march to Zion's land.

3 It sets my heart all in a flame
 A soldier brave to be;
I will enlist, gird on my arms
 And fight for liberty.

4 We want no cowards in our bands,
 Who will our colors fly,
We call for valiant-hearted men,
 Who're not afraid to die.

5 To see our armies on parade,
 How martial they appear!
All armed and dressed in uniform,
 They look like men of war.

6 They follow their great General,
 The great Eternal Lamb;
His garments stained in His own blood,
 King Jesus is His name.

7 The trumpets sound, the armies shout,
    They drive the hosts of hell,
How dreadful is our God, our King,
    The great Emanuel.

8 Sinners enlist with Jesus Christ,
    Th' eternal Son of God,
And march with us to Zion's land,
    Beyond the swelling flood.

9 There on a green and flowery mount,
    Where fruits immortal grow,
With angels all arrayed in white,
    We'll our Redeemer know.

10 We'll shout and sing for evermore,
    In that eternal world,
While Satan and his army too
    Shall down to hell be hurled.

11 Lift up your heads, ye soldiers bold,
    Redemption now is nigh;
We soon shall hear the trumpet sound,
    That shakes the earth and sky.

12 In fiery chariots we shall rise,
    And leave the world on fire,
And all surround the throne of love,
    And join the heavenly choir.

HYMN 254. (P.M.)

1 The pure testimony poured forth in the Spirit,
  Cuts like a keen two-edged sword,
And hypocrites now are most sorely tormented,
  Because they're condemned by the word.
The pure testimony discovers the dross,
While wicked professors make light of the cross,
But Babylon trembles for fear of her loss.

2 Is not the time come for the Church to be gathered
  Into the one Spirit of God ?
Baptized by one Spirit into the one body,
  Partaking of Christ's flesh and blood ?
They drink in one spirit, which makes them all see
The're one in Christ Jesus wherever they be,
The Jew and the Gentile, the bond and the free.

3 Then blow ye the trumpet in pure testimony,
  And let the world hear it again!

O, come ye from Babylon, Egypt and Sodom,
   And make your way over the plain,
And gird on your armor, ye Saints of the Lord,
For Christ will direct you by His living word—
The pure testimony will cut like a sword.

4 The great prince of darkness is must'ring his forces
   To make you his captives again,
By flatteries, insults or vile persecution,
   That you in his cause may remain.
But shun his temptations wherever they lay,
And mind not his servants whatever they say—
The pure testimony will give you the day.

5 The world will not persecute those who are like them,
   But hold them the same as their own;
The pure testimony cries out, separation,
   And calls you your lives to lay down.
Come out from their spirit, and practices too,
The track of your Savior keep still in your view—
The pure testimony will cut the way through,

6 A battle is coming between the two kingdoms,
The armies are gathering round,
The pure testimony and vile persecution,
Will soon in close battle be found.
Then wash all your robes in the Lamb's cleansing blood,
And keep, as did Jesus, the Spirit of God.
By pure testimony are all things subdued.

HYMN 255. (L.M.)

1 Afflicted Saint, to Christ draw near,
Thy Savior's gracious promise hear;
His faithful word declares to thee
That "as thy day, thy strength shall be."

2 Let not thy heart despond and say,
"How shall I stand the trying day?"
He has engaged by firm decree
That "as thy day, thy strength shall be."

3 Should persecution rage and flame,
Still trust in thy Redeemer's name;
In fiery trials thou shalt see
That "as thy day, thy strength shall be."

4 If faith be weak and foes be strong,
And if the conflict should be long,

Thy Lord will make the tempter flee,
For "as thy day, thy strength shall be."

5 When called to bear the weighty cross
Of sore affliction pain or loss,
Or deep distress, or poverty,
Still "as thy day, thy strength shall be."

6 When ghastly death appears in view,
Christ's presence shall thy fears subdue;
He comes thy spirit to set free,
And "as thy day, thy strength shall be."

HYMN 256. (6-7's.)

1 Daniel's wisdom may I know,
Stephen's faith and patience show,
John's divine compassion feel,
Moses' meekness, Joshua's zeal,
Run like persevering Paul,
Win the prize and conquer all.

2 Mary's love may I possess,
Lydia's tender-heartedness,
Peter's ardent spirit feel,
James' faith by works reveal;
Like young Timothy may I
Every sinful passion fly.

3 Job's submission let me show,
　David's true devotion know,
　Samuel's call, O may I hear,
　Lazarus' happy portion share;
　Let Isaiah's hallowed fire
　All my new-born soul inspire.

4 Mine be Jacob's wrestling prayer,
　Gideon's valiant steadfast care,
　Joseph's purity impart,
　Isaac's meditative heart;
　Abram's friendship let me prove,
　Faithful to the God of love.

5 Most of all, may I pursue
　That example Jesus drew,
　In my life and conduct show
　How He lived and walked below;
　Day by day through grace conferred,
　Imitate my dearest Lord.

6 Then shall I these worthies meet,
　With them bow at Jesus' feet,
　With them praise the God of love,
　With them share the joys above,
　With them range the blissful shore,
　Meet them all to part no more.

HYMN 257. (L.M.)

1 When Joseph saw his brethren moved
    With keenest sorrow and distress,
He could no longer hide his love,
    No more his feelings could supress.

2 The mystery he did unfold,
    Then fell upon their necks in tears—
I am your brother whom you sold,
    Dismiss your doubts, dispel your fears.

3 'Twas God that sent me by command
    To save you from the famine sore,
To bring you into Egypt's land,
    Where you shall never hunger more.

4 What mingled feelings seized their breasts!
    Surprise and grief, and joy and love,
And shame and sorrow and distress,
    Alternate did their feelings move.

5 Lo! this a vivid type shall be
    Of Joseph's remnant long unknown;
The Gentiles shall their glory see,
    When to their brethren they are known.

6 A curse, a by-word they have been,
    Afflicted by the Gentile race,
  Despoiled and driven, sold and slain,
    Or brought to shame and deep disgrace.

7 But lo! their origin revealed
    Brings blessings on the Gentile world;
  Their ancient records long concealed,
    Are, like a banner, now unfurled.

HYMN 258. (C.M.)

1 Ye wond'ring nations, now give ear
    Unto the angel's cry,
  For lo! from heaven he does appear,
    To bring salvation nigh.

2 He brought the ancient records forth,
    Unloosed the mighty seal;
  His glory soon shall fill the earth,
    And wondrous things reveal.

3 The things of worth in ages gone,
    Its pages clear unfold,
  And things to come, now rolling on,
    The wise may well behold.

4 Its opening wonders burst to view,
    All glorious and sublime,
  Point out the path that men pursue,
    Down to the end of time.

5 The meek and humble shall rejoice,
    The wise shall understand;
  All Israel now shall know His voice,
    And gather to their land.

HYMN 259. (C.M.)

1 I saw a mighty angel fly,
    To earth he bent his way,
  A message bearing from on high,
    To cheer the sons of day.

2 Truth is the tidings which he bears,
    The Gospel's joyful sound,
  To calm our doubts, to chase our fears,
    And make our joys abound.

3 He cries, and with a mighty voice,
    Ye nations, lend an ear,
  And isles and continents rejoice,
    The great Redeemer's near!

4 He cries, let every tongue attend,
    And thrones and empires all!
  Fear God, and make the Lord your friend,
    The King, the Lord of all!

5 Fear God, and worship Him who made
    The heavens, earth and sea!
Fear Him on whom your sins were laid,
    Who died to make you free!

HYMN 260. (8's, 7's & 4.)

1 Go, ye messengers of glory,
    Run, ye legates of the skies,
Go and tell the pleasing story,
    That a glorious angel flies,
      Great and mighty,
    With a message from the skies.

2 Go to every tribe and nation,
    Visit every land and clime,
Sound to all the proclamation,
    Tell to all the truth sublime:
      That the Gospel
    Does in ancient glory shine.

3 Go! to all the Gospel carry,
    Let the joyful news abound;
Go! till every nation hear ye,
    Jew and Gentile hear the sound;
      Let the Gospel,
    Echo all the earth around.

4 Bearing seed of heavenly virtue,
   Scatter it o'er all the earth;
Go! Jehovah will support you,
   Gather all the sheaves of worth,
     Then, with Jesus,
Reign in glory on the earth.

HYMN 261. (4-6's & 2-8's.)

1 All hail the glorious day,
   By Prophets long foretold,
When, with harmonious lay,
   The sheep of Israel's fold
On Zion's hill his praise proclaim,
And shout hosanna to His name.

2 When Israel from afar
   And Judah scattered wide
Shall to their land repair,
   And there in peace abide,
Directed by Jehovah's hand,
Shall dwell in peace in Zion's land.

3 From Zion's heavenly mount
   Shall healing waters flow,
And near this holy fount
   Will trees immortal grow,
Whose heavenly balm the kingdoms feel
Whose leaves will all the nations heal.

Jerusalem shall be
  Our great Redeemer's throne,
O'er all the earth and sea,
  His glory be made known,
And nations, kings Messiah greet,
And lay their honors at his feet.

5 Strike, strike the golden lyre,
  And ye, His angels, sing,
Let joy your bosoms fire,
  And heaven with glory ring;
From earth, and air, and sea, and skies,
Let our Redeemer's praise arise.

HYMN 262. (L.M.

1 The glorious plan which God has given,
To bring a ruined world to heaven,
Was framed in Christ by the new birth,
Was sealed in heaven, was sealed on earth.

2 As in the heavens they all agree,
The record's given there by Three,
On earth three witnesses are given,
To lead the sons of earth to heaven.

3 Jehovah, God the Father's one,
Another, His Eternal Son,
The Spirit does with them agree,
The witnesses in heaven are three.

4 Nor are we in the second birth,
  Left without witnesses on earth,
  To grope, as in eternal night,
  About the way to endless light.

5 Buried beneath the liquid wave,
  To know the Spirit's power to save,
  And feel the virtue of His blood,
  Are witnesses ordained of God.

6 In heaven they all agree in One,
  The Father, Spirit and the Son,
  On earth these witnesses agree:
  The water, blood, and Spirit three.

7 One great connecting link is given
  Between the sons of earth and heaven:
  The Spirit seals us hear on earth,
  In heaven records our second birth.

8 If we on earth possess these three,
  Mysterious, saving unity,
  The Book of Life will record bear,
  Our names are surely written there.

HYMN 263. (8's & 7's.)

1 Truth reflects upon our senses,
 Gospel light reveals to some,
If there still should be offenses,
 Woe to them by whom they come.

2 Judge not, that you be not judged,
 Was the counsel Jesus gave,
Measure given, large or grudged,
 Just the same you must receive.

3 Jesus said, be meek and lowly,
 For 'tis high to be a judge;
If I would be pure and holy,
 I must love without a grudge.

4 It requires a constant labor,
 All His precepts to obey;
If I truly love my neighbor,
 I am in the narrow way.

5 Once I said unto another,
 In thine eye there is a mote,
If thou art a friendly brother,
 Hold, and let me pull it out.

6 But I could not see it fairly,
    For my sight was very dim,
When I came to search more clearly,
    In mine eye there was a beam.

7 If I love my brother dearer,
    And his mote I would erase,
Then the light should shine the clearer,
    For the eye's a tender place.

8 Others I have oft reproved,
    For an object like a mote,
Now I wish this beam removed,
    O! that tears would wash it out.

9 Charity and love are healing,
    These will give the clearest sight;
When I saw my brother's failing,
    I was not exactly right.

10 Now I'll take no farther trouble,
    Jesus' love is all my theme,
Little motes are but a bubble,
    When I think upon the beam.

HYMN 264. (3-7's & 4.)

1 Stars of morning, shout for joy,
Sing redemption's mystery,
Holy, holy, holy, cry,
    And praise the Lamb!

2 Ethiopia, stretch thy hand;
  Come, ye tribes of every land,
  Countless as the ocean's sand,
    To praise the Lamb.

3 Bend thy bow and come, good Lord,
  Send Thy Spirit with Thy word,
  Be Thy saving work restored,
    Thou bleeding Lamb.

4 My believing spirit fill,
  Faith demands, it is Thy will,
  All things now are possible,
    It shall be done.

5 Thus may we each moment feel,
  Love Him, serve Him, praise Him still,
  Till we meet on Zion's hill,
    To praise the Lamb.

6 Savior, let Thy kingdom come,
  Now the man of sin consume,
  Bring the blest Millennium,
    Exalted Lamb!

HYMN 265. (11's.)

1 Let Judah rejoice in this glorious news,
  The sound of glad tidings will soon reach
    the Jews.

And save them far, far from oppression and fear,
Deliv'rance proclaim to their sons far and near.

2 Long, long thou hast wandered an exile forlorn,
And all that have seen thee have laughed thee to scorn,
Thou nought but affliction and sorrow hast seen [been.
Heartrending and cheerless thy pathway has

3 In vain 'midst the nations for friends didst thou seek, [thou wast weak,
They robbed thee and spoiled thee because
No bosom has pitied, no friend has been near,
Thy woe-stricken spirit, to comfort and cheer.

4 But thy days of mourning are near at an end,
Messiah will come, thy Redeemer and friend,
To cheer thee, and bless thee, and dry up thy tears, [fears.
And calm thy sad bosom, and chase all thy

5 Messiah, the hope of all Israel will come,
To lead thee from islands and continents home.

Whom thou hast rejected, thy Savior shall
    be; [free.
He'll strike off thy fetters, and bid thee be

6 Thou shalt from affliction forever be free,
The sons of oppressors shall bow down to
    thee; [Jew,
Ten men shall take hold of the skirt of the
And say, "We will go, for Jehovah's with
    you."

7 Old Israel shall come from his place of
    retreat
And worship Messiah and bow at his feet,
And Abraham's seed from the nations shall
    come
And find in the land of their fathers a home.

8 As once the Red Sea was dried up by the
    rod, [God;
So thou shalt again see the power of thy
Thy Moses shall speak, and the waters shall
    flow,
Thy tribes shall in glory on dry land pass
    through.

9 Again thou shalt plant, and inhabit, and
    eat,
Thy soul shall be fed on the finest of wheat;

In beautiful valleys thy herds shall lie down,
And thou on the earth be a plant of renown.

10 Thy olive shall flourish, thy fig tree shall grow, [shall flow;
With wine, milk and honey thy mountains
Beneath the fig trees, in their cool spreading shade,
Thou shalt worship God, and none make thee afraid.

11 Mesiah will come, and His right will maintain,
Over thee and all nations, in majesty reign;
Thou shalt with His presence forever be blest,
From pain and from sorrow eternally rest.

HYMN 266. (L. M.)

1 When earth in bondage long had lain,
And darkness o'er the nations reigned,
And all man's precepts proved in vain,
A perfect system to obtain,

2 A voice resounded from on high.
Hark, hark! it is the angel's cry,

Descending from the throne of light,
His garments shining clear and white.

3 He comes to show the Gospel plan
In fulness to benighted man;
Lo! from Cumorah's lonely hill,
There comes a record of God's will.

4 Translated by the power of God,
His voice bears record to his word;
Again an angel did appear,
As witnesses do record bear,

5 Restored the Priesthood, long since lost,
In truth and power as at the first;
Thus men, commissioned from on high,
Came forth and did repentance cry,

6 Baptizing those who did believe,
That they the Spirit might receive,
In fulness, as in days of old,
And have one Shepherd and one fold.

HYMN 267. (L.M.)

1 Ye Gentile nations, cease your strife,
And listen to the words of life;
Turn from your sins with one accord,
Prepare to meet your coming Lord.

2 Let Judah's remnants, far and near,
  The glorious proclamation hear;
  For Israel and the Gentiles, too,
  The way to Zion shall pursue.

3 Their voices and their tongues employ
  In songs of everlasting joy,
  The mountains and the hills rejoice,
  Let all creation hear His voice.

4 From north to south, from east to west,
  In Thee all nations shall be blest,
  When Abram and his seed shall stand,
  Unnumbered on the promised land.

HYMN 268. (L.M.)

1 The solid rocks were rent in twain,
  When Christ the Lamb of God was slain;
  The sun in darkness vailed his face,
  The mountains moved, and left their place.

2 The whole creation groaned in pain,
  Till the Messiah rose again.
  Then nature ceased her dreadful groan,
  The sun unveiled his face and shone.

3 The righteous that were spared alive,
With joy and wonder did believe,
And soon together they convene,
Conversing on the things they'd seen,

4 Which had been given for a sign,
When lo! they heard a voice divine,
And as the heavenly voice they heard,
The Lord of glory soon appeared.

5 With joy and wonder, all amazed,
Upon their glorious Lord they gazed,
And wist not what the vision meant,
But thought it was an angel sent,

6 While in their midst He smiling stood,
Proclaimed Himself the Son of God,
And said, "Come forth and feel and see,
That you may witness bear of me."

7 And when they all had looked and seen
Where once the nails and spear had been,
Hosanna! rose with loud acclaim,
They blessed and praised His holy name.

8 He then proceeded to make plain
His Gospel to the sons of men;
The prophecies He did unfold,
Yea, things that were in days of old,

9 And every thing that should transpire,
Till elements should melt with fire;
Gave them commandments to record
The sayings of their risen Lord.

10 That generation should be blest,
And with Him in His kingdom rest.
But O! what scenes of sorrow rolled
When He the future did unfold!

11 Four generations should not pass,
Until they'd turn from righteousness,
The Nephite nation be destroyed,
The Lamanites reject His word.

12 The Gospel taken from their midst,
The record of their fathers hid,
They dwindle long in unbelief,
And ages pass without relief.

13 Until the Gentiles from afar,
Should smite them in a dreadful war,
And take possession of their land,
And they should have no power to stand.

14 But as their remnants wander far,
In darkness, sorrow and despair,
Lo! from the earth their record comes
To gather Israel to their homes.

15 First to the Gentiles 'tis revealed;
The prophecy must be fulfilled,
That they may know and understand
His Gospel, and no more contend.

16 Hear, O ye Gentiles! and repent!
To you is this salvation sent;
God to the Gentiles lifts his hand
To gather Israel to their land.

HYMN 269. (11's & 8's.)

1 O, who has not searched in the records of
old,
And read of the last scenes of woe?
With Mormon were left twenty-four to behold
Their nation lie crumbling below.

2 The Nephites destroyed, the Lamanites then
Were roaming for ages unknown,
And centuries passed till the Gentiles again
Divided their lands as their own.

3 O, who has not seen, on the wide spreading
plain,
The Lamanites wander forlorn,
While Gentiles in pride and oppression obtain
The land they could once call their own?

4 And who that believes does not long for the hour
   When sin and oppression shall cease,
  And truth, like the rainbow, display through the shower,
   That bright written promise of peace?

5 O, thou sore afflicted and sorrowful race,
   The days of thy sorrow shall end!
  The Lord soon will shower upon you His grace
   Once promised to Abram His friend.

6 The stones of thy cities in glory shall stand,
   With sapphires all shining around;
  Thy windows of agates, in this blessed land,
   Thy gates with carbuncles abound.

7 With songs of rejoicing to Zion return,
   And sorrow and sighing shall flee,
  The powers of heaven among you come down
   And Christ in the centre will be.

8 And then all the watchmen shall see eye to eye,
   The Lord bringing Zion again,

The wolf and the kid down together shall lie;
The lion shall dwell with the lamb.

9 The earth shall be filled with the knowledge of God,
And nothing shall hurt nor destroy,
And these are the tidings we have to proclaim,
Glad tidings abounding with joy.

HYMN 270. (L.M.)

1 Hark! listen to the gentle strain,
O'er hill and valley, grove and plain!
It echoes from the heights above
The voice of freedom, peace and love.

2 The flowers that bloom o'er all the land
In harmony and order stand,
Nor hatred, pride, nor envy know;
In freedom, peace and love they grow.

3 The birds their numerous notes resound
In songs of praise the earth around;
Their voices and their tongues employ
In songs of freedom, love and joy.

4 And then behold the crystal stream
  With multitudes of fishes teem;
  In silent joy they live and move
  In freedom, union, peace and love.

5 The mountains high, the rivers clear,
  Where heaven sheds the dewy tear,
  In silence or with gentle roar,
  The God of love and peace adore.

6 The earth and air, the sea and sky,
  The Holy Spirit from on high,
  And angels who above do reign,
  Cry "Peace on earth, good will to men."

7 But most of all, a Savior's love
  Was manifested from above;
  He died, and rose to life again,
  Our freedom, love and peace to gain.

8 But man, vile man, alone seems lost,
  With hatred, pride and envy tossed,
  His hardened soul does seldom move
  In freedom, union, peace and love.

9 For Him let all creation mourn,
  O'er Him did Enoch's bosom yearn,
  Till He was promised from above,
  A day of freedom, peace and love.

HYMN 271. (L.M.)

1 Another day has fled and gone,
    The sun declines in western skies,
  The birds retired have ceased their song,
    Let ours, in pure devotion rise.

2 The moon her beauteous course resumes,
    And sheds her light o'er land and sea;
  The gentle dews in soft perfumes
    Fall sweetly over herb and tree.

3 While here in meditation sweet,
    Those happy hours I call to mind
  When with the Saints I oft did meet,
    Our hearts in pure devotion joined.

4 Those friends afar I call to mind—
    When shall we meet again below?
  Their hearts affectionate and kind—
    How did they soothe my grief and woe!

5 As flow'rets in their brightest bloom,
    Are withered by the chilling blast,
  So man's fond hopes are like a dream—
    His days, how fleet, how swift they pass!

6 But why this melancholy moan,
    Or sigh for those who will not come?
  For Israel surely will return
    To Zion and Jerusalem.

7 There is a source of pure delight,
    Which ever shall support my heart;
In Zion's land revealed to sight,
    Where Saints will meet, no more to part.

HYMN 272. (L.M.)

1 How fleet the precious moments roll!
    How soon the harvest will be o'er!
The watchmen seek their final rest,
    And lift a warning voice no more!

2 Another year has rolled away,
    And taken thousands to the tomb;
Its sorrows and its joys are fled,
    To hasten on the general doom.

3 The moments that we labor here
    Are passing swiftly on the wing,
And soon the leaves and tendrils thrive,
    A token of returning spring.

4 The fulness of the Gospel shines
    With glorious and resplendent rays,
While earth and heaven show forth their signs
    As tokens of the latter days.

HYMN 273. (L.M.)

1 Ye chosen Twelve, to you are given
   The keys of this last ministry,
To every nation under heaven,
   From land to land, from sea to sea.

2 First to the Gentiles sound the news,
   Throughout Columbia's happy land,
And then, before it reach the Jews,
   Prepare on Europe's shores to stand.

3 Let Europe's towns and cities hear
   The Gospel tidings, angels bring,
Let Gentile nations far and near
   Prepare their hearts His praise to sing.

4 Both Africa's and India's plains
   Must hear the tidings as they roll,
Where darkness rules and sorrow reigns,
   And tyranny has held control.

5 Give ear, ye isles in every zone,
   For every land must hear the sound!
And tongues and nations long unknown,
   Since they were lost, shall soon be found.

6 And then again shall Asia hear,
   Where angels first the news revealed,
Eternity the record bear,
   And earth a joyful tribute yield.

7 The nations catch the pleasing sound,
    And Jew and Gentile swell the strain,
Hosanna o'er the earth resound—
    Messiah then will come to reign.

HYMN 274. (C.M.)

1 Lift up your heads, ye scattered Saints,
    Redemption draweth nigh;
Our Savior hears the orphan's plaints,
    The widow's mournful cry.

2 The blood of those who have been slain
    For vengeance cries aloud;
Nor shall its cries ascend in vain
    For vengeance on the proud.

3 The signs in heaven and earth appear,
    And blood, and smoke, and fire;
Men's hearts are failing them for fear,
    Redemption draweth nigher.

4 Earthquakes are bellowing 'neath the ground,
    And tempests through the air,
The trumpet's blast, with fearful sound,
    Proclaims the coming war.

5 The Saints are scattered to and fro
   Through all the earth abroad,
The Gospel trump again to blow,
   And then behold their God.

6 Rejoice, ye servants of our Lord,
   Who to the end endure,
Rejoice, for great is your reward,
   And your defence is sure.

7 Although this body should be slain,
   By cruel, wicked hand,
I'll praise my God in higher strain,
   And on Mount Zion stand.

8 To God be glory! Saints rejoice,
   And sigh and groan no more,
But listen to the Spirit's voice,
   Redemption's at the door.

HYMN 275. (L.M.)

1 Torn from our friends and captive led
   By armed legions, bound in chains,
That peace for which our fathers bled
   Is gone, and dire confusion reigns.

2 Our peaceful Zion, happy home,
    Where oft we joined in praise and prayer,
  A desolation has become,
    And grief and sorrow linger there.

3 Her virgins sigh, her widows mourn,
    Her children for their parents weep,
  In chains her Priests and Prophets groan,
    While some in death's dark shadow sleep.

4 Exultingly her savage foes
    Now ravage, steal and plunder, where
  A virgin's tears, a widow's woes,
    Became their song of triumph there.

5 How long, O Lord, wilt Thou forsake
    The Saints who tremble at Thy word?
  Stretch forth Thy arm, O Lord! Awake
    And teach the nations Thou art God.

6 Descend with all Thy holy throng,
    The year of Thy redeemed bring near,
  Haste, haste the day of vengeance on,
    B d Zion's children dry their tear.

7 Deliver, Lord, Thy captive Saints,
    And comfort those who, suffering, moan
  Bid Zion cease her dire complaints,
    And all creation no more to groan.

HYMN 276.   (11's.)

1 This morning in silence I ponder and mourn
 O'er scenes that have passed and will no
    more return;
 How vast is the labor, the trouble and fear,
 Of hundreds of millions who toiled through
    the year.

2 How many ten thousands were slain by
    their foes,   [sad woes;
 While widows and orphans bewailed their
 Dire pestilence, famine and earthquakes
    appear,   [past year!
 And signs in the heavens throughout the

3 How many were murdered and plundered
    and robbed,   [mobbed!
 How many forsaken were driven and
 How oft have the heavens bedewed with
    a tear,
 The earth, o'er the scenes they beheld the
    past year.

4 But now has appeared o'er the land of the
    blest   [rest,
 The first beam of morning, the morning of
 When, cleansed from pollution, the earth
    shall appear   .   [year.
 As beautiful Eden, and peace crown the

5 Then welcome the new year, I hail with
    delight [flight!
The season approaching with time's rapid
While each fleeting moment brings near
    and more near,
The day long foretold, the Millennial year.

6 I praise and adore the eternal I Am;
Hosanna, hosanna, to God and the Lamb!
Who order the seasons that glide o'er the
    sphere,
And crown with such blessings each happy
    new year.

HYMN 277. (11's.)

1 'Mid scenes of confusion and creature com-
    plaints,
How sweet to my soul is communion with
    Saints,
To find at the banquet of mercy there's room,
And feel, in the presence of Jesus, at home.
    Home, home, sweet, sweet home!
Receive me, dear Savior, in glory, my home.

2 Sweet bonds, that unite all the children of
    peace, [not cease,
And thrice precious Jesus, whose love can-

Though oft from Thy presence in sadness I roam,
I long to behold Thee in glory at home.

3 I sigh from this body of sin to be free,
Which hinders my joy and communion with Thee; [may foam,
Though now my temptations like billows
All, all will be peace when I'm with Thee at home.

4 While here in this valley of conflict I stay,
O, give me submission and strength as my day,
In all my afflictions to Thee would I come,
Rejoicing in hope of my glorious home.

5 Whate'er Thou deniest, O give me Thy grace, [Thy face,
The Spirit's sure witness, and smiles of
Indulge me with patience to wait at Thy throne, [home.
And find, even now, a sweet foretaste of

6 I long, dearest Lord, in Thy beauties to shine,
No more as an exile in sorrow to pine,
And in Thy fair image arise from the tomb,
With glorified millions to praise Thee at home.

HYMN 278. (6-8's.)

1 Down by the river's verdant side,
Low by the solitary tide,
There, while the peaceful waters slept,
We pensively sat down and wept,
And on the bending willows hung
Our silent harps, through grief unstrung.

2 For they who wasted Zion's bowers,
And laid in dust her ruined towers,
In scorn their weary slaves desire
To strike the chords of Israel's lyre,
And in their impious ears to sing
The sacred songs to Zion's King.

3 How shall we tune those lofty strains
On Babylon's polluted plains,
When low in ruin on the earth
Remains the place that gave us birth,
And stern destruction's iron hand
Still sways our desolated land!

4 O, never shall our harps awake,
Laid in the dust for Zion's sake,
Forever on the willows hung,
Their music hushed, their chords unstrung;
Lost Zion! city of our God,
While groaning 'neath the tyrant's rod.

5 Still mould'ring lie thy levelled walls,
And ruin stalks along thy halls,
And brooding o'er thy ruined towers,
Such desolation sternly lowers,
That when we muse upon thy woe,
The gushing tears of sorrow flow!

6 And while we toil through wretched life,
And drink the bitter cup of strife,
Until we yield our weary breath,
And sleep, released from woe, in death,
Will Zion in our memory stand—
Our lost, our ruined native land.

HYMN 279. (L.M.)

1 O Zion, when I think of thee,
  I long for pinions like the dove,
And mourn to think that I should be,
  So distant from the land I love.

2 A captive exile, far from home,
  For Zion's sacred walls I sigh,
With ransomed kindred there to come,
  And see Messiah eye to eye.

3 While here, I walk on hostile ground;
  The few that I can call my friends
Are, like myself, in fetters bound,
  And weariness our steps attends.

4 But yet we hope to see the day
    When Zion's children shall return,
When all our grief shall flee away,
    And we again no more shall mourn.

5 The thoughts that such a day will come,
    Makes e'en the exile's portion sweet;
Though now we wander far from home,
    In Zion soon we all shall meet.

HYMN 280. (6-11's.)

1 Children of Zion, awake from your sadness,
    For soon all your foes shall oppress you no more;
Bright o'er your hills shines the day-star of gladness,
    Arise! for the night of your sorrow is o'er;
Children of Zion, awake from your sadness,
    For soon all your foes will oppress you no more!

2 Strong are your foes, but His arm will subdue them,
    And scatter their armies to regions afar;

Then they will flee from the scourge that pursues them,
For vain are their strength and their chariots of war.
Children of Zion, awake from your sadness,
For soon all your foes shall oppress you no more.

3 Children of Zion, His power will save you,
O, loudly extol it o'er land and o'er sea;
Shout! for the foe will be slain that enslaved you,
Oppressions shall vanish, and Zion be free.
Children of Zion, awake from your sadness,
For soon all your foes shall oppress you no more.

HYMN 281. (L.M.)

1 I have no home, where shall I go?
While I am left to weep below,
My heart is pained, my friends are gone,
And here I'm left on earth to mourn.

2 I see my people lying round,
All lifeless here upon the ground,
Young men and maidens in their gore,
Which does increase my sorrows more.

3 My father looked upon this scene
  And in his writings has made plain
  How every Nephite's heart did fear
  When he beheld his foe draw near.

4 With axe and bow they fell upon
  Our men and women, sparing none,
  And left them prostrate on the ground;
  Lo! here they now are bleeding, round.

5 Ten thousand that were led by me
  Lie round this hill called Cumorah;
  Their spirits from their bodies fled,
  And they are numbered with the dead.

6 Well might my father, in despair,
  Cry, All ye fair ones, once how fair,
  How is it that you've fallen? O!
  My soul is filled with pain for you.

7 My life is sought, where shall I flee?
  Lord, take me home to dwell with Thee,
  Where all my sorrows will be o'er,
  And I shall sigh and weep no more!

8 Thus sang the son of Mormon, when
  He gazed upon his Nephite men
  And women, too, who had been slain,
  And left to moulder on the plain.

HYMN 282. (11's & 10's.)

1 Praise to the man who communed with Jehovah!
  Jesus anointed "that Prophet and Seer"—
Blessed to open the last dispensation;
  Kings shall extol him and nations revere.

CHORUS.

Hail to the Prophet, ascended to heaven!
  Traitors and tyrants now fight him in vain ;
Mingling with Gods, he can plan for his brethren,
  Death cannot conquer the hero again.

2 Praise to his memory, he died as a martyr,
  Honored and blest be his ever great name!
Long shall his blood, which was shed by assassins,
  Stain Illinois, while the earth lauds his fame.
                    Hail to the Prophet, etc.

3 Great is his glory, and endless his Priesthood,
  Ever and ever the keys he will hold;

Faithful and true, he will enter his kingdom,
Crowned in the midst of the Prophets of old.
Hail to the Prophet, etc.

4 Sacrifice brings forth the blessings of heaven;
Earth must atone for the blood of that man;
Wake up the world for the conflict of justice;
Millions shall know "brother Joseph" again.
Hail to the Prophet, etc.

HYMN 283.   (12's.)

1 Come to me, will ye come to the Saints that have died,
To the next, better world, where the righteous reside,
Where the angels and spirits in harmony be,
In the joys of a vast Paradise? Come to me.

2 Come to me, where the truth and the virtues prevail,
Where the union exists, and the years never fail;

For no heart can conceive, and no human
  eye see
What the Lord has prepared for the just.
  Come to me.

3 Come to me, where there is no destruction
    nor war,   [ajar;
Neither tyrants, nor mobbers, nor nations
Where the system is perfect, and happiness
    free,
And the life is eternal with God. Come to me.

4 Come to me; will ye come to the mansions
    above,
Where the bliss and the knowledge, the
    light and the love,
And the glory of God shall eternally be?
Death, the wages of sin, is not here. Come
    to me.

5 Come to me; here are Adam and Eve at the
    head   [the dead;
Of a multitude quickened and raised from
Here's the knowledge that was, or that is,
    or will be,   me.
In the gen'ral assembly of worlds. Come to
6 Come to me; here are mysteries man hath
    not seen,   [the Queen,
Here's our Father in heaven, and Mother,

> Here are worlds that have been, and the worlds yet to be,
> Here's eternity, endless; Amen. Come to me.

7 Come to me, all ye faithful and blest of Nauvoo,
> Come, ye Twelve, and ye High Priests, and Seventies, too,
> Come, ye Elders, and all of the great company,
> When your work you have finished on earth, come to me.

8 Come to me; here's the future, the present and past;
> Here is Alpha, Omega, the first and the last;
> Here's the "Fountain," the "River of Life," and the "Tree!"
> Here's your Prophet and Seer, Joseph Smith. Come to me.

HYMN 284. (8's & 9's.)

1 The Lord imparted from above
> · The "Word of Wisdom" for our blessing,
> But shall it unto many prove
> A gift that is not worth possessing

2 Have we not been divinely taught
    To heed its voice and highly prize it?
Then who shall once indulge the thought,
    It can be better to despise it?

3 Has self-denial grown a task?
    Or has that word been vainly spoken?
Or why, I fain would humbly ask,
    Why is that word so often broken?

4 It is a straight and narrow way
    That leads to the celestial city;
That high-taught Saints should go astray,
    Through gentile customs, is a pity.

5 O, that the Saints would all regard
    Each gracious word that God has given,
And prize the favor of the Lord
    Above all things beneath the heaven!

HYMN 285. (L.M.)

1 Awake, ye Saints of God, awake!
    Call on the Lord in mighty prayer,
That He will Zion's bondage break,
    And bring to naught the fowler's snare.

2 He will regard His people's cry,
    The widow's tear, the orphan's moan;
The blood of those that slaughtered lie,
    Pleads not in vain before His throne.

3 Though Zion's foes have counseled deep,
    Although they bind with fetters strong,
The God of Jacob does not sleep;
    His vengeance will not slumber long.

4 Then let your souls be stayed on God,
    A glorious scene is drawing nigh;
Though tempests gather like a flood,
    The storm, though fierce, will soon pass by.

5 With constant faith and fervent prayer,
    With deep humility of soul,
With steadfast mind and heart prepare,
    To see th' eternal purpose roll.

6 Our God in judgment will come near,
    His mighty arm He will make bare,
For Zion's sake He will appear;
    Then O, ye Saints, awake, prepare

7 Awake to righteousness, be one,
    Or, saith the Lord, you are not mine!
Yea, like the Father and the Son,
    Let all the Saints in union join.

HYMN 286. (C.M.)

1 The glorious Gospel light has shone
    In this the latter day,
With such intelligence, that none
    From truth need turn away.

2 Important truths which had been sealed,
    And from the world kept hid,
  The Lord has to His Saints revealed
    As anciently He did;

3 And through the Priesthood, now restored,
    Again prepared the way
  Through which the dead may hear His word,
    And all its truths obey.

4 As Christ to spirits went to preach
    Who were in prison laid,
  So many Saints have gone to teach
    The Gospel to the dead.

5 And we for them can be baptized,
    Yes, for our friends most dear,
  That they can with the just be raised,
    When Gabriel's trump they hear.

6 That they may come with Christ again
    When He to earth descends,
  A thousand years with Him to reign,
    And with their earthly friends.

  Now, O ye Saints, rejoice to-day
    That you can saviors be,
  For all your dead who will obey
    The Gospel and be free.

8 Then let us rise without restraint
And act for those we love,
For they are giving their consent,
And wait for us to move.

HYMN 287. (8's & 7's.)

1 Wake, O wake, the world from sleeping!
Watchman, watchman, what's the hour?
Hark ye, only hear him saying,
'Tis the last, eleventh hour!

CHORUS.

Let the true born sons of Zion
Gather in from lands afar,
To the royal branch of Joseph,
Israel's glorious morning star.

2 Lo! the lion leaves his thicket,
Up, ye watchmen, be in haste;
The destroyer of the Gentiles
Goes to lay their cities waste.
Let the true born sons, etc.

3 Bring the remnants from their exile
For the promise is to them;
Japhet's time to rule is ended,
He must leave the "tents of Shem."
Let the true born sons, etc.

4 Comfort ye the house of Israel,
    They are pardoned, gather them;
  Hear the watchman's proclamation:
    "Jews, rebuild Jerusalem!"
            Let the true born sons, etc.

5 Soon the Jews will know their error—
    How they killed the Holy One;
  They will turn and shout "Hosanna!
    This is THE BELOVED SON!"
            Let the true born sons, etc.

6 Sound the trumpet with the tidings,
    Call in all of Abram's seed,
  Though the Gentiles may reject it,
    Christ will come in very deed.
            Let the true born sons, etc.

HYMN 288. (9's & 8's.)

1 Ho, ho, for the Temple's completed,
    The Lord hath a place for His head;
  The Priesthood in power now lightens
    The way of the living and dead!

2 See, see, 'mid the world's dreadful splendor;
    Religions and folly and sword,
  The "Mormons," the diligent "Mormons,"
    Have reared up this house to the Lord!

3 By seeking the wisdom of Joseph
   Whose blood stains the honor of state,
 By tithing and sacrifice daily,
   The poor learn the way to be great.

4 Mark, mark (for the Gentiles are fearful),
   The work of the Lord is begun;
 Already, this monument finished
   Is counted one miracle done.

5 Gaze, gaze at the flight of the righteous
   From fire-showers of ruin at hand;
 Their prayers and their sufferings are moving,
   Jehovah to sweep off the land.

6 Sing, sing, for the hour of redemption,
   The day for the poor Saints' reward,
 Is coming, and richest of blessings,
   Are showering down from the Lord.

7 Watch, watch, for the blessing of Jesus,
   Is richer the harder 'tis gained,
 The wonderful chain of our union
   Is tightened the longer 'tis strained.

8 Shout, shout, for the armies of heaven
   Will purify earth at a word,
 The "Twelve," with the Saints that are faithful,
   Shall enter the House of their Lord!

HYMN 289. (4-8's & 10's.)

1 Weep, weep not for me, Zion,
   Rejoice and sing ye aloud,
  Pray, pray that Judah's fierce lion
   May quickly descend in a cloud.
  Haste, haste; O, quickly descend in a cloud!

2 He wields the rod of His power,
   And lays our enemies low;
  While frowns His countenance lower,
   They sink in perdition and woe.
  Yes, yes, they sink to perdition and woe.

3 Long, long, dear Saints, we have wandered,
   Yet, yet we will not complain,
  Though oft our all has been plundered,
   The loss is our infinite gain.
  Yes, yes, the loss is our infinite gain.

4 Cease, cease your sighing and weeping,
   Mourn, mourn not, neither repine,
  Now I'm in heaven's blest keeping,
   With Jesus I ever shall shine.
  Yes, yes, with Jesus I ever shall shine.

5 Mobs, mobs, of all you've bereft me,
  Home, friends, and pleasures so sweet,
 Now, from your power I'm set free,
  And you and I never shall meet.
 No, no; you and I never shall meet.

6 Go, go ye wretches who've slain me;
  Now, now your power is o'er;
 Though in the tomb they have laid me,
  I'm resting on Zion's bright shore.
 Yes, yes, I'm resting on Zion's bright shore.

7 Weep, weep not, Zion's fair maidens;
  Brave sons, weep, weep not for me;
 Crowned now, with glory I'm laden,
  Now happy I ever shall be.
 Yes, yes, now happy I ever shall be.

8 Sad, sad was that hour of parting,
  Then, then fell many a tear;
 Soon you'll be over the smarting,
  And meet with the holy ones here.
 Haste, haste, to meet with the holy ones here.

9 Heaves, heaves each bosom with sorrow,
  Anguish, how fervent the pain!
 Soon, soon will come the blest morrow,
  When you will see JOSEPH again.
 Yes, yes, then you will see JOSEPH again.

O   Then, then how happy the meeting!
    Joy, joy, each bosom will fill!
  Joseph and Hyrum then greeting,
    On Zion's thrice sanctified hill.
  Yes, yes, on Zion's thrice sanctified hill.

HYMN 290. (P.M.)

1 The Seer, the Seer, Joseph the Seer!
  I'll sing of the Prophet ever dear;
  His equal now cannot be found,
  By searching the wide world around.
  With Gods he soared in the realms of day,
  And men he taught the heavenly way.
  The earthly Seer! the heavenly Seer!
  I love to dwell on his memory dear;
  The chosen of God and the friend of man,
  He brought the Priesthood back again;
  He gazed on the past, and the present too,
  And opened the heavenly world to view.

2 Of noble seed, of heavenly birth,
  He came to bless the sons of earth;
  With keys by the Almighty given,
  He opened the full rich stores of heaven;
  O'er the world that was wrapt in sable night,
  Like the sun, he spread his golden light;

He strove, O, how he strove to stay
The stream of crime in its reckless way!
With a mighty mind and a noble aim,
He urged the wayward to reclaim;
'Mid the foaming billows of angry strife,
He stood at the helm of the ship of life.

3 The Saints, the Saints, his only pride,
For them he lived, for them he died!
Their joys were his, their sorrows too,
He loved the Saints, he loved Nauvoo.
Unchanged in death, with a Savior's love
He pleads their cause in the courts above.
The Seer, the Seer! Joseph the Seer!
O, how I love his memory dear!
The just and wise, the pure and free,
A father he was and is to me.
Let fiends now rage in their dark hour—
No matter, he is beyond their power.

4 He's free! he's free! the Prophet's free!
He is where he ever more will be,
Beyond the reach of mobs and strife,
He rests unharmed in endless life.
His home's in the sky, he dwells with the Gods,
Far from the furious rage of mobs.
He died! he died for those he loved,
He reigns, he reigns in the realms above.

He waits with the just who have gone before,
To welcome the Saints to Zion's shore.
Shout, shout, ye Saints; this boon is given:
We'll meet our martyr'd Seer in heaven.

HYMN 291. (C.M.)

1 When all thy mercies, O my God,
    My rising soul surveys,
Transported with the view, I'm lost
    In wonder, love and praise.

2 O, how shall words with equal warmth,
    The gratitude declare,
That grows within my ravished heart!
    But Thou canst read it there.

3 Thy providence my life sustained,
    Thou didst my wants supply,
Before I drew my earliest breath,
    And through my infancy.

4 To all my weak complaints and cries
    Thy mercy lent an ear,
Ere yet my feeble thoughts had learned
    To form themselves in prayer.

5 Unnumbered comforts to my soul
    Thy tender care bestowed,

Before my infant heart conceived
From whom those comforts flowed.

6 When in the slippery paths of youth
With heedless steps I ran,
Thine arm unseen conveyed me safe,
And led me up to man.

7 Through hidden dangers, toils and death,
It gently cleared my way,
And through the pleasing snares of vice,
More to be feared than they.

PART SECOND.

8 When worn by sickness, oft hast Thou,
With health renewed my face,
And, when in sin and sorrow sunk,
Revived my soul with grace.

6 Thy bounteous hand with worldly bliss
Has made my cup run o'er,
And, in a kind and faithful friend,
Has doubled all my store.

10 Ten thousand thousand precious gifts
My daily thanks employ,
Nor is the least a cheerful heart
That tastes those gifts with joy.

11 Through every period of my life
   Thy goodness I'll pursue,
 And after death in distant worlds
   The glorious theme renew.

12 When nature fails, and day and night
   Divide their works no more,
 My ever grateful heart, O Lord,
   Thy mercy shall adore.

13 Through all eternity, to Thee
   A joyful song I'll raise,
 But O, eternity's too short
   To utter all thy praise.

HYMN 292. (7's & 6's.)

1 O, stop and tell me, Red Man,
   Who are you, why you roam,
 And how you get your living;
   Have you no God, no home?

2 With stature straight and portly,
   And decked in native pride,
 With feathers, paints and brooches,
   He willingly replied:

3 "I once was pleasant Ephraim,
   When Jacob for me prayed;
But O, how blessings vanish,
   When man from God has strayed!

4 Before your nation knew us,
   Some thousand moons ago,
Our fathers fell in darkness,
   And wandered to and fro.

5 And long they've lived by hunting
   Instead of work and arts,
And so our race has dwindled
   To idle Indian hearts.

6 Yet hope within us lingers,
   As if the Spirit spoke,
He'll come for your redemption,
   And break your Gentile yoke,

7 And all your captive brothers
   From every clime shall come,
And quit their savage customs,
   To live with God at home.

8 Then joy will fill our bosoms,
   And blessings crown our days,
To live in pure religion,
   And sing our Maker's praise."

HYMN 293. (12's & 11's.)

1 The time is far spent, there is little remaining
To publish glad tidings by sea and by land,
Then hasten, ye heralds! go forward proclaiming:
Repent, for the kingdom of God is at hand.

2 Shrink not from your duty, however unpleasant,
But follow the Savior, your pattern and friend,
Our little afflictions, though painful at present,
Ere long, with the righteous, in glory will end.

3 What though, if the favor of Ahman possessing,
This world's bitter hate you are called to endure,
The angels are waiting to crown you with blessings,
Go brethren! be faithful, the promise is sure.

4 All, all things are known to the mind of
    Jehovah,
  There's nothing concealed from His all-
    searching eye,
  Then, fear not! the hairs of your heads are
    all numbered,
  And even the ravens are heard when they
    cry.

5 Be fixed in your purpose, for Satan will
    try you,
  The weight of your calling he perfectly
    knows,
  Your path may be thorny, but Jesus is nigh
    you,
  His arm is sufficient, though demons op-
    pose.

6 Press on to the mark of eternal perfection,
  Determined to reap the celestial reward,
  That you may come forth in the first resur-
    rection,
  And feast at the supper of Jesus, the
    Lord.

HYMN 294. (13's.)

1 Ye who are called to labor and minister for God,
Blest by the royal Priesthood, appointed by His word
To preach among the nations the news of Gospel grace,
And publish on the mountains, salvation, truth and peace,

2 O let not vain ambition nor worldly glory stain
Your minds so pure and holy—acquit yourselves like men;
While lifting up your voices like trumpets long and loud,
Say to the slumbering nations, "Prepare to meet your God!"

3 Then cease from all light speeches, light-mindedness and pride,
Pray always, without ceasing, and in the truth abide;
The Comforter will teach you, His richest blessings send,
Your Savior will be with you always unto the end.

4 And while you roam as pilgrims and strangers on this earth,
O do not be discouraged, with songs of joy go forth;
Rejoice in tribulation, for your reward is sure,
Remember that your Savior like sorrows did endure.

5 Rich blessings do await you, and God will give you faith,
You shall be crowned with glory and triumph over death,
And soon you'll come to Zion, and bear your many sheaves,
No more to taste of sorrow, but glorious crowns receive.

HYMN 295. (4-6's & 2-8's,)

1 All hail, the new-born year!
   Thrice welcome to the Saints,
Whose coming Lord is near,
   To end their long complaints,
Sweet hope, still perching on thy wing,
Anticipates a happier spring.

2   When life shall spring anew,
        And vegetation bloom,
    And flowers of varied hue
        Will spread a rich perfume,
While happy birds fill every grove
With songs of joy and life and love.

3   These but a type shall be
        Of glories more sublime;
    A wondrous jubilee
        Hangs on the wings of time,
Near and more near redemption comes,
Near and more near, the sinner's doom.

4   Come, tune your harps anew,
        And join in hymns of praise
    To Him whose power we view
        In these eventful days!
Whose arm shall make the nations yield,
Shall conquer death, and win the field.

5   All hail the glorious King
        Of righteousness and peace!
    Thy promises we sing,
        And hope for quick release;
Let Zion find her promised rest,
And nations in her courts be blest.

HYMN 296. (L.M.D.)

O, give me back my Prophet dear,
    And Patriarch, O give them back,
The Saints of Latter-days to cheer,
    And lead them in the Gospel track!
But O, they're gone from my embrace,
    From earthly scenes their spirits fled,
Two of the best of Adam's race,
    Now lie entombed among the dead.

2 Ye men of wisdom, tell me why—
    No guilt, no crime in them were found—
Why now their blood doth loudly cry
    From prison walls and Carthage ground?
Your tongues are mute, but pray attend,
    The secret I will now relate,
Why those whom God to earth did lend,
    Have met the suffering martyrs' fate.

3 It is because they strove to gain,
    Beyond the grave, a heaven of bliss,
Because they made the Gospel plain
    And led the Saints in righteousness;
It is because God called them forth,
    And led them by His own right hand,
Christ's coming to proclaim on earth,
    And gather Israel to their land.

4 It is because the priests of Baal
   Were desperate, their craft to save,
And when they saw it doomed to fall,
   They sent the Prophets to their grave.
Like scenes the ancient Prophets saw,
   Like these, the ancient Prophets fell,
And, till the resurrection dawn,
   Prophet and Patriarch, farewell.

HYMN 297. (7's & 8's.)

1 Beautiful Zion for me!
   Down in the valley reclining;
Memories sacred to thee,
   Close round my heart are entwining,
Clasped in the mountains embrace,
   Safe from the spoiler for ever,
Chased are the tears from thy face,
   Joy shall depart from thee never.
When from thy presence I roam,
   Midst the world's grandeur, I see
Nought like my own mountain home"
   Beautiful Zion for me!

2 Beautiful queen of the west!
   Reigning o'er mountain and valley;
Hosts of the purest and best,
   Under thy standard shall rally.
Robed in the garments of peace,
   Virtue the crown of thy glory,

God shall thy kingdom increase,
  Angels delight in the story.
When through this wide world I roam,
  Nought on the land or the sea,
Charms like "my own mountain home,"
  Beautiful Zion for me!

HYMN 298. (C.M.D.)

1 Should solemn cov'nants be forgot,
  Or lightly sway the mind?
Should "Mormons" have a sinful spot,
  That Satan's eye can find?
Oh no! dear Saints, we must be pure,
  And ne'er our vows forget;
Temptation's power is great, 'tis sure,
  But we shall conquer yet.

2 Should Passion's peace-destroying flame
  Escape from Will's strong guard?
Or should the fiend Impure Desire
  Our heav'nly course retard?
Oh no! to quench the *first* we will
  A stream of patience get;
With holy love the *other* kill,
  And we shall conquer yet.

3 Should Selfishness pinch up the heart,
  And close Compassion's door?
Or whisper, when we should impart,
  "Remember you are poor?"

Oh no! the cringing elf we'll fight,
   The deed we'll ne'er regret;
We will resist with all our might,
   And we shall conquer yet.

4 Should "Mormon" hearts be filled with pride
   Or e'er rebellious be?
Should they the Priesthood's word deride,
   Or ever disagree?
Oh no! all sin we will oppose,
   Our hearts on virtue set;
We'll struggle with our inward foes,
   And we shall conquer yet!

HYMN 298. (11's.)

1 O thou who hast promised in love to receive
The children of those who in Jesus believe,
Thy Spirit impart and our blessings bestow
On those, to thy service we dedicate now.

2 Receive them, our Father, as lambs that
      were lost,
   The blood of Thy Son is the price they
      have cost,
   By the power of the Priesthood Thy good
      ness has given,
   We bless them as Thine in the Kingdom
      of heaven.

3 Let mercy surround them, Thou Father
      adored,

To do the commands of our crucified Lord,
Thy Spirit forever their bosoms inspire,
And seal them Thine own with Thine unction and fire.

4 May they to Thy glory be jewels of worth,
When Jesus shall come to be King on the earth,
And stand in their lot, with the sanctified crowned,
When all shall adore Thee, the universe round.

HYMN 299. (P.M.)

1 O! wouldst thou from bondage and strife be free
And dwell in a happier clime?
Then away o'er the breast of the beautiful sea,
The storm spirit's breath shall be gentle on thee,
When he rides in his wrath sublime.
Away, though the threat'ning billows rise,
And the thunder-browed clouds look down.
Jehovah controls the seas and the skies,
He speaks, and the death-laden tempest dies,
And the elements cease to frown.

2 Then hasten away with a fearless breast
    And follow the course of the sun;
But when you land in the mighty West,
Oh! tarry not there, nor pause to rest
    Till the prize you are seeking is won;
For the boasted "Shrine of Liberty"
    Holds nought but her tattered dress.
To the mountain valleys she's had to flee;
Her home is there, and she calls on thee
    To come through the wilderness!

3 Then on to the plains through the waving grass,
    Where the red man roams in his pride;
O'er the sandy hill and the rocky pass,
By the rushing stream and the crumbling mass,
    And the heights which Old Time have defied.
Press on till the peaceful valleys lie
    At your feet, in their loveliness,
And the grand old mountains rise on high,
Pointing above to the cloudless sky,
    Blue, gentle and fathomless.

4 Then down to the city, spread out below,
    Where the glistening steamlets glide,
Through the spacious streets where the shade trees grow,

And the arbored dwellings and orchards show
Where the children of freedom abide.
Abundant gifts to labor, there,
The ransomed wilderness yields,
And the sunbeams smile, with a beauty rare,
In the smokeless breath of the mountain air,
And shimmer in grassy fields.

5 Oh! this is the place where the poor may stand
Unshackled in limb or soul,
And diligence grasp, in its strong, right hand,
The wealth it has wrung from the toil-bought land,
Nor yield to a tyrant's control.
Then haste to the valleys of Deseret,
While the dying world goes to its grave.
There the stars of virtue and peace have met
With truth and liberty, never to set,
The glory and light of the brave!

HYMN 300. (8's & 7s.

1 Earthly happiness is fleeting,
　Earthly prospects quickly fade,
　Oft the heart, with pleasure beating,
　Is to bitterness betrayed!

2 Scenes of sorrow most distressing,
   Scenes that fill the heart with pain,
Often yield the choicest blessing—
   Present loss is future gain.

3 In the darkest dispensation,
   O, remember God is just;
'Tis the richest consolation
   In His faithfulness to trust.

4 Let the heart oppressed with sorrow,
   Let the bosom filled with grief,
Let the wounded spirit borrow
   From His promise kind relief.

5 While affliction's surge comes o'er you
   Look beyond the roaring wave,
See a brighter scene before you.
   Hail the triumph o'er the grave.

6 Though your darling child is taken
   From your bosom to the urn,
Soon the sleeping dust will waken
   And the spirit will return.

7 Yes, again we will behold it,
   Fairer than the morning ray,
In your arms you will enfold it,
   When all tears are wiped away.

HYMN 301. (11's & 10's.)

1 Hail to the brightness of Zion's glad morning,
  Joy to the lands that in darkness have lain!
 Hushed be the accents of sorrow and mourning,
  Zion in triumph begins her glad reign.

2 Hail to the brightness of Zion's glad morning,
  Long by the Prophets of Israel foretold!
 Hail to the millions from bondage returning!
  Gentiles and Jews the glad vision behold.

3 Lo! in the desert the rich flowers are springing,
  Streams ever copious are gliding along,
 Loud from the mountain-tops echoes are ringing,
  Wastes rise in verdure and mingle in song.

4 Hark! from all lands, from the isles of the ocean,
  Praise to Jehovah ascending on high;
 Fallen are engines of war and commotion,
  Shouts of salvation are rending the sky.

HYMN 302. (L.M.)

Thou dost not weep, to weep alone;
   The broad bereavement seems to fall
Unheeded and unfelt by none:
   He was beloved, beloved by all.

2 But lo! what joy salutes our grief!
   Bright rainbows crown the tearful gloom
Hope, hope eternal, brings relief;
   Faith sounds a triumph o'er the tomb.

3 It soothes our sorrow, says to thee,
   The Lord in chastening comes to bless:
God is thy God, He says He'll be
   A father to the fatherless.

4 'Tis well with the departed one;
   His heaven-lit lamp was shining bright;
And when his mortal day went down,
   His spirit fled where reigns no night.

5 'Tis meet to die as he has died;
   He smiled amid death's conquered gloom,
While angels waited by his side,
   To bear a kindred spirit home.

6 Vain are the trophies wealth can give!
   His memory needs no sculptor's art;
He's left a name—his virtues live,
   Graved on the tablets of the heart.

HYMN 303. (C.M.)

1 Prayer is the soul's sincere desire,
  Uttered or unexpressed;
 The motion of a hidden fire
  That trembles in the breast.

2 Prayer is the burden of a sigh,
  The falling of a tear,
 The upward glancing of an eye,
  When none but God is near.

3 Prayer is the simplest form of speech
  That infant lips can try;
 Prayer, the sublimest strains that reach
  The Majesty on high.

4 Prayer is the Christian's vital breath,
  The Christian's native air;
 His watchword at the gates of death;
  He enters heaven with prayer.

5 Prayer is the contrite sinner's voice,
  Returning from his ways,
 While angels in their songs rejoice,
  And say, "Behold, he prays!"

6 The Saints in prayer appear as one
  In word and deed and mind,
 While with the Father and the Son
  Their fellowship they find.

7 Nor prayer is made on earth alone;
   The Holy Spirit pleads,
 And Jesus on the Father's throne,
   For sinners intercedes.

8 O Thou by whom we come to God,
   The Life, the Truth, the Way!
 The path of prayer, Thyself hast trod;
   Lord, teach us how to pray.

HYMN 304. (11's.)

1 Ye Elders of Israel, come join now with me,
 And search out the righteous, wherever they be,
 In desert or mountain, on land or the sea,
 And bring them from Babel to Zion so free.

   O Babylon, O Babylon, we bid thee farewell;
   We go to the mountains of Ephraim to dwell.

2 The harvest is great and the laborers few,
 But if we're united, we all things can do;

We'll gather the wheat from the midst of the tares,
And bring them from bondage, deep sorrows and snares.

                    O Babylon, etc.

3 We'll go to the poor, like our Captain of old,
And visit the weary, the hungry and cold;
We'll heal all their wounds, and we'll dry up their tears,
And lead them to Zion to spend future years.

                    O Babylon, etc.

4 We'll visit the feeble, the halt, dumb and blind,
And preach them the Gospel of Jesus so kind;
We'll cheer up their hearts with the news that He bore,
And point them to Zion for life evermore.

                    O Babylon, etc.

5 And when we have finished the work we've begun,
The Priesthood in Zion shall say, '"Tis well done"

With friends, wives and children, how happy we'll be,
And shout, when the trumpet sounds, "Zion is free!"

O Babylon, etc.

HYMN 305. (11's.)

1 The shepherds have lifted their sweet warning voice,
And called us to flee to the land of God's choice;
As Prophets of old, they have warned us to flee
To Ephraim's mountains where happy we'll be.

O Babylon, O Babylon, we bid thee farewell,
We go to the mountains of Ephraim to dwell.

2 Prepare for your journey, ye Saints of the Lord;
Although it is tedious, you'll have your reward;
You've done His commands and you've bowed to His will;
Your rest now remaineth on Zion's fair hill.

O Babylon, etc.

3 Though now persecuted, the Saints will be free,
While Babylon under God's anger shall be.
Come out from the wicked, ye meek-hearted ones,
And flee to the mountains, the place of your homes.
                    O Babylon, etc.

4 The time's quickly coming, though now you say nay,
When you will remember the Saints gone away
To dwell on the mountains, where they will be free,
While judgments of God all the wicked shall see.
                    O Babylon, etc.

5 Then hasten, ye Saints, to the refuge prepared,
That Israel's salvation by you may be shared;
Leave Babel, her woe and her troubles behind,
A covert of safety in Zion, to find.
                    O Babylon, etc.

HYMN 306. (C.M.D.)

1 Our Father, in the sacred name
  Of Jesus Christ, Thy Son,
The blessing that has been pronounced
  These little ones upon,
We pray Thee, own, confirm and seal
  In Thy most holy place,
That they may constantly receive
  Of Thy celestial grace.

2 May Thy good Spirit fall on them,
  From this auspicious hour,
As dew upon the tender plant,
  As the refreshing shower,
That by its genial influence
  They may, in infancy,
In youth, and in life's vig'rous prime
  Be holy unto Thee.

3 Protect them in their tender years
  From seen and unseen ills;
And may they, as their days increase,
  Have Thy kind watch-care still.
May they grow up in health and strength
  Of body and of mind,
Be filled with pure intelligence,
  And wisdom's treasures find.

4 O, may they with a righteous zeal
   Be thoroughly imbued,
To o'ercome evil and to tread
   The path of rectitude.
Yea, Lord, may they, at home, abroad,
   Valiant for Thee remain
With tongue, and pen, in word and deed,
   And endless lives obtain.

HYMN 307. (11's & 10.)

1 Cheer, Saints! cheer, we are bound for
      peaceful Zion!   [happy land!
   Cheer, Saints! cheer, for that free and
Cheer, Saints! cheer, we will Israel's God
      rely on;
   We will be led by His Almighty hand.
            Cheer Saints, cheer etc.

2 Long, long in Babel we have lived in
      sorrow,
   But God in mercy opened up our way!
"Hope points before, and shows the bright
      to-morrow;
   Let us forget the darkness of to-day."
            Cheer, Saints, cheer! etc.

3 See, see the judgment on the earth extending,
   With plagues and earthquakes, famine,
   fire and sword;

365

Soon shall the rulers of this world come bending, [Lord.
Shorn of their glory, for thus saith the
  Cheer, Saints, cheer! etc.

4 Come, come away unto the hill of Zion;
 Come, enter now the temples of the Lord;
Come ye and hear the roaring of the Lion,
 Where Ephraim's children tremble at the word.
    Cheer, Saints, cheer! etc.

5 Away, far away to Zion's sacred mountains;
 Away to her fairest valleys in the West;
Away, far away to yonder gushing fountains,
 Where faithful Saints in latter days are blest.
    Cheer, Saints, cheer etc.

6 Sing, sing aloud the song of adoration;
 Yea, praise aloud the goodness of our King;
Ye who are blest to see this great salvation,
 Lift up your voice and make the mountains ring.
    Cheer, Saints, cheer! etc.

HYMN 308. (8's & 7's.)

1 Welcome, best of all good meetings;
   Welcome, brothers, sisters true;
Gifts and blessings, happy greetings,
   Heavenly treasures, old and new.

2 Gladly young and old assemble;
   Sweetest songs rise from the soul;
Saints rejoice and sinners tremble;
   Power unseen pervades the whole.

3 Prayer and praise and testimony,
   Tongues unknown and prophecy,
Burning words of inspiration—
   O, how swift the moments fly!

4 Faithful Saints refreshed and strengthened,
   Drooping ones revived and cheered;
Thus their happy days are lengthened,
   Thus Jehovah's name's revered.

5 Where is heaven? who can tell it?
   Answer, ye who only know,
Where abides the Holy Spirit?
   Where its fruits and graces show?

6 Blessed people! pure religion!
   Godlike, priceless, simple, free,
Loved and held up in derision,
   'Twill be truth eternally.

HYMN 309. (C.M.D.)

1 I'll serve the Lord while I am young,
    And, in my early days,
Devote the music of my tongue
    To my Redeemer's praise.
I'll praise His name, that He has given
    Me parentage and birth
Among the most beloved of heaven
    That dwell upon the earth.

2 O Lord, my parents here preserve,
    To teach me righteousness,
That my young feet may never swerve
    From paths of holiness;
And, like the faithful ones of old
    Who now behold Thy face,
May I be formed in virtue's mould
    To fill a holy place.

3 While youth and beauty sweetly twine
    Their garlands round my head,
I'll seek, at wisdom's sacred shrine,
    The gems that never fade.
Long may I sing Thy praises here
    Among thy Saints below,
And in eternity appear
    With them in glory too.

HYMN 310. (C.M.)

1 A Saint! and is the title mine,
Or have I but the name?
Have I the lineaments divine
Which can this honor claim?

2 Have I believed that God is God,
And, as a sovereign Lord,
To all who need and serve Him right
Will give a free reward?

3 Have I to penitence been brought,
Marked with a godly woe,
That needs not one repentant thought,
Or single tear to flow?

4 Humbled for sin, have I been led
To seek the wat'ry tomb,
Whence, through our great exalted Head,
Remission's blessings come?

5 Have I the heavenly gift received
From Apostolic hands,
Bestowed on those who first believed,
And kept the Lord's commands?

6 Have I the faith divine and pure—
Gift of celestial birth—
That warms the heart and keeps it pure,
And shows a Savior's worth?

7 If so, the body broke for sin
  To me is living bread;
 The Spirit's power is felt within;
  For me the blood was shed.

8 Nor must I here presume to rest,
  But, leaving these behind,
 Perfection ever keep in view,
  For which the Saint's designed.

9 Celestial crowns await the day,
  For conq'rors in the war,
 When Jesus will His power display,
  And sin be banished far.

HYMN 311. (P. M.)

1 My Father in heaven, and dear kindred there,
  How long shall my spirit exist
 In this sphere of sorrow, this world of despair,
  Where men in rebellion persist?

2 Yet let me not murmur, nor scorn Thy design—
  Thy purpose intended in me;
 Thou sent me, a spirit eternally Thine,
  To dwell in a body, for Thee.

3 And when through Thy help I have finished the course
  Thy love has appointed for me,

That spirit again will return to its source,
  And then with the Gods ever be.

4 Thou author of life! Thou art truth, Thou art love,
  The first, and the last, unto me;
O Thou who art worshiped by angels above,
  The Spirit of truth send to me.

HYMN 312. (C. M.)

1 "The silver, gold and precious stones,"
  Thus saith the Lord, "are Mine;
The cattle on a thousand hills
  I own by right divine.

2 "The forest, rich-stored mountains, plains,
  The fertile valleys too,
The earth and all that is therein
  Are but My righteous due.

3 "And men themselves belong to Me—
  They hold from Me a lease
Of health and strength, and even life,
  Which at My word may cease."

4 Then why should men so much desire
  To seize on all they see—
Cheat, covet and appropriate
  To self so greedily?

5 The Saints have learned a purer faith;
   They own the Lord's just claim;
   They're stewards o'er what they possess,
   And hold it in His name.

6 Their flocks and herds and lands and wealth,
   Their wives and children dear,
   Their all, themselves, they bring to Him;
   Thus they His love revere.

HYMN 313. (10's.)

1 "Great Spirit, listen to the red man's wail!
   Thou hast the power to help him in his woe,
   Thy mighty arm was never known to fail;
   Great Chieftain, save him from the pale-faced foe!

2 "His broad, green hunting-grounds, where buff"loes roam,
   His bubbling streams, where finny thousands play,
   The waving prairies, once his happy home,
   Are fast departing to the Christian's sway.

3 "With cursed firewater's stupefying flame,
   (Which lulled the senses of our chiefs to rest,)
   And soft-mouthed words, the cheating paleface came
   And stole our lands and drove us to the west.

4 "Our gray-haired med'cine men, so wise and good,
All are confounded with the dread disease,
Which ne'er was known to flow in Indian blood
Till white men brought it from beyond the seas.

5 "And shall our nation, once so great, decay?
Our children perish, and our chieftains die?
Great Spirit, help! Thy glorious power display,
Subvert our foes! O! hear the Indian's cry."

SECOND PART.

6 The red man ceased and trembled with delight,
For, brighter far than the meridian sun,
A dazzling vision burst upon his sight—
A glorious angel from the Holy One!

7 "Your prayers are heard," he said, "and I am here
To tell you what will shortly come to pass;
A day of joy for all your tribes is near,
Your foes shall perish like the sun-scorched grass.

8 "The Holy Book your fathers hid is found,
Your 'Mormon' brothers will the truth reveal;

Though troubles press, and all seems black around, [will heal.
Obey their words--your soul's deep wounds

9 "Not many moons shall pass away, before
The curse of darkness from your skin shall flee;
Your ancient beauty will the Lord restore,
And all your tribes shall dwell in unity.

10 "The arts of peace shall flourish, ne'er to die; [shall cease;
The war-whoop and the deadly strife
Disease shall then depart, and every sigh,
And health and life shall flow in every breeze.

11 "Farewell! remember I was once on earth,
And served the Lord of Hosts on this fair land,
Observed His sacred precepts from my birth,
And now I dwell in bliss at His right hand."

12 The angel left, and darkness came again,
But light and joy dwelt in the Indian's soul. [reign,
Oh! may the day soon dawn for Ephraim's
When all the "glorious land" he shall control.

HYMN 314. (L.M.)

1 Though deep'ning trials throng your way,
  Press on, press on, ye Saints of God!
Ere long the resurrection day
  Will spread its light and truth abroad.

2 Though outward ills await us here,
  The time at longest is not long
Ere Jesus Christ will re-appear,
  Surrounded by a glorious throng.

3 Lift up your hearts in praise to God,
  Let your rejoicings never cease;
Though tribulations rage abroad,
  Christ says, "In me ye shall have peace."

4 What though our rights have been assailed?
  What though by foes we've been despoiled?
Jehovah's promise has not failed,
  Jehovah's purpose is not foiled.

5 His work is moving on apace,
  And great events are rolling forth;
The kingdom of the latter days—
  The "little stone—" must fill the earth.

6 Though Satan rage, 'tis all in vain;
  The words the ancient Prophets spoke,
Sure as the throne of God remain,
  Nor men nor devils can revoke.

7 All glory to His holy name,
  Who sends His faithful servants fortl
To prove the nations—to proclaim
  Salvation's tidings through the earth.

HYMN 315. (P.M.)

1 Sons of Michael, He approaches!
    Rise, the Eternal Father greet;
  Bow, ye thousands, low before Him
    Minister before His feet;
  Hail the Patriarch's glad reign,
    Spreading over sea and main!

2 Sons of Michael, 'tis His chariot
    Rolls its burning wheels along!
  Raise aloft your voices million
    In a torrent power of song;
  Hail our Head with music soft!
    Raise sweet melodies aloft!

3 Mother of our generations,
    Glorious by great Michael's side,
  Take thy children's adoration,
    Endless with thy Lord preside;
  Lo, to greet Thee now advance
    Thousands in the joyous dance!

4 Raise a chorus, sons of Michael,
    Like old Ocean's roaring swell,

Till the mighty acclamation
  Through rebounding space doth tell
That the Ancient One doth reign
  In His paradise again!

HYMN 316. (P.M.)

1 O, ye mountains high, where the clear blue sky
  Arches over the vales of the free,
 Where the pure breezes blow and the clear streamlets flow,
  How I've longed to your bosom to flee.
 O Zion! dear Zion! home of the free,
  Now my own mountain home, unto thee I have come—
 All my fond hopes are centered in thee.

2 Though the great and the wise all thy beauties despise,
  To the humble and pure thou art dear;
 Though the haughty may smile and the wicked revile,
  Yet we love thy glad tidings to hear.
 O Zion! dear Zion! home of the free,
  Though thou wert forced to fly to thy chambers on high,
 Yet we'll share joy and sorrow with thee.

3 In thy mountain retreat, God will strengthen
 thy feet;
On the necks of thy foes thou shalt tread;
And their silver and gold, as the Prophets
 foretold,
Shall be brought to adorn thy fair head.
O Zion! dear Zion! home of the free,
 Soon thy towers shall shine with a splendor
 divine
And eternal thy glory shall be.

4 Here our voices we'll raise, and we'll sing
 to thy praise,
Sacred home of the Prophets of God;
Thy deliv'rance is nigh, thy oppressors
 shall die,
And the Gentiles shall bow 'neath thy rod.
O Zion! dear Zion! home of the free,
 In thy temples we'll bend, all thy rights
 we'll defend
And our home shall be ever with thee.

HYMN 317. (C. M.)

1 Sweet is the peace the Gospel brings
 To seeking minds, and true;
With light refulgent on its wings,
 It clears the human view.

2 Its laws and precepts are divine,
    And show a Father's care;
  Transcendent love and mercy shine
    In each injunction there.

3 Tradition flees before its power,
    And unbelief gives way;
  The gloomy clouds, which used to lower,
    Submit to reason's sway.

4 May we who know the Sacred Name
    From every sin depart;
  Then will the Spirit's constant flame
    Preserve us pure in heart.

5 Ere long the tempter's power will cease,
    And sin no more annoy,
  No wrangling sects disturb our peace,
    Or mar our heart-felt joy.

6 That which we have in part received
    Will be in part no more;
  For He in whom we have believed
    To us will all restore.

7 In patience, then, let us possess
    Our souls, till He appear;
  On to our mark of calling press;
    Redemption draweth near.

HYMN 318. (3-8's & 6.)

1 With cheerful hearts and willing hands,
We'll labor for the just demands
Our God now makes on various lands,
    His Temple to uprear.

2 Where Saints may meet, His will to know,
Whence all the choicest gifts shall flow,
Which on them freely he'll bestow,
    Their willing hearts to cheer.

3 The sacred claims to kindred due,
The Priesthood's power will then pursue,
And every Gospel rite renew,
    Till Jesus doth appear

4 To break death's adamantine chain,
And o'er His ransomed people reign,
While Ephraim's sons return again,
    Messiah to revere.

5 Respond, ye nations, to His call;
Know now salvation's free to all,
Before Jehovah's mandate fall,
    For judgment draweth near.

6 Seek ye the Son, His laws obey,
Lest He in anger turn away,
Nor own you in the coming day;
    To meet your God, prepare.

HYMN 319. (C.M.)

1 O Thou, at whose supreme command
    The hosts of darkness fly,
Upheld by whose eternal hand,
    Thy Saints can dare to die;

2 Thou, at whose word the trackless deep
    Must curb each flashing wave,
And own Thy voice when surges sweep
    Destruction round the brave;

3 O hear us for the pilgrim band
    Who, o'er yon dark blue sea,
Self-exiled from their native land,
    Are borne to worship Thee!

4 Father of men! Almighty Power!
    Guard them from every ill,
And in temptation's trying hour,
    O keep them faithful still!

5 Be Thou their guide, till, peril past,
    Where rest and joy belong,
On Zion's distant hills, at last
    They join Thy ransomed throng.

6 To Thee we call, the Lofty One!
    Light of the pure and free!
O, never may their hearts be won,
    Thou God of Truth, from thee.

HYMN 320. (13's & 14's.)

1 There is a place in Utah, that I remember well,
And there the Saints in joyful peace and plenty ever dwell,
My Mountain Home, so dear to me! to thee I fondly cling,
While here I roam, far from my home, my Mountain Home I sing.
My Valley Home, my Mountain Home,
The dear and peaceful Valley.

2 When wintry winds are storming, and snow is falling deep,
Then rich supplies are forming among the mountains steep,
The fertilizing crystal streams, when sunny skies illume,
Make nature's verdant bosom teem within my Mountain Home.
. My Valley Home, etc.

3 The storm-king has no terrors when wintry winds blow cold;
We lighten all life's sorrows in our calm Mountain Fold;

We worship there, we dance and sing among
    the joyful throng,
And there our tithes and offerings bring,
    which to the Lord belong.
                My Valley Home, etc.

4 We plow, we sow and irrigate, to raise the
    golden grain;
And diligently labor, to independence gain;
Some haul the wood from canyons wild,
    some tend the flocks and herds,
And all our moments are beguiled by in-
    dustry's rewards.
                My Valley Home, etc.

5 All kinds of fruit and flowers we cultivate
    with care,
And strive our tastes to elevate by products
    choice and rare;
The desert blossoms as the rose in many a
    mountain vale,
And rich abundance ever flows, on which
    the Saints regale.
                My Valley Home, etc.

6 Our leaders, who are valiant, love truth
    and justice too;
They lead our righteous battles with glory
    full in view;

The people are united all our leaders to sustain,
And cheerfully obey each call with all their might and main.

     My Valley Home, etc.

HYMN 321. (P.M.)

1 Deseret, Deseret! 'tis the home of the free,
And dearer than all other lands 'tis to me;
Where the Saints are secure from oppression and strife,
And enjoy to the full the rich blessings of life.
'Tis a land which for ages has been lying waste,
Where the savage has wandered, by darkness debased,
Where the wolf and the bear unmolested did roam,
Away, far away! Deseret is my home.

2 Deseret, Deseret! she has long been oppressed.
But now, for a while, she is taking her rest,
She feels like a giant, refreshed with new wine,   [benigns
And enjoys from Jehovah his blessing.

There are hearts that can feel for another's
  deep woe,
And with charity, blessings on others
  bestow,
Return good for evil to those who oppress,
And await the time coming to give them
  redress.

3 Deseret, Deseret! O, I love to be there,
  With my brethren and sisters each blessing
    to share,
  Nor regret I've forsaken the land of my
    birth,
  To dwell on that sweet, favored spot of the
    earth,
  Where men full of wisdom and honor
    preside,
  With all the full quorums of Priesthood
    beside;
  Where the law of the Lord is the standard
    of life,
  Apart from foul Babylon's darkness and
    strife.

4 Deseret, Deseret! she's the pride of the
    world,
  Where the banner of freedom is wildely un-
    furled,

Where oppression is hated and liberty loved,
And truth and sincerity highly approved;
Where labor is honored, nor the workmen oppressed;
Where youth is instructed and age finds a rest;
Where society frowns upon vice and deceit,
And adulterers find Heaven's laws they must meet.

Deseret, Deseret shows the pattern to all,
That they may take warning ere Bab'lon shall fall,
And flee to the mountains when trouble shall come,
To be free from the plagues, in this beautiful home,
O, how my heart yearns for the time to draw near,
When earth will be freed from oppression and fear,
And the truth rule triumphant o'er sea and o'er land,
And Jesus as King of the nations will stand.

HYMN 322. (C. M.)

1 Thou, earth, wast once a glorious sphere
    Of noble magnitude,
And didst with majesty appear
    Among the worlds of God.

2 But thy dimensions have been torn
    Asunder, piece by piece,
And each dismembered fragment borne
    Abroad to distant space.

3 When Enoch could no longer stay
    Amid corruption here,
Part of thyself was borne away
    To form another sphere.

4 That portion where his city stood
    He gained by right approved;
And nearer to the throne of God
    His planet upward moved.

5 And when the Lord saw fit to hide
    The "ten lost tribes" away,
Thou, earth, wast severed to provide
    The orb on which they stay.

6 And thus, from time to time, thy size
    Has been diminished, till
Thou seemst the law of sacrifice
    Created to fulfil.

SECOND PART.

7 The curse of God on man was placed;
    That curse thou didst partake,
And thou hast been by turns disgraced
    And honored for his sake.

8 The vilest wretches hell will claim,
    Now breathe thy atmosphere;
The noblest spirits heaven can name,
    Have been embodied here.

9 Lord Jesus Christ, thy surface graced;
    He fell a sacrifice;
And now within thy cold embrace
    Thy martyred Joseph lies.

10 When Satan's hosts are overcome,
    The martyred, princely race
Will claim thee, their celestial home—
    Their royal dwelling-place.

11 A "restitution" yet must come,
    That will to thee restore,
By that grand law of worlds, thy sum
    Of matter heretofore.

12 And thou, O earth, will leave the track
    Thou hast been doomed to trace;
The Gods with shouts will bring thee back
    To fill thy native place.

HYMN 323. (C.M.)

I long to breathe the mountain air
  Of Zion's peaceful home,
Where, free from sorrow, strife and care,
  The Saints of God may roam;

2 Where hearts may glow with feeling warm,
  Nor fear suspicion's blight,
To chill each thought with worldly form,
  And shade affection's light.

3 Where want and misery's piteous strain
  Shall ne'er an echo find,
And where oppression's icy chain
  Shall cease to crush the mind;

4 Where Truth shall reign with Godlike power,
  And shed its heavenly ray,
To brighten up each passing hour
  And sanctify each day;

5 Where voice with voice shall sweetly tell
  The joys in Zion found,
Till every mountain, hill and dell
  Shall vibrate back the sound;

6 Where unity and peace shall blend
  In prayer and songs of praise';
And where one object, aim and end
  Shall strengthen all our ways.

7 O God of Israel, look down
   And bless Thy faithful band,
Who fain would win a glorious crown
   And in Thy presence stand.

8 In mercy light each honest mind
   That strives to do Thy will,
And grant that all who seek may find
   A home on Zion's hill.

HYMN 324. (C.M.)

1 Come, all ye Saints throughout the earth,
   And join with one accord;
Come, brethren, let us rise and build
   A Temple to the Lord.

2 Our tithes and free-will offerings
   The Lord doth now require;
By keeping this and other laws
   We'll bide the day of fire.

3 From thence the law of God will spread
   In majesty abroad,
And over nations all shall rule
   The "LION OF THE LORD."

4 'Tis there, the precious things of old
   Which but the righteous know,
Which unbelieving Gentiles scorn,
   God will again bestow.

5 Life's ordinances all are there—
　　Endowments of great worth—
　Anointings, washings, keys and powers,
　　Perfecting man on earth.

6 There, in the great Baptismal Font,
　　Built to our living Head,
　Anointed ones to God baptize
　　The LIVING for the DEAD.

7 Thus every dispensation past
　　In this will be assured—
　The last and first, the first and last,
　　By welding links secured.

HYMN 325. (P.M.)

1 When first the glorious light of truth
　　In this last age burst forth,
　How few they were, with heart and soul
　　Could feel its real worth!
　Yet of those few how many
　　Have passed from earth away,
　And in their graves are sleeping
　　Till the Resurrection day!

2 How many on Missouri's plains
　　Were left in death's embrace—
　Pure, honest hearts, too good to live
　　In such a wicked place.
　And are they left in sorrow
　　And doubt to pine away?

Oh, no; in peace they're sleeping
   Till the Resurrection day.

3 And in Nauvoo, the city where
   The Temple cheered the brave,
Have hundreds of the faithful found
   A cold, yet peaceful grave;
And there they now are sleeping
   Beneath the silent clay,
But soon they'll share the glories
   Of a Resurrection day.

4 Our Patriarch and Prophet, too,
   Were massacred; they bled
To seal their testimony, they
   Are numbered with the dead.
Ah, tell me, are they sleeping?
   Methinks I hear them say,
"Death's icy chains are bursting!
   'Tis the Resurrection day!"

5 And here in this sweet, peaceful vale,
   The shafts of death are hurled,
And many faithful Saints are called
   To find a better world.
And friends are often weeping
   For those who've passed away
And in their graves are sleeping
   Till the Resurrection day.

6 Why should we mourn because we leave
   These scenes of toil and pain?

O happy change! the faithful go
　Celestial joys to gain;
And soon we all shall follow
　To realms of endless day,
And taste the joyous glories
　Of a Resurrection day.

HYMN 326. (8's & 6's.)

1 Though pride may show some nobleness
　　When honor's its ally,
　Yet there is such a thing on earth,
　　As holding heads too high!
　The sweetest bird builds near the ground,
　　The loveliest flower springs low:
　And we must stoop for happiness,
　　If we its worth would know,

2 Like water that encrusts the rose,
　　Still hard'ning to its core,
　So pride encases human hearts
　　Until they feel no more.
　Shut up within themselves they live,
　　And selfishly they end
　A life, that never kindness did
　　To kindred, or to friend!

3 Whilst virtue, like the dew of heaven
　　Upon the heart, descends,
　And draws its hidden sweetness out,
　　The more—*as more it bends!*

For there's a strength in lowliness
  Which nerves us to endure,
A heroism in distress,
  Which renders victory sure!

4 The humblest being born, is great,
  If true to his degree;
His virtue illustrates his fate,
  Whatever that may be!—
Thus, let us daily learn to love
  Simplicity and worth:—
For not the eagle, but the DOVE,
  Brought peace unto the earth!

HYMN 327. (9's & 8s.)

1 Think not, when you gather to Zion,
  Your troubles and trials are through,
That nothing but comfort and pleasure
  Are waiting in Zion for you:
No, no; 'tis designed as a furnace,
  All substance, all textures to try,
To burn all the "wood, hay and stubble,"
  The gold from the dross purify.

2 Think not, when you gather to Zion,
  That all will be holy and pure;
That fraud and deception are banished,
  And confidence wholly secure:
No, no; for the Lord our Redeemer
  Has said that the tares with the wheat

Must grow, till the great day of burning
Shall render the harvest complete.

3 Think not, when you gather to Zion,
The Saints here have nothing to do
But look to your personal welfare,
And always be comforting you.
No; those who are faithful are doing
What they find to do, with their might;
To gather the scattered of Israel
They labor by day and by night.

4 Think not, when you gather to Zion,
The prize and the victory won.
Think not that the warfare is ended,
The work of salvation is done.
No, no; for the great Prince of Darkness
A tenfold exertion will make,
When he sees you go to the fountain
Where freely the truth you may take.

HYMN 328. (C.M.)

1 O God, Thou God that rules on high,
Bow down Thine ear to me:
O listen to my humble cry,
O hear my fervent plea.

2 Rebuke the heartless, wicked clan
That seek thy servant's harm;
Protect him from the power of man,
By Thy almighty arm.

3 Let unseen watchmen wait around
   To shield Thy servant's head;
Let all his enemies be found
   Caught in the net they spread.

4 Thy grace, like morning dews distilled,
   To all his needs apply;
And let his upright heart be filled
   With comfort from on High.

5 The work is Thine—Thy promise sure,
   Though earth and hell oppose:
Roll, roll it on! but oh! secure
   Thy Prophet from his foes.

6 O hide him in Thy secret hold
   When on his path they tread,
Safe as Elijah, who of old
   Was by the ravens fed.

7 Bring our accusers' deeds to light,
   And give Thy people rest;
Eternal God, gird on Thy might
   And succor the oppressed.

HYMN 329. (6-8's.)

1 Cease, ye fond parents, cease to weep,
   Let grief no more your bosoms swell;
For what is death? 'Tis nature's sleep;
   The trump of God will break its spell,

For He, whose arm is strong to save,
Arose in triumph o'er the grave.

2 Why should you sorrow? Death is sweet
   To those that die in Jesus' love;
Though called to part you soon will meet
   In holier, happier climes above;
For all the faithful, Christ will save,
And crown with vict'ry o'er the grave.

3 There's consolation in the blow,
   Although it crush a tender tie;
For while it lays its victims low,
   Death opens to the worlds on high;
Celestial glories proudly wave
Above the confines of the grave.

4 Let heathen nations clothe the tread
   Of death in faithless, hopeless gloom,
While vain imaginations spread
   Terrific forms around the tomb;
For human science never gave
A light to shine beyond the grave.

5 But where the light, the glorious light
   Of revelation freely flows,
Let reason, faith and hope unite
   To hush our sorrows to repose.
Through faith in Him who died to save,
We'll shout hosannas o'er the grave.

HYMN 330. (P. M.)

1 Come, go with me beyond the sea
    Where happiness is true,
Where Joseph's land, blest by God's hand,
    Inviting waits for you.
With joyful hearts you'll understand
    The blessings that await you there.
I know it is the promised land,
    My home, my home is there.

2 There, on those everlasting hills,
    And in the valleys fair,
Beside the gurgling fountain rills,
    We'll bow in humble prayer,
And praise our God in joyful strains,
    That we are safely gathered there.
                      I know, etc.

3 There Israel's sons, so long oppressed,
    Are pure, free, happy, too;
And daughters, in true virtue dressed,
    Do wait to welcome you,
To greet you with a kindred hand,
    And with you every good to share.
                      I know, etc.

4 There, too, are Prophets, Priests and Seers
    Who have the Holy Priesthood's powers,
To guide our souls through endless years,
    And light our darkest hours;

Yea, truth, which lighted Enoch's band,
Is freely to them given there.
I know, etc.

HYMN 331. (C.M.)

1 Though nations rise, and men conspire,
   Their efforts will be vain ;
Jehovah mocks their vile desire
   His Zion to defame.

2 In vain they'll look and strive to show
   Defilement in her laws ;
The thought of God they ne'er can know
   While they oppose His cause.

3 He will make bare His mighty arm ;
   His messengers shall come,
To gather home His Saints as sheaves
   Unto the harvest home.

4 Let Zion's converts now arise ;
   Our Father will defend,
And arm them for each glorious war,
   Till vict'ry's triumphs end.

5 Armed with His truth, before our face
   The people feel dismayed,
And all their treasure and their wealth
   Jehovah's purpose aid.

6 Thrice happy Saints, who bow beneath
    The banner of the Lord;
Celestial crowns your brows shall wreathe—
    Endurance' sure reward.

HYMN 332. (L.M.)

1 Again we meet around the board
Of Jesus, our redeeming Lord,
With faith in His atoning blood,
Our only access unto God.

2 He left His Father's courts on high,
With man to live, for man to die,
A world to purchase and to save,
And seal a triumph o'er the grave.

3 Help us, O God, to realize
The great atoning sacrifice,
The gift of Thy Beloved Son,
The Prince of Life, the Holy One.

4 We're His, who has the purchase made;
His life, His blood, the price He paid;
We're His, to do His sacred will,
And His requirements all fulfil.

5 Jesus the great fac-simile
Of the Eternal Deity,
Has stooped to conquer, died to save
From sin and sorrow and the grave.

6 Bless us, O Lord, for Jesus' sake;
   O may we worthily partake
   These emblems of the flesh and blood
   Of our Redeemer, Savior, God.

HYMN 333. (L.M.)

1 Behold the great Redeemer die,
   A broken law to satisfy;
   He dies, a sacrifice for sin,
   That man may live and glory win.

2 While guilty men His pains deride,
   They pierce His hands and feet and side,
   And with insulting scoffs and scorns,
   They crown His head with plaited thorns.

3 Although in agony He hung,
   No murm'ring word escaped His tongue;
   His high commission to fulfil,
   He magnified His Father's will.

4 "Father, from me remove this cup,
   Yet if Thou wilt, I'll drink it up,
   I've done the work Thou gavest me,
   Receive my spirit unto Thee."

5 He died, and at the awful sight
   The sun in shame withdrew its light!
   Earth trembled, an all nature sighed
   In dread response, "A God has died!"

6 He lives—He lives: we humbly now
Around these sacred symbols bow,
And seek, as Saints of latter-days,
To do His will and live His praise.

HYMN 334. (C.M.)

1 How great the wisdom and the love,
  That filled the courts on high,
And sent the Savior from above
  To suffer, bleed and die!

2 His precious blood He freely spilt,
  His life He freely gave;
A sinless sacrifice for guilt,
  A dying world to save.

3 By strict obedience Jesus won
  The prize with glory rife:
"Thy will, O God, not mine, be done,"
  Adorned His mortal life.

4 He marked the path and led the way,
  And every point defines,
To light and life and endless day,
  Where God's full presence shines.

5 How great, how glorious and complete,
  Redemption's grand design,
Where justice, love and mercy meet
  In harmony divine!

6 Remembering the broken flesh
   We eat the broken bread;
And witness with the cup, afresh,
   Our faith in Christ, our head.

HYMN 335. (C.M.)

1 O Lord of Hosts, we now invoke
   Thy Spirit most divine,
To cleanse our hearts while we partake
   The broken bread and wine.

2 May we forever think of Thee,
   And of Thy suffering sore,
Endured for us on Calvary,
   And praise Thee evermore.

3 Prepare our minds that we may see
   The beauties of Thy grace;
Salvation purchased on that tree
   For all who seek Thy face.

4 As brethren let us ever live,
   In fellowship and peace,
Forgive, that God may us forgive,
   That love may still increase.

5 May union, peace and love abound,
   And perfect harmony,
And joy in one continual round,
   Through all eternity

HYMN 336. (L.M.)

1 While of these emblems we partake,
In Jesus' name and for His sake,
Let us remember and be sure
Our hearts and hands are clean and pure.

2 For us the blood of Christ was shed,
For us on Calvary's cross He bled,
And thus dispelled the awful gloom,
That else were this creation's doom.

3 Man broke the law of His estate
And Jesus came to expiate,
Atone and rescue fallen man,
According to Jehovah's plan.

4 The law was broken, Jesus died
That justice might be satisfied,
That man might not remain the slave
Of death, of hell, or of the grave,

5 But rise triumphant from the tomb,
And in eternal splendor bloom;
Freed from the power of death and pain
With Christ, the Lord, to rule and reign.

HYMN 337. (L. M.)

1 "Come, follow me," the Savior said;
Then let us in His footsteps tread,
For thus alone can we be one
With God's own loved, begotten Son.

2 Come, follow me, a simple phrase.
Yet truth's sublime, effulgent rays
Are in these simple words combined
To urge, inspire the human mind.

3 Is it enough alone to know
That we must follow Him below,
While traveling through this vale of tears?
No, this extends to holier spheres.

4 Not only shall we emulate
His course while in this earthly state,
But when we're freed from present cares,
If, with our Lord, we would be heirs,

5 We must the onward path pursue
As wider fields expand to view,
And follow Him unceasingly,
Whate'er our lot or sphere may be.

6 For thrones, dominions, kingdoms, powers
And glory great and bliss are ours
If we, throughout eternity,
Obey His words, "Come, follow me."

HYMN 338. (7's.)

1 School thy feelings, O my brother,
   Train thy warm, impulsive soul;
Do not its emotions smother,
   But let wisdom's voice control.

2 School thy feelings; there is power
   In the cool, collected mind;
Passion shatters reason's tower,
   Makes the clearest vision blind.

3 School thy feelings; condemnation
   Never pass on friend or foe,
Though the tide of ACCUSATION
   Like a flood of truth may flow.

4 Hear DEFENSE before deciding,
   And a ray of light may gleam,
Showing thee what filth is hiding
   Underneath the shallow stream.

5 Should affliction's acrid vial
   Burst o'er thy unsheltered head,
School thy feelings to the trial,
   Half its bitterness hath fled.

6 Art thou falsely, basely slandered?
   Does the world begin to frown?
Gauge thy wrath by wisdom's standard,
   Keep thy rising anger down.

7 Rest thyself on this assurance:
    Time's a friend to innocence,
And that patient, calm endurance
    Wins respect and aids defense.

8 Noblest minds have finest feelings,
    Quiv'ring strings a breath can move,
And the Gospel's sweet revealings,
    Tune them with the key of love.

9 Hearts so sensitively moulded,
    Strongly fortified should be,
Trained to firmness, and enfolded
    In a calm tranquility.

10 Wound not wilfully another;
    Conquer haste with reason's might;
School thy feelings, sister, brother,
    Train them in the path of right.

HYMN 339. (6's & 7.)

1 Rest for the weary soul,
    Rest, for the aching head,
Rest, on the hill-side, rest
    With the great uncounted dead.

2 Rest, for the battle's o'er,
    Rest, for the race is run,
Rest, where the gates are closed
    With each evening's setting sun.

3 Peace, where no strife intrudes,
  Peace, where no quarrels come,
Peace, for the end is there
  Of our wild life's busy hum.

4 Peace, the oppressed are free,
  Rest, óh, ye weary, rest;
For angels guard those well
  Who sleep on their mother's breast.

5 Peace, there is music's sound,
  Peace, till the rising sun
Of the resurrection morn
  Proclaims life's victory won.

HYMN 340. (L.M.D.)

1 We here approach Thy table, Lord,
  At Thy command through chosen men;
O may each heart, with one accord,
  Thy Spirit feel, inspiring them.
This peaceful Sabbath day we come,
  To drink this cup, and eat this bread,
In memory of the days to come,
  When we shall sit with our great Head.

2 Here, as we eat and drink, we show
  His death, until He comes again,
And feel, within, that sacred glow
  Revivify love's purest flame.

We here renew, with earnest heart,
  The covenants of the latter day,
To choose, for life, that "better part,"
  Which none can give, or take away.

3 As earthly Sabbaths roll along,
    O Father, give us grace in store,
  That, like a glad perennial song,
    Our lips and lives for evermore
  May honor all that Thou hast given,
    Thyself,Thy Son,Thy Priesthood's power,
  Thy Gospel, Spirit, which hath striven,
    And heaven for our eternal dower.

HYMN 341. (P.M.)

1 How swift the months have passed away,
    'tis Conference again,
  And Zion's untold thousands come to swell
    the joyous strain;
  To wake the echoes slumbering through
    Utah's blest domain,
  As the Saints are marching on victorious.

CHORUS.
Hurrah, hurrah, for this our jubilee,
Hurrah, hurrah, the truth has made us free,
We'll make the chorus ring, from the east to
    western sea,
And march through the earth victorious.

2 We have heard, have prophesied, the Priest-
    hood yet shall hold
  (As 'twas ordained before the stars, to-
    gether sung of old,)
  The rule of right, and truth impart, more
    precious far than gold,
As the Saints are marching on victorious.
                    Hurrah, hurrah, etc.

3 The world may laugh, and madly rave, may
    deem the truth a lie,
  And seek to bring upon the Saints, the
    vengeance they decry,
  But they proudly raise their banner, and
    bid it wave on high,
As the Saints are marching on victorious.
                    Hurrah, hurrah, etc.

4 Still we trust our faithful Head, and the
    God who doth inspire
  The Twelve, and each authority who
    guards the sacred fire,
  And every man in every land who hath a
    pure desire,
For the Saints are marching on victorious.
                    Hurrah, hurrah, etc.

5 Each day we ask our Father, give Thy
    Spirit from on high,
  That in the day of trial, from the track we
    may not fly,
  But for the Kingdom of our God, contented
    live or die,
  Like Saints who are marching on victorious.
            Hurrah, hurrah, etc.

6 When this time shall come to earth, and God
    doth truly reign,
  The hallelujas of the Saints, shall in un-
    broken strain,
  Sweep earth and sea, as now they do glad
    Utah's hill and plain,
  With the Saints still marching on victorious.
            Hurrah, hurrah, etc.

HYMN 342. (C.M.)

1 This house we dedicate to Thee,
    "Our God, our Fathers' God."
  Wilt Thou accept, and deign to bless
    The paths our feet have trod.

2 Wilt Thou Thy servants here inspire,
    When in Thy name they speak?
  And wilt Thou bless each contrite soul,
    Who here thy face doth seek?

3 Here may our sons and daughters come,
  And find that peace which swells
From grateful hearts, when touched by Thee,
  Wherein Thy Spirit dwells.

4 And may pollution ne'er have place
  Within this shrine we give;
And in it, through the years to come,
  Awake the dead to live;

5 Live to Thy Kingdom, live to Thee,
  While life shall pass away,
Then greet again with praise and song,
  In heaven's eternal day.

HYMN 343. (C.M.)

1 We'll sing all hail to Jesus' name!
  And praise and honor give
To Him who bled on Calvary,
  And died that we might live.

2 He passed the portals of the grave,
  Salvation was His song!
He called upon the sin-bound soul
  To join the heavenly throng.

3 He seized the keys of death and hell
   And bruised the serpent's head;
   He bid the prison doors unfold,
   The grave yield up her dead!

4 The bread and wine now represent
   His sacrifice for sin;
   Ye Saints, partake, and testify
   Ye do remember him.

5 The sacrament the soul inspires,
   And calms the human breast;
   Points to the time when faithful Saints
   Shall enter into rest.

6 Then, hail, all hail, to such a Prince
   Who saves us by his blood!
   He's marked the way, and bids us tread
   The path that leads to God.

HYMN 344. (L. M.)

1 How dark and gloomy was the night
   When Satan did his powers array
   Against the Prince of life and light,
   And Judas did his Lord betray!

2 O how each heart did throb with fear
  When He proclaimed the solemn word,
  "There's one of you assembled here
  Who will this night betray his Lord!"

3 The hour arrived, He took the cup,
  Likewise the bread, and brake and blest;
  "If I," said He, "be lifted up,
  The penitent shall share my rest."

4 "When you shall meet, do this," He cried,
  "United in my doctrine be,
  In union, love and peace abide,
  And then, always remember Me.

5 "Though I'm betrayed I will return,
  For all the dead shall hear My word,
  And all My Saints shall cease to mourn
  When heaven reveals their living Lord.'

6 May we be of the chosen few
  Who ever faithful will remain;
  And eat and drink with Christ anew,
  And with Him in His Kingdom reign.

HYMN 345. (C.M.D.)

1 O Lord, preserve Thy chosen seed,
  They've keenly felt the stroke
  Of vile oppression's iron grasp,
  And every Gentile yoke.

Sustain their name, make bare thine arm,
  Their rightful claims maintain,
And bring Thy long-since scattered band
  Unto their lands again.

2 Thy servants, too, preserve from harm
  As through the earth they roam
With joyful news of heavenly birth,
  To gather Israel home.
And guide their feet in paths that lead
  To Israel's chosen race,
And let their remnants now behold
  The plan of saving grace.

3 May light divine shed forth its ray,
  And with the pure remain;
Jesus return to dwell on earth,
  Whose right it is to reign !
O, hasten on the glorious time
  When Israel shall sing :
Hail ! Prince of Peace, Zion's redeemed,
  Jesus is sovereign King.

HYMN 346. (L.M.)

Oh what a boon ! the Sabbath day,
  To Saints who meet, its bliss to share;
To honor God's eternal way,
  Of Sabbath rest from worldly care.

2 For when they meet, they drink the cup,
   And eat the broken bread again,
In memory of One, lifted up—
   A Savior, once on Calvary slain.

3 'Twas His command, to celebrate,
   His blood, His death upon the tree;
And here we humbly congregate,
   Glad His disciples yet to be.

4 Until He comes to earth again,
   As King, among His Saints to dwell,
We will this sacred rite maintain,
   'Gainst all His foes of earth or hell!

5 He is our Lord, our Savior He;
   And we His Gospel will revere,
So shall we claim His love, and be
   True subjects of His kingdom here!

HYMN 347. (C.M.)

1 Throughout this congregation, Lord,
   Wilt thou thy presence give,
Thy Spirit drawing heavenward—
   Its life—that we may live!

2 In psalm and song, may we as one,
   With praise on each glad tongue,
Feel as 'twere heaven already won
   And songs by angels sung.

3 In prayer may we uplifted be,
  Petition flow as flood;
 Yet trusting all and leave to thee,
  What is for our best good!

4 In breaking bread, and tasted cup
  May we discern aright
 That Savior who when lifted up,
  Redemption brought to light!

5 And when Thy word distils, as rain
  Refresheth all the earth,
 Wilt thou not help us to maintain
  Its truth, its living worth!

6 Thus all our worship shall inspire
  To consecrate to Thee
 Our time, our talent, each desire,—
  Time and eternity!

HYMN 318. (10's.)

1 Spirit of heaven, all pervading love,
  Deign to accept our off'ring here to-day;
 Take home our hearts to purer realms above,
  Hear holy Father while meek souls do pray! [kind,
 Teach us to love with gracious hearts and
  Better and kinder than our souls have known.
 Teach us a deep forgiveness; that we, blind,
  May feel the sweet forgiveness at Thy throne.

2 Spirit descend! The emblem of thy pain
    With tearful hearts together we partake;
  Let us not fall beneath thy dark disdain,
    Give pow'r the sins of earth to e'er forsake.
  Ah, weary is the heart with sin and woe,
    Oft do we pray for peace amid our tears;
  Deep sobs despair, when o'er our spirits, lo,
    Steals hope's sweet harmony from God's own sphere.

HYMN 349. (11's.)

1 Sweet friend of the needy, kind helper of youth, [truth,
  Firm guardian of virtue, bright lover of
  Thy sleep shall be peaceful, unbroken thy rest, [breast.
  Thy spirit, disburdened, shall sleep on God's

2 Oh, well we remember, sweet spirit, the light [night—
  God lent us awhile ere it sank in the
  The night we call death, yet in vain do we see—
  The day spring of glory envelopeth thee.

3 In songs with the angels thou takest thy part,
  The glory of heaven now filleth thine heart;

Earth's woes now may languish—no more
   for thy brow
Their thorns shall they weave—thou art
   slumbering now.

4 The river of heaven now laveth thy feet;
  Fair angels shall twine thee a bridal wreath,
     sweet,
  And am'ranth immortal shall crown thy
     fair head—
  In heaven they deem thee not, loved one,
     as dead.

  Sweet, sweet be thy slumber, unbroken thy
     rest,
  Sleep sweet as a babe on the Savior's kind
     breast,
  God grant we may meet thee on heaven's
     bright shore,
  To part with thee, dear one, in grief, never-
     more.

HYMN 350. (C.M.

1 The bodies of our dead are laid
   In earth's inviting crust,
  Confirming what the Lord hath said:
   They must return to dust.

2 Not so the beaming spirits bright;
　They go not 'neath the sod,
　But upward take their glorious flight,
　　To paradise of God.

3 They there, in active, peaceful state,
　Await the final hour,
　When Christ will open wide the gate,
　　By His redeeming power.

4 The dead shall spring forth from the earth,
　Redeemed, immortal souls,
　No more again to taste of death,
　　While time eternal rolls.

5 With them we'll meet in realms of love,
　And everlasting joy;
　In mansions, of the Lord above,
　　Where peace hath no alloy.

HYMN 351. (C.M.D.)

1 What voice salutes the startled ear,
　And wakes the stricken heart,
　Yet seems to chide each childish fear,
　　And life again impart?
　Is it an echo of the past,
　　To which we silent cling?
　"O grave, where is thy victory!
　　O death, where is thy sting!"

This doth not spring from earthly soil,
  Nor from its wisdom grow!
'Tis not evoked by student's toil,
  Though years hath crowned with snow!
No! rich experience bids this swell,
  Divine, its precious ring—
"Oh grave, where is thy victory!
  Oh death, where is thy sting!"

3 Here, where the open bier sustains
  The friend just passed away,
We know that glad relief obtains
  From its encumb'ring clay!
While by the ready grave we stand,
  Exulting faith we bring—
"Oh grave, where is thy victory!
  Oh death, where is thy sting!"

4 And so we thank Thee, Father, God,
  Thy voice will raise the dead!
E'en though a thorny path they trod,
  Or were by Calv'ry led!
'Twas there Thy Son, our Savior, went,
  And man by this can sing:
"Oh grave, where is thy victory!
  Oh death, where is thy sting!"

HYMN 352. (P.M.)

1 Weep, weep for the early dead,
   Tears for the one we miss,
 E'en now by the angels led
   To realms of perfect bliss.

2 Gone, gone from the home of earth,
   Followed by deepest love,
 To taste of the higher birth,
   To dwell in the courts above!

3 Lost, lost shall we tearfully say,
   When sure of heaven and God?
 It is but the house of clay
   Which rests in the eager sod!

4 Soft, soft let the footsteps fall,
   The murmuring heart be still,
 'Till the trump of angels call
   The dead from the crowded hill;

5 Then, then we shall surely know,
   What'er we meet is best,
 For God will again bestow,
   The loved, in His tearless rest!

HYMN 353. (8's, 6's & 10's.)

1 We lay thee softly down to sleep
    Among the silent hills,
Where angels solemn vigils keep,
    'Til time its measure fills.
Tenderly parting, O, sweet be thy rest;
Joyous the meeting in realms of the blest.

2 We sadly part with one we love,
    And breathe a last farewell;
We lift our hearts to God above,
    Who "doeth all things well."
We lay thee away, in the silent tomb,
'Til eternal day, shall lighten its gloom.

3 We gently strew thy grave with flow'rs,
    While our tears fall like rain;
Lonely will be the dreary hours,
    'Til we see thee again;
Then gladly we'll meet when time is no more,
And our weary feet touch "the golden shore."

HYMN 354. (8's & 7's D.)

1 Resting now from care and sorrow,
    Resting from fatigue and pain;
Faithfully she's fought life's battle—
    Death to such is endless gain.

God hath gather'd home her spirit,
    God hath taken what He gave ;
Friend and sister, sweetly slumber
    In the quiet, peaceful grave.

2 All her warfare is accomplished ;
    Bid her now a fond adieu ;
Brief the parting, glad the meeting,
    That shall nearest ties renew ;
True and tender, self-denying,
    One of Truth's disciples brave—
Let her sleep, she needs to slumber
    In the quiet, peaceful grave.

3 Shall we mourn for one who's left us?
    Yes, our tears we needs must blend ;
Love's own offering, this, we owe thee,
    Faithful mother, faithful friend ;
While we look for consolation
    Unto Him, "The strong to save"—
Friend and sister, sweetly slumber
    In the quiet, peaceful grave.

HYMN 355. (8's & 7's.)

1 Sing ye of a home immortal,
    Where there's no more grief or pain,
Where there dwelleth love eternal,
    And there is no sad refrain.

2 No more weeping, no more sighing,
    No more agonizing fears,
And no requiem for the dying,
    Chanted 'mid the falling tears.

3 There the righteous live forever
    In the beauteous "better land,"
And no parting scenes shall sever
    Happy hearts in household band.

4 Sweetest strains of music ringing,
    Echo through the wide domain;
Choirs of heavenly voices singing,
    "Nevermore to part again!"

5 O! the rapt'rous joy of meeting,
    Just beside the heavenly gate,
With a sweet and tender greeting,
    Those for whom we fondly wait!

6 Angel escorts, bearing banners,
    Every entrance watch to see,
One, who cometh with hosannas,
    Marching on to victory,

7 Coming up through tribulation,
    Where the Savior's feet have trod;
Christ the guide to exaltation,
    Upward to the throne of God.

HYMN 356. (6's.)

1 Come! Saints of latter days,
    Unite in cheerful songs ;
  Come! sing our Father's praise—
    To whom all praise belongs.

2 Sing, for the joyful time,
    By prophets long foretold,
  The age of truths sublime
    Our mortal eyes behold.

3 Look down, ye bards, and seers,
    Who sang in ages past,
  The Zion of your dreams
    Established is at last.

4 Zion is famed afar,
    And more renowned shall be;
  Behold! the rising star
    Whose brightness kings shall see.

5 Let Zion's foes combine
    To hold her sons in thrall;
  Zion, by help divine,
    Will triumph over all.

6 God, in His own good time,
    Will crown the pure and true;
  God will be glorified,
    Whate'er the nations do.

HYMN 357. (P. M.)

1 The day of redemption, so near is at hand—
    We can sing in spite of oppression;
But never, to meet e'en a nation's demand
    Will we feign either fear, or depression;
The foes of our faith, like the billows, may foam
    "But a rest for the Saints yet remaineth,"
So we'll sing and rejoice in our own mountain home,
    That "the Lord God Omnipotent reigneth."

2 Proscribed, for opinion, in liberty's land—
    Face we bondage, misrule and disaster;
Yet e'en unto death, by the truth may we stand,
    And be leal to our Lord and our Master.
But sooner the ocean may quieted be,
    And sooner may mortals enchain it,
Than souls can be fettered, whom truth maketh free,
    While "the Lord God Omnipotent reigneth."

3 The heralds of truth yet shall compass the earth;
    And gather "the wheat" to the garner;
The honest will welcome the tidings of worth,
    Undismay'd by the wrath of the scorner.

The law of Jehovah we needs must fulfil,
  We cannot reject or disdain it;
'Tis "the hour of His judgment," and scoffers will feel
  That "the Lord God Omnipotent reigneth."

4 "From the wise and the prudent," the haughty and high
  The loftiest truths are oft hidden;
To "the feast of the Bridegroom" whose coming is nigh,
  The halt and the humble are bidden;
Through obedience, the Lord doth a witness bestow;
  Which any one seeking obtaineth;
And thus do His people assuredly know
  That "the Lord God Omnipotent reigneth."

5 Shall we barter our souls for a nation's applause,
  That denies us fair representation?
Are we traitors? Nay, verily, just is our cause;
  'Twill survive e'en unjust legislation.
The faith of the Saints shall astonish the world,
  And puzzle the wise to explain it;
Hosanna! hosanna! Truth's flag is unfurled;
  And "the Lord God Omnipotent reigneth."

HYMN 358. (P. M.)

1 The Truth has come forth in the last dispensation,
The Truth which has ever been anarchy's rod;
And its friends, in the midst of a wild, rampant nation,
Sing praises and honor and glory to God.
We will sing! we must sing! though the scorner may scoff it,
And hypocrites rage around God's people free;
He hath said in His word, by the voice of His Prophet,
"The song of the righteous is a prayer unto me."

2 King Pharaoh strove, in the time of good Moses,
To keep ancient Israel in bondage to him;
And to-day, in like manner, a nation proposes,
To render our prospects, as hopeless and grim:
But we'll stand! as they stood! and we'll see the salvation,
Which bore them triumphantly through the Red Sea;

And we'll sing! for 'tis written in God's revelation,
"The song of the righteous is a prayer unto me."

3 And blessings shall follow, yea, blessings unnumbered
Shall answer this token, "the song of the heart:"
Oh voices long silent! oh muse that hath slumbered!
Awake! and in union sweet praises impart.
We will sing of His grace in this imminent hour,
Whose love is our refuge, and ever shall be;
Who hath said to His Saints, in this day of His power,
"The song of the righteous is a prayer unto me."

HYMN 359. (P.M.)

1 Oh! blest was the day when the Prophet and Seer,
(Who stands at the head of this last dispensation,)
Inspir'd from above by "The Father" of Love,

Form'd the Daughters of Zion's great
organization.
Its purpose, indeed, is to comfort and
feed
The honest and poor in distress and in
need.
Oh! the Daughters of Zion, the friends
of the poor, [pure.
Are exemplars of faith, hope and charity,
CHORUS.
Oh! the Daughters of Zion, the friends of
the poor,
Are exemplars of faith, hope and charity,
pure.

2 Oh! Daughters of Truth, ye have cause
to rejoice,
Lo! the key of advancement is placed in
your keeping;
To help with your might whatsoever is right,
To gladden their hearts who are weary of
weeping.
By commandment divine, Zion's daughters must shine,
And all of the sex, e'en as one, should
combine; [ensure,
For a oneness of action success will
In resisting the wrongs that 'tis wrong
to endure. CHORUS.

3 Oh, woman! God gave thee the longing
to bless,
Thy touch like Compassion's, is warm and
caressing; [distress,
There is power in thy weakness to soften
To brighten the gloom and the darkness
depressing :
And not in the rear, hence, need woman
appear; [near;
Her star is ascending, her zenith is
Like an angel of mercy, she'll stand in
the van,
The joy of the world, and the glory of
man.
CHORUS.

4 Oh! be of good cheer, far-extending we see
The rosy-hued dawn like a vision of
beauty ;
Its glory and light can interpreted be :
Go on, in the pathway of love and of duty!
The brave earnest soul will arrive at its
goal; [unroll ;
True heroes are crowned as the ages
There is blessing in blessing, admit it
we must,
And there's honor in helping a cause
that is just.
CHORUS.

HYMN 360. (8's & 6's & 8's.)

1 Oh that my soul in joy might meet
   My lov'd Redeemer's face,
In blessed confidence might greet
   The throne of heav'nly grace!
That, as my soul ascends on high,
The happy pæans of the sky
Might ring a glad farewell to earth
And welcome to a heav'nly birth.

2 Oh that my soul might learn to live
   The laws that are most high;
Learn sweetly, meekly to forgive
   And grandly how to die!
That with its last farewell to earth,
A gem of bright, celestial worth,
'Twould find its mansion 'mong the blest—
The happy souls whom Christ loves best!

3 Oh teach me, Lord, within my heart,
   The law that leads to Thee;
And give me pow'r to choose the part
   That leaves the soul most free.
To Thee my dimmed, blurred life would rise
To purer realms beyond the skies;
My every hope and wish shall be
To still live nearer, Lord, to Thee.

HYMN 361. (10's.)

1 Take courage, Saints, and faint not by the way.
 Though storm clouds thick and fast be hov'ring nigh,
 The sun proclaims the glory of the day
 Behind the cloud as in the cloudless sky.

2 The darkest hour is just before the dawn,
 Yet who shall doubt the fast approaching morn;
 Or when we see the snow-clad hedge and lawn
 Who dares to say that spring will ne'er return.

3 'Tis meet that some should now and then be left
 To blindly grope in life's sequestered shade;
 To feel their breast of life and hope bereft,
 Till all their sins are on the altar laid.

 No vain aspiring can the soul afford;
 God's searching eyes will ev'ry vice assail;
 The wrong must perish like the miser's hoard,
 Or as the chaff before the passing gale.

5 God knows the proper path to lead us in,
   And what is best that we should do and know
 To win the vict'ry over death and sin,
   And fit us for the reign of peace below.

6 Let not the heart be sad at trials here,
   But sense how e'en the Savior suffered ill;
 He bore the cruel thorn, the galling spear
   To glorify His Father's holy will.

HYMN 362. (8's & 6's D.)

1 Uphold the right, tho' fierce the fight,
   And pow'rful is the foe;
 As freedom's friend, her cause defend,
   Nor fear nor favor show.
 No coward can be called a man—
 No friend will friends betray;
 "Who would be free," alert must be;
 Indifference will not pay.

2 Note how they toil whose aim is spoil,
   Who plundering plots devise;
 Yet time will teach, that fools o'erreach
   The mark, and lose the prize.
 Can justice deign to wrong maintain,
   Whoever wills it so?
 Can honor mate with treach'rous hate?
   Can figs on thistles grow?

3 Dare to be true, and hopeful too ;
   Be watchful, brave and shrewd ;
 Weigh every act ; be wise, in fact,
   To serve the general good.
 Nor basely yield, nor quit a field—
   Important is the fray ;
 Scorn to recede, there is no need
   To give our rights away.

4 Left handed fraud let those applaud
    Who would by fraud prevail ;
  In freedom's name, contest their claim,
    Use no such word as fail ;
  Honor we must each sacred trust,
    And rightful zeal display;
  Our part fulfil, then, come what will,
    High heaven will clear the way.

HYMN 363.   (7's.)

1 Rev'rently and meekly now
  Let thy head most humbly bow ;
  Think of Me, thou ransom'd one;
  Think what for thee I have done;
  With My blood that dripp'd like rain,
  Sweat in agony of pain ;
  With My body on the tree,
  I have ransom'd even thee.

2 In this bread now blest for thee,
　Emblem of My body see;
　In this water or this wine,
　Emblem of My blood divine.
　Oh, remember what was done
　That the sinner might be won—
　On the cross at Calvary
　I have suffered death for thee!

3 Bid thine heart all strife to cease;
　With thy brother be at peace;
　O forgive, as thou wouldst be
　E'en forgiven now by Me.
　In the solemn faith of prayer
　Cast upon Me all thy care,
　And My Spirit's grace shall be
　Like a fountain unto thee!

4 At the throne I intercede;
　For thee ever do I plead;
　I have loved thee as thy friend
　With a love that cannot end.
　Be obedient, I implore,
　Prayerful, watchful evermore,
　And be constant unto Me
　That thy Savior I may be.

HYMN 364. (L. M.)

All-wise, Eternal, Loving One,
  Our friend, our guide, in days gone by,
Sustain us till our race is run
  To serve Thee with a single eye.

2 We feel our weakness day by day,
  Unless Thy grace our bosoms fill;
O, grant us wisdom, Lord, we pray,
  To learn and love Thy holy will.

3 Prone as the sparks to upward fly
  Are we to choose the paths of sin,
But with Thy grace forever nigh
  The narrow gate we enter in.

4 The arm of flesh we dare not trust,
  Man's purpose turns, his love grows cold;
But, Thou, O Lord, unchanging, just,
  Thy truth, Thy love were never told.

5 O help us then to trust in Thee,
  In life, in death, in weal or woe,
And fill our hearts with charity,
  And love, and peace to all below.

HYMN 365. (2 6's & 4, 3 6's & 4.)
1 Our mountain home so dear,
  Where crystal waters clear
    Flow ever free,
  While thro' the valleys wide,
  The flowers on every side,
  Blooming in stately pride,
    Are fair to see.
2 We'll roam the verdant hills,
  And by the sparkling rills
    Pluck the wild flowers;
  The fragrance on the air,
  The landscape bright and fair,
  And sunshine everywhere,
    Make pleasant hours.
3 In sylvan depth and shade,
  In forest and in glade,
    Where'er we pass,
  The hand of God we see,
  In leaf, and bud, and tree,
  Or bird or humming bee,
    Or blade of grass.
4 The streamlet, flower and sod
  Bespeak the works of God,
    And all combine,
  With most transporting grace,
  His handiwork to trace,
  Through nature's smiling face,
    In heart divine.

HYMN 366. (8's & 7's D.)

1 In remembrance of Thy suffering,
   Lord, these emblems we partake,
When Thyself Thou gav'st an off'ring—
   Dying for the sinner's sake.
We've forgiven as Thou biddest
   All who've trespassed against us,
Lord, forgive as we've forgiven,
   All Thou seest amiss in us.

2 Purify our hearts, our Savior,
   Let us go not far astray,
That we may be counted worthy
   Of Thy Spirit, day by day.
When temptations are before us,
   Give us strength to overcome ;
Always guard us in our wanderings,
   Till we leave our earthly home.

3 When Thou comest in Thy glory
   To this earth to rule and reign,
And with faithful ones partakest
   Of the bread and wine again,
May we be among the number
   Worthy to surround the board,
And partake anew the emblems
   Of the sufferings of our Lord.

HYMN 367. (8's & 7's.)

1 Sing the sweet and touching story,
    Of the babe in Beth'lem born;
How the morning star with glory
    Lighted that auspicious morn.

2 What more beautiful and tender
    Than the blessed Savior's birth?
Cradled in a lowly manger,
    Was the King of all the earth.

3 Birds had nests, the foxes roaming
    Had their refuge free from care;
Jesus had no safe abiding—
    Homeless pilgrim everywhere.

4 Come to do His Father's bidding,
    Fresh from brilliant courts on high,
Holy missions thus fulfilling—
    Here to suffer and to die.

5 Now for us He's interceding
    In bright mansions up above,
"Father, guide them," thus He's pleading,
    "Save them through redeeming love."

HYMN 368. (8-8's.)

1 When dark and drear the skies appear,
    And doubt and dread would thee enthrall,
Look up nor fear, the day is near,
    And Providence is over all.
From heav'n above, His light and love,
    God giveth freely when we call;
Our utmost need is oft decreed,
    And Providence is over all.

2 With jealous zeal God guards our weal,
    And lifts our wayward thoughts above;
When storms assail life's bark so frail,
    We seek the haven of His love.
And when our eyes transcend the skies.
    His gracious purpose is complete,
No more the night distracts our sight—
    The clouds are all beneath our feet.

3 The direst woe that mortals know,
    Can ne'er the honest heart appall,
Who holds the trust—that God is just,
    And Providence is over all.
Should foes increase to mar our peace,
    Frustrated all their plans shall fall.
Our utmost need is oft decreed,
    And Providence is over all.

HYMN 369. (L. M.)

1 The nations bow to Satan's thrall;
   He fills with strife the souls of men;
He seeks to blind them one and all,
   Lest they the way of life obtain.

2 Soon shall the crash of war resound!
   Hark, hark, it spreads from land to land!
Alone on earth can peace be found
   With Zion's favor'd faithful band.

3 Behold the gloom and strife dispelled!
   The glorious day succeeds the night,
And Satan's powers have all been quelled—
   See, see the clear millennial light!

4 Now peace and love o'er earth extend,
   The air resounds with sweet refrains;
The voices of the righteous blend
   In praise of Christ who o'er them reigns.

INDEX TO FIRST LINES.

A

PAGE.
Adieu, my dear brethren, adieu.................... 233
Adieu to the city, etc........... ....*P. P. Pratt.* 244
Afflicted Saint, to Christ draw near........*Fawcett.* 287
Again we meet around the board ......*E. R. Snow.* 399
A holy angel from on high......... ...*P. P. Pratt.* 216
All hail the glorious day............. 294
All hail! the new-born year ....*P. P. Pratt.* 346
All praise to our Redeeming Lord.....*Wesley's Col.* 117
All-wise, Eternal, Loving One..........*J. Chrystal.* 437
All you that love Immanuel's name.......*Fellowes.* 172
An angel came down, etc ....*W. W. Phelps.* 251
An angel from on high.................*P. P. Pratt.* 218
And are we yet alive ....*Wesley's Col.* 116
Another day has fled and gone.........*P. P. Pratt.* 311
A poor, wayfaring man of grief ....*Montgomery.* 254
Arise! arise! with joy survey................*Kelly.* 26
Arise, my soul, arise ....*Wesley's Col.* 152
Arise, O glorious Zion ....*W. G. Mills.* 29
A Saint! and is the title mine........*M. A. Morton.* 368
As the dew, from heaven distilling.....*P. P. Pratt.* 103
At first the babe of Bethlehem......... *do.* 208
Author of faith, Eternal Word........ *Wesley's Col.* 56
Awake! O ye people, etc.............*W. W. Phelps.* 190
Awake! ye Saints of God, awake.......*E. R. Snow.* 329
Away with our fears, etc. . ...*Wesley's Col.* 68

B

Beautiful Zion for me..............*C. W. Penrose.* 349
Before all lands in east or west............*A. Ross.* 82
Before Jehovah's glorious throne.....*Wesley's Col.* 97
Behold the Great Redeemer die........*E. R. Snow.* 400
Behold, the Great Redeemer comes....*P. P. Pratt.* 201
Behold the Lamb of God..... 174
Behold the Mount, etc................*P. P. Pratt.* 203
Behold, the mountain of the Lord..........*Logan.* 219
Behold, the Savior comes.............*P. P. Pratt.* 202
Behold thy sons and daughters, Lord.. *do.* 162
Behold! the harvest wide extends.....*P. P. Pratt.* 243
Be it my only wisdom here............*Wesley's Col.* 36
Beloved brethren, sing His praise................ 24

C

Captain of Israel's host, etc.... ......*Wesley's Col.* 86
Cease, ye fond parents, etc............*E. R. Snow.* 395
Cheer, Saints, cheer, etc.............. .....*J. F. Bell.* 364
Children of Zion, awake from our sadness........ 322
Come, all ye Saints, etc..................*J. Jaques.* 389
Come, all ye Saints who, etc.........*W. W. Phelps.* 19
Come, all ye sons of God, etc.........*T. Davenport.* 180
Come, all ye sons of Zion............*W. W. Phelps* 257
Come, come, ye Saints, etc.............*W. Clayton.* 58
Come, dearest Lord, etc.....................*Watts.* 101
Come, follow me, the Savior said......*J. Nicholson.* 404
Come, go with me, etc............ *C. H. Wheelock.* 397
Come hither, all ye weary souls.......... ...*Watts.* 96
Come, Holy Ghost, etc............... .....*Wesley's Col.* 54
Come, let us anew, our journey, etc.... *do.* 51
Come, let us purpose with one heart.......*J. Lyon.* 123
Come, let us sing, etc................*W. W. Phelps.* 227

	PAGE.
Come, listen to a prophet's voice	266
Come, O thou King of kings.........*P. P. Pratt.*	209
Come, Saints of latter days.....*E. H. Woodmansee.*	425
Come, thou Desire of all Thy Saints........*Steele.*	101
Come, thou glorious day of promise	246
Come to me, will ye come, etc........*W. W. Phelps.*	326
Come we that love the Lord..............*Watts.*	36
Creation speaks with awful voice......*P. P. Pratt.*	185

D

Daniel's wisdom may I know	288
Dark is the human mind...............*E. L. Sloan.*	98
Deseret! Deseret! 'Tis the home, etc....*W. Willes.*	383
Do we not know that solemn word..........*Watts.*	168
Do what is right, the day dawn is breaking	165
Down by the river's verdant side.	320

E

Earth is the place where, etc..........*P. P. Pratt.*	203
Earth, with her, etc................*W. W. Phelps.*	258
Earthly happiness is fleeting...........*E. R. Snow.*	354
Ere long the vail will, etc.............*P. P. Pratt.*	17
Except the Lord conduct, etc..........*Wesley's Col.*	136

F

Farewell all earthly honors	210
Farewell, my kind, etc................*P. P. Pratt.*	242
Farewell, our friends, etc............*W. W. Phelps.*	234
Farewell, ye servants of the Lord......*P. P. Pratt.*	246
Father, how wide Thy glories shine.........*Watts.*	72
Father in heaven, we do believe.......*P. P. Pratt.*	177
For the strength, etc.........*Altd. by E. L. Sloan.*	92
From all that dwell below the skies.........*Watts.*	89
From Greenlands's icy mountains..........*Heber.*	235
From the regions of glory...........*W. W. Phelps.*	191

G

Gently raise the sacred strain........ *W. W. Phelps.* 160
Give us room that we may dwell.................... 57
Glorious things are sung of Zion..... *W. W. Phelps.* 79
Glorious things of thee are spoken......... *Newton.* 7
Glory to God on high....................... *Boden.* 149
Glory to Thee, my God, this night........... *Kenn.* 228
God moves in a mysterious way............ *Cowper.* 28
God of all consolation, take .... *Wesley's Col.* 140
God spake the word, etc............. *W. W. Phelps.* 20
Go, ye Gospel heralds, go................ *M. Travis.* 99
Go, ye messengers of glory...... ....*John Taylor.* 293
Go, ye messengers of heaven...................... 88
Great God, attend while Zion sings.......... *Watts.* 146
Great God, indulge my humble claim........ *do.* 62
Great God, to Thee my evening song .... *Steele.* 230
Great is the Lord! 'tis good, etc....... *E. R. Snow.* 10
Great Spirit, listen, etc.............. *C. W. Penrose.* 371
Guide us, O thou Great Jehovah.......... *Robinson.* 259

H

Hail! bright millennial day of rest........ *J. Lyon.* 74
Hail to the brightness of, etc........... *T. Hastings.* 356
Happy the man who finds, etc......... *Wesley's Col.* 39
Happy the souls who first believed.... *do.* 40
Hark! from afar a funeral knell....... *E. R. Snow.* 193
Hark! listen to the gentle strain....... *P. P. Pratt.* 309
Hark! listen to the trumpeters..................... 283
Hark! the song of Jubilee............ *Montgomery.* 107
Hark! ten thousand, etc......... .....*Dr. Raffles.* 170
Hark! ye mortals. Hist! be still...... *P. P. Pratt.* 85
Haste glorious day, when, etc............. *W. Clegg.* 230
He died! the great Redeemer died.... ...... *Watts.* 155

		PAGE
High on the mountain top............*J. H. Johnson.* 134
Ho, ho, for the Temple's, etc........*W. W. Phelps,* 333
Hosanna to the great Messiah..........*P. P. Pratt.* 204
How are Thy servants blest! O Lord......*Addison.* 61
How beauteous are their feet................ *Watts.* 118
How dark and gloomy, etc.............*R. Alldridge.* 412
How firm a foundation, etc................*Kirkham.* 260
How fleet the precious moment, etc....*P. P. Pratt.* 312
How foolish to the carnal mind........   *do.*   178
How great the wisdom, etc..............*E. R. Snow.* 401
How great the joy, that promised day.............. 131
How often in sweet meditation, etc. ..*P. P. Pratt.* 237
How pleasant 'tis to see......................*Watts.* 261
How pleased and blessed was I.............. *do.* 262
How sweet communion is on earth. 125
How swift the months, etc...........*H. W. Naisbitt.* 408
How will the Saints rejoice to tell................ 43

I

If you could hie to Kolob............*W. W. Phelps.* 252
I have no home, Where shall I go......*Lucy Smith.* 323
I know that my Redeemer lives............ *Medley.* 158
I'll praise my Maker while I've breath.. ....*Watts.* 66
I'll serve the Lord while, etc...........*E. R. Snow.* 367
I long to breathe, etc.............*M. A. Johnstone.* 388
In ancient times a man of God. ....*P. P. Pratt.* 176
In Jordan's tide, etc................*Rippon's Col.* 164
In remembrance of Thy............. .. *E. Stephens.* 439
Inspirer of the ancient Seers.........*Wesley's Col.* 55
In the sun and moon and stars............*Heber.* 214
I saw a mighty angel fly   292
Israel, Israel, God is calling............*R. Smyth.* 154
Israel, awake from thy, etc............*J. McGregor.* 89

J

	PAGE.
Jehovah, Lord of heaven and earth................	25
Jesus, from whom all, etc... .... Wesley's Col.	41
Jesus, mighty King of Zion...............Fellowes.	163
Jesus, once of humble birth. ....P. P. Pratt.	206
Jesus, thou all-redeeming Lord....... Wesley's Col.	50
Joy to the World! the Lord will come....... Watts.	15
Judges, who rule the world by laws......... Watts.	222

K

Know this that every soul is free................... 263

L

Let earth and heaven agree........... Wesley's Col. 48
Let every mortal ear attend................. Watts. 6
Let Judah rejoice in this glorious news............. 299
Let sinners take their course............... Watts. 18
Let earth's inhabitants rejoice............ W. Clegg. 188
Let us pray, gladly pray .... W. W. Phelps. 194
Let Zion in her beauty rise........................ 195
Let those who would be Saints, etc......E. R. Snow. 182
Lift up your heads, etc....,..............P. P. Pratt. 314
Lo! on the water's brink we stand................. 179
Lo! the Gentile chain is broken.... ..P. P. Pratt. 102
Lo! the mighty God appearing..................... 64
Lord, let Thy Holy Spirit now..........E. L. Sloan. 224
Lord, when iniquities abound............ .... Watts. 221
Lord, dismiss us with Thy blessing.........Burder. 107
Lord, make Thy mercy known..................... 86
Lord, Thou hast searched, etc............. ... Watts. 122
Lord, Thou wilt hear me when I pray........ do. 231
Lord, we come before Thee now........Hammond. 100

M

May the grace of Christ our Savior.........Newton. 148

	PAGE.
May we, who know the joyful sound......	108
Men of God! go take your stations............*Kelly.*	94
'Mid scenes of confusion, etc........................	318
Mortals awake! with angels join......... ...*Medley.*	21
Mourn not for those who, etc...........*E. L. Sloan.*	172
My Father in heaven, etc.......... ..*M. A. Morton.*	369
My God, the spring of all my joys...........*Watts.*	61
My soul is full of peace and love	197

N

Now he's gone, we'd not recall him.................	169
Now, is the voice, etc..............;...*Mrs. Sigourney.*	141
Now let us rejoice in the day, etc....*W. W. Phelps.*	198
Now we'll sing with one accord...... *do.*	189

O

O awake! my slumbering minstrel.....*E. R. Snow.*	133
O'er the gloomy hills of darkness ....*Williams.*	95
O fear not, brother, etc.............*C. W. Wandell.*	135
O give me back my prophet dear..........	348
O God! our help in ages past.........*Wesley's Col.*	147
O God! the Eternal Father..........*W. W. Phelps.*	156
O God, Thou God, that rules on high....*E.R. Snow.*	394
O God, Thou great, Thou good, Thou wise.........	112
O God, we raise to Thee.................. *B. Snow.*	46
O! happy is the man who hears....................	31
O happy home! O blest abode!.........*M. Morton.*	76
O happy souls who pray..;...........*W. W. Phelps.*	12
Oh, blest was the day, etc.......*E. H. Woodmansee.*	429
Oh, that my soul in joy might meet..*M.M. Johnson.*	432
Oh, what a boon.......... ....*H. W. Naisbitt.*	414
O Jesus! the giver of all we enjoy...*W. W. Phelps.*	22
O Lord, do Thou in heaven seal ....*J. Lyon.*	129
O Lord, do Thou Thy gifts bestow.......... *do.*	91

	PAGE.
O Lord of Hosts, we now invoke.....*A. Dalrymple.*	402
O Lord, our Father, let Thy grace..................	167
O Lord, our sovereign King........................	84
O Lord! responsive to Thy call....................	60
O Lord, preserve Thy chosen seed....*R. Alldridge.*	413
O, my father, Thou that dwellest.......*E. R. Snow.*	143
Once more, my soul, the rising day..........*Watts.*	224
Once more we come before our God..........*Lyte.*	105
On the mountain's top appearing..........*Kelly.*	115
O Saints, have you seen, etc...........*P. P. Pratt.*	70
O say what is truth, etc.................*J. Jaques.*	71
O, stop and tell me, Red Man........*W. W. Phelps.*	341
O Thou, at whose almighty word..........*Newton.*	104
O Thou, at whose supreme, etc......*I. E. Reading.*	380
O Thou who hast promised in love to receive.......	351
Our Father, in the sacred name..........*J. Jaques.*	363
Our mountain home...................*E. B. Wells.*	438
O who has not searched, etc...........*P. P. Pratt.*	307
O, wouldst thou from bondage......*C. W. Penrose.*	352
O ye mountains high, etc.........*C. W. Penrose.*	376
O Zion, when I think of thee.................*Kelly.*	321

P

Peace, troubled soul! thou need'st not fear........	32
Praise God from whom all blessings flow.....*Kenn.*	149
Praise to God, immortal praise.......*Stewart's Col.*	13
Praise to the man, etc...................*W. W. Phelps.*	325
Praise ye the Lord, my heart shall join......*Watts.*	119
Praise ye the Lord, 'tis good to raise........ *do.*	67
Prayer is the soul's sincere desire.....*Montgomery.*	358

R

Redeemer of Israel................*W. W. Phelps.*	212
Repent, ye Gentiles all................*P. P. Pratt.*	181

Rest for the weary soul............H. W. *Naisbitt.* 406
Resting now from care, etc.....E. H. *Woodmansee.* 422
Rev'rently and meekly now.........J. L. *Townsend.* 435

S

Salvation, sacred word of love........E. *Hanham.* 120
Satan's empire long has flourished.....E. L. *Sloan.* 99
School thy feelings, O my brother...C. W. *Penrose.* 405
See! all creation joins................W. W. *Phelps.* 11
See how the morning sun............. do. 225
See, the mighty angel flying.......R. B. *Thompson.* 114
Shall I, for fear of feeble man... ....*Wesley's Col.* 77
Should you feel inclined to censure............... 66
Should solemn covenants, etc.......C. W. *Penrose.* 350
Sing the sweet and touching ....E. B. *Wells.* 440
Sing to the great Jehovah's praise..... *Wesley's Col.* 142
Sing ye of a home immortal............E. B. *Wells.* 423
Sister, thou wast mild and lovely ......S. F. *Smith.* 184
Softly beams the sacred dawning ....J. *Jaques.* 33
Sons of Michael, he approaches..E. L. T. *Harrison.* 375
Spirit of faith come down............... *Wesley's Col.* 53
Spirit of heaven...................................... 416
Stars of morning, shout for joy 298
Sweet friend of the needy.......................... 417
Sweet is the peace, etc. ....M. A. *Morton.* 377
Sweet is the work, my God, my King .... *Watts.* 132
Sweetly may the blessed Spirit 60

T

Take courage, Saints, etc.............. J. *Crystal.* 361
The bodies of our dead 418
The curse of God on man was placed...E. R. *Snow.* 387
The day is past and gone.................P. P. *Pratt* 232
The day of redemption, etc.....E. H. *Woodmansee.* 426

	PAGE.
The gallant ship is under way........ *W. W.Phelps*.	239
The glorious day is rolling on... ....*E. R. Snow*.	199
The Gospel standard high is raised................	85
The glorious Gospel light, etc........*J. H. Johnson*.	330
The glorious plan, which, etc.............*J. Taylor*.	295
The great and glorious Gospel light...	265
The happy day has rolled on......................	266
The Lord imparted from above........*E. R. Snow*.	328
The Lord my pasture shall prepare.......*Eddison*.	27
The morning breaks, etc...............*P. P. Pratt*.	5
The morning flowers, etc....... ......*Wesley's Col*.	186
The nations bow to Satan's thrall.......*J. Nicholson*.	442
The night is wearing fast away.............	145
The pure testimony poured forth in the Spirit.....	285
The red man ceased, etc............*C. W. Penrose*.	372
There is a place in Utah................. *W. Willes*.	381
There is now a feast for the, etc..... ·. *W. Phelps*.	273
The rising sun has chased the night...............	109
The Seer, the Seer, Joseph the Seer.....*J. Taylor*.	337
The shepherds have lifted, etc ....,*W. Ross*.	361
The silver, gold and precious stones.....*J. Jaques*.	370
The solid rocks were rent in twain......*P. P. Pratt*.	304
The Spirit of God, etc..... .... *W. W. Phelps*.	268
The sun that, etc..... ..*T. B. Marsh & P. P. Pratt*.	270
The time is far spent, etc......... .... *E. R. Snow*.	343
The time is nigh, that happy time..................	9
The towers of Zion soon, etc........ *W. W. Phelps*.	272
The trials of the present day..........*E. R. Snow*.	138
The truth has come forth, etc.....*L. L. G. Richards*.	428
Think gently of the erring one......*Miss Fletcher*.	184
Think not when you gather to Zion....*E. R. Snow*.	393
This child we dedicate to Thee...... *Plymouth Col*.	223

		PAGE.
This earth shall be a blessed place....	P. P. Pratt.	206
This earth was once, etc	W. W. Phelps.	277
This God is the God we adore	Stewart's Col.	94
This house we dedicate to Thee	H. W. Naisbitt.	410
This morning in silence, etc	P. P. Pratt.	317
Thou dost not weep to weep alone	E. R. Snow	357
Thou earth, wast once, etc	E. R. Snow.	386
Though deep'ning trials, etc	E. R. Snow.	374
Though in the outward Churc below		277
Though now the nations sit beneath		109
Though nations rise, etc	M. A. Morton.	398
Though pride may show		392
Throughout this congregation, Lord	H. W. Naisbitt.	415
To Father, Son and Holy Ghost	Stewart's Col.	150
To Him who rules on high	W. Clegg.	253
To Him who made the world	W. W. Phelps.	16
To leave my dear friends	P. P. Pratt.	249
Torn from our friends, etc	P. P. Pratt.	315
To Thee, O God, we do approach	J. Lyon.	121
Truth reflects upon our senses		297
'Twas on that dark, that solemn night	Watts.	155
'Twas the commission of our Lord	do.	171

U

Unveil thy bosom, faithful tomb	Watts.	220
Up, arouse thee, O beautiful Zion	E. M.	127
Up, awake, ye defenders of Zion	C. W. Penrose.	73
Uphold the right, etc	E. H. Woodmansee.	434

W

Waked from my bed, etc	P. P. Pratt.	226
Wake, O wake the world, etc	W. W. Phelps.	332
Weep for the early dead	H. W. Naisbitt.	421
Weep not for him that's dead and gone.		144

	PAGE.
Weep, weep not for me, Zion.......*C. W. Wandell.*	335
We have met, dear friends and brethren...........	85
We here approach, etc....... ......*H. W. Naisbitt.*	407
We lay thee softly down to sleep......*E. B. Wells.*	422
Welcome, best of all good meetings..*T. J. Dawson.*	366
We'll sing the songs of Zion...........*W. G. Mills.*	110
We'll sing all hail to Jesus' name.....*R. Alldridge.*	411
We're not ashamed, etc............*W. W. Phelps.*	14
We thank Thee, O God, etc. ... .*W. Fowler.*	166
What fair one is this, etc............ *W. W. Phelps.*	279
What, though the Gentiles, etc....*W. H. Shearman.*	83
What voice salutes....... ....*H. W. Naisbitt.*	419
What was witnessed in the heavens..'........:..*J. D.*	38
What wondrous scenes mine eyes behold.....	217
What wondrous things we now behold..............	213
When all Thy mercies, O my God.........*Addison.*	339
When dark and drear the skies...*E. H. Woodmansee*	441
When earth in bondage, etc.........\.... *P. P. Pratt.*	302
When first the glorious light, etc........*W. Clayton.*	390
When God's own people stand in need.............	128
When Joseph his brethren, etc.......*W. W. Phelps.*	281
When Joseph saw his brethren, etc..... *P. P. Pratt.*	290
When quiet in my house I sit..........*Wesley's Col.*	87
When restless on my bed I lie.....................	282
When shall we all meet again..........*P. P. Pratt.*	247
When sickness clouds, etc..................*J. Lyon.*	96
When time shall be no more........... *P. P. Pratt.*	250
When worn by sickness, oft hast Thou.....*Addison.*	340
Where the voice of friendship's heard.....*J. Lyon.*	63
While of these emblems, etc...... ....*J. Nicholson.*	403
Who are these arrayed in white..........*De Courcy.*	52
With all the powers of heart and tongue..... *Watts.*	124

		PAGE.
With cheerful hearts, etc............	M. A. Morton	379
With joy we own Thy servants, Lord................		106

Y

Ye children of our God................	P. P. Pratt.	161
Ye chosen Twelve, to you are given....	do.	313
Ye differing, jarring sects attend..........	W. Clegg.	188
Ye Elders of Israel, etc	C. H. Wheelock.	359
Ye Gentile nations, cease your strife...	do.	303
Ye ransomed of our God...............	do.	215
Ye Saints who dwell, etc...............	E. R. Snow.	47
Ye simple souls who stray.............	Wesley's Col.	44
Yes, my native land, I love thee.......	S. F. Smith.	241
Ye sons of men, a feeble race...............	Watts.	126
Ye who are called to labor and minister for God....		345
Ye wond'ring nations, now give ear		291
Your sweet little rosebud, etc..........	E. R. Snow.	150

Z

Zion stands with hills surrounded...........	Kelly.	168

INDEX TO SUBJECTS.

THE FIGURES REFER TO NUMBER OF HYMN.

A
Address to earth—322.
Agéncy of man—240.
American Indians—292, 313.
Anointing and prayer for the sick—84.
Atonement—141.

B
Baptismal—149, 150, 154, 160, 161, 162, 163, 164, 165, 167, 262.
Baptism for the dead—286.
Believer's assurance in God—48, 80, 152, 237, 314.
Blessing of children—69, 205, 298, 306.
Book of Mormon—175, 199, 200, 230, 258, 266.

C
Charity—54, 170, 263.
Christ's appearance to His disciples in America after His resurrection—268.
Coming of Christ—10, 12, 176, 180, 181, 182, 183, 184, 185, 186, 187, 188, 189, 190, 191, 192, 196, 212.
Completion of the Temple in Nauvoo—288.
Conference—341.
Confession of Christ—9, 13.

Confirmation—78, 148.
Consolation of believers—35, 50, 108, 255, 271, 274, 277, 285, 314, 317.
Consecration—312.
Crucifixion of Christ—143, 268.

D

Dedication—342.
Defence of Zion—61, 68, 87, 117, 155.
Deseret—320, 321.
Desire to serve the Lord—28, 193, 256.
Destruction of the Nephites—269, 281.
Doxologies—76, 98, 135, 136, 138.

E

Evening hymns—210, 211, 213, 214, 215, 271.
Excellence of heavenly wisdom—24, 31.
Excellence of the Word of God—74.

F

Faith—15, 45, 86.
Fall of Babylon, and triumph of the kingdom o Christ—4, 27, 77, 321, 369.
Fall of man—103.
Farewell hymns—216, 217, 220, 221, 222, 223, 224, 226, 227, 228, 229.
Fellowship meeting—308.
Final triumph of the Saints—41, 126, 127, 253, 280.
Follow Christ—337.
Forsaking all for Christ—63.
Forbearance—338.
Funeral hymns—70, 131, 139, 156, 159, 169, 171, 172, 178, 202, 300, 302, 329, 339, 349, 350, 351, 352, 365, 366.

G

Gathering—47, 52, 142, 166, 254, 304, 305, 319, 323, 327, 330.

Glory of Zion—3, 23, 46, 53, 65, 102, 105, 122, 246, 297, 299, 301, 316, 365.

God, the strength of His Saints—7, 67, 116, 133, 134, 203, 204, 237.

Gospel—317.

H

Hymns in memory of the Prophet Joseph—282, 290.

I

Invitation to sinners—2, 83, 116, 158, 176, 258, 267.

J

Joseph made known to his brethren—251, 257.

Juvenile hymn—309.

L

Lamentation of Zion—278, 289, 296.

M

Marriage—119.

Millennial—1, 4, 20, 26, 34, 62, 71, 97, 132, 157, 173, 180, 190, 201, 244, 261, 264, 315.

Ministers' hymns—57, 64, 66, 96, 219, 247.

Miscellaneous—73, 92, 100, 120, 125, 128, 168, 204, 231, 233, 239, 245, 270, 279, 307, 361, 364.

Mission of the Twelve—273.

Morning hymns—101, 207, 208, 209.

N

New Year—40, 129, 272, 276, 295.

O

Omniscience and Omnipresence of God—112.
Opening hymns—206, 347.

P

"Peace be to this house"—72.
Plan of salvation—262.
Practical religion—99, 113, 310, 362.
Praise offered to God—8, 11, 29, 36, 51, 55, 56, 79, 85, 109, 111, 114, 137, 232, 235, 241, 368.
Praise to the Savior—6, 14, 16, 17, 38, 106, 107, 145, 177, 367.
Prayer—303.
Prayer for Israel—414.
Prayers for the Holy Spirit—42, 43, 44, 49, 90, 93, 94, 95, 348.
Prayer for the Prophet—328.
Preaching of the Gospel and missionary hymns—19, 39, 75, 81, 82, 88, 218, 247, 260, 293, 294.
Pre-existence of man—130, 311.
Pride—326.
Providence—21, 22, 25, 118, 291, 368.

R

Redemption at hand—357.
Restoration of Israel—153, 194, 195, 197, 225, 234, 265.
Restoration of the earth—183, 248, 322 (Second Part).
Restoration of the Gospel—5, 18, 29, 104, 175, 198, 242, 243, 250, 259, 358, 359.
Resurrection—171, 179, 325, 367.

S

Sabbath—121, 146, 346.

Sacramental—115, 140, 141, 144, 147, 332, 333, 334, 335, 336, 340, 343, 344, 363, 366.
Salvation—110.
Saints' prayers—89, 91, 236, 275, 360.
Scenes in the eleventh hour—287.
Standard of Zion—58, 123.

T
The Temple—288, 318, 324.

U
Unity of the Saints—32, 33, 37, 107, 174, 238, 285.

V
Voice from Joseph—283, 289.

W
What is truth—59.
Wheat and tares—249.
Word of Wisdom—284.

METRICAL INDEX.

The figures refer to number of Hymn. C. M. means Common Meter; L. M. means Long Meter; S. M. means Short Meter; P. M. means Peculiar Meter; D. means Double.

C. M.—2, 5, 9, 10, 14, 16, 18, 19, 22, 24, 34, 37, 39, 43, 50, 60, 66, 91, 95, 96, 99, 103, 107, 116, 127, 129, 131, 134, 138, 148, 159, 163, 165, 168, 170, 183, 201, 203, 206, 207, 210, 214, 232, 243, 253, 258, 259, 274, 286, 291, 303, 310, 312, 317, 319, 322, 323, 324, 328, 331, 334, 335, 342, 343, 347, 350.

C. M. D.—71, 78, 84, 111, 180, 220, 298, 306, 309, 345, 351.

L. M.—1, 4, 12, 15, 20, 25, 31, 32, 33, 45, 48, 51, 56, 57, 64, 76, 83, 85, 86, 90, 94, 100, 101, 109, 110, 112, 114, 115, 118, 119, 120, 121, 124, 133, 136, 140, 143, 145, 153, 154, 158, 161, 162, 164, 171, 172, 173, 174, 181, 184, 186, 187, 188, 195, 198, 199, 202, 205, 209, 211, 212, 213, 222, 223, 226, 240, 241, 242, 246, 252, 255, 257, 262, 266, 267, 268, 270, 271, 272, 273, 275, 279, 281, 285, 302, 314, 332, 333, 336, 337, 344, 346, 364, 442.

L. M. D.—296, 340.

L. P. M.—204.

P. M.—40, 47, 58, 59, 68, 77, 79, 88, 117, 139, 151, 152, 166, 177, 190, 194, 230, 248, 254, 290, 299, 311, 315, 316, 321, 325, 330, 341, 352, 357, 358, 359.

S. M.—6, 13, 42, 72, 106, 108, 147, 185, 208, 215.

S. M. D.—35.

6's.—368.

4-6's & 2-8's.—11, 38, 69, 123, 141, 160, 167, 192, 197, 200, 229, 261, 295.

6, 6, 8 D.—238, 239.

3-7's & 4.—264.

6's & 7's D.—179, 193, 234.

7's.—8, 46, 89, 97, 175, 189, 196, 338, 363.

7's D.—41.

8-7's.—52.

7's & 6's D.—102, 144, 218.

4-7's & 4.—146.

7's & 8's.—297.

8's.—80, 216, 233, 251.

8-8's.—368.

8's & 7's.—3, 26, 30, 49, 54, 65, 70, 75, 92, 93, 104, 122, 130, 132, 135, 149, 156, 169, 263, 287, 300, 308, 367.

8's & 7's D.—366.

8's & 7's, 6 lines.—87.

3-8's & 7's.—126.

8's & 6's.—128.

8's & 6's, 8 lines.—326, 362, 366,

8's & 7's, 10 lines.—157.

3-8's & 6.—318.

8's & 9's.—284.

4-8's & 10's.—289.

10's.—313, 348, 361.

12's & 13's.—176, 224, 293.

12 & 11's D.—182, 250.

11's & 12's.—244.

12's, 11's & 10's.—247.

11's & 8's.—269.

11's & 5.—277.

6-11's.—280.

11's & 10's.—282, 301, 307.

12's.—283.

13's.—294.

13's & 14's.—320.

4-11's.—17, 219, 228, 237, 245, 265, 276, 298 304, 305, 349.

6-8's.—21, 44, 55, 74, 150, 249, 278, 329.

7's & 6's.—23, 191, 217, 231, 292.

6-7's.—27, 227, 235, 256, 339.

8's & 6's & 8's.—360.

8-8-6's—28.

8's, 6's & 10's.—365.

2-6's & 4, & 3-6 & 4.—36, 137.

8's, 7's & 4.—53, 82, 98, 105, 142, 155, 221, 225, 236, 260.

9's & 8's.—62, 288, 327.

2-8's & 6's.—26, 63, 113, 125, 178.

2-8's & 7.—67.

2-6's & 4, 3-6's & 4.—365.

www.ingramcontent.com/pod-product-compliance
Lightning Source LLC
Chambersburg PA
CBHW022115300426
44117CB00007B/720